SPOILED PRIEST

GABRIEL LONGO TRIED DESPERATELY
TO RECONCILE HIS LIFE
AS A PRIEST WITH HIS LIFE AS A MAN.

THIS IS THE INTIMATE STORY
OF HIS STRUGGLE—

AGAINST DISHONESTY

"You see, Gabe, it's wonderful to be an honest man. But in your—our—Holy Roman Catholic Church, being an honest priest is absolute *hell* . . . Come on," Father Basil said, "I want you to meet my wife."

AGAINST BIGOTRY

"I had never heard a priest use words like 'guinea' and 'wop' until [Monsignor] Powers came on the scene."

AGAINST CARNAL TEMPTATION

"The rectory seemed always to be filled with young women . . . Reading or music had been able to dispel sex fantasies before, now I could only rid myself of such thoughts by plunging into an ice cold shower. And my trips to the shower gradually increased."

AND AGAINST TORTUROUS DOUBT

Viewing Da Vinci's The Last Supper, "my subconscious was caught up on the mysterious figure near the end of the table, the most despicable traitor who ever lived—the first spoiled priest."

SPOILED PRIEST

The Autobiography of an Ex-Priest

BY GABRIEL LONGO

BANTAM BOOKS
TORONTO · NEW YORK · LONDON

SPOILED PRIEST

*A Bantam Book / published by arrangement with
University Books, Inc.*

PRINTING HISTORY

*University Books edition published July 1966
2nd printing .... September 1966
3rd printing .... December 1966*

Mystic Arts Book Society edition published August 1966

A portion of this book appeared in
DOMINION MAGAZINE *March 1967*

Bantam edition published October 1967

*Bantam Books are published by Bantam Books, Inc., a subsidiary
of Grosset & Dunlap, Inc. Its trade-mark, consisting of the words
"Bantam Books" and the portrayal of a bantam, is registered in the
United States Patent Office and in other countries. Marca Registrada.
Bantam Books, Inc., 271 Madison Avenue, New York, N.Y. 10016.*

mcmxxxiv

The history of Our Lady of Mt. Carmel Parish records like a symphony with its theme, the promotion of God's kingdom on earth, and its keynote, the salvation of souls here in the Marion Section of Jersey City. The opening strains reveal how in April, 1905, the Rev. Ernest Monteleone, upon his arrival from Italy, purchased a discarded Baptist Church on the corner of Broadway and Giles Avenue in Marion and transformed it into a Catholic Church. The Church was officially opened on July 16, 1905, under the title of Our Lady of Mt. Carmel. The late Monsignor Sheppard, the Vicar-General of the Diocese blessed this New House of God. Father Monteleone then celebrated the first Solemn Mass here at which Monsignor Arcese preached on the start of another parish in the vineyard of the Lord. The heart of the Catholics of Marion swelled with pride and gratitude. Those were the pioneer days for Mt. Carmel—a handful of parishioners with two Masses scheduled for Sundays and meagre collections. But the Providence of God blessed these modest beginnings and soon the parish made rapid advancement in spiritual and social progress. From 1913 to 1916, Father Monteleone served the needs of Mt. Carmel parish and another newly organized Church, Our Lady of Sorrows, in Greenville, Jersey City, with the assistance of Fathers Schianese and Basile.

Upon his return to America in 1916, after having served his native country in the First World War, Father Monteleone devoted all his time to Our Lady of Sorrows Parish. He recommended the appointment of Father Julius Moscati whom he had left in charge of Mt. Carmel during the war, as its Pastor. Consequently, the late Bishop O'Connor assigned Father Moscati to his post on January 6, 1917. Father Moscati had been ordained a priest on December 17, 1905, in Italy, and was formerly an assistant pastor at St. Lucy's Church in Paterson. Guided by the apostolic zeal of Father Moscati, Mt. Carmel grew in leaps and bounds. More masses were added to the Sunday schedule. The Pallottine Sister of Charity from Kearney conducted Sunday Schools for the children. The Rectory was built on April 25, 1917. Church property expanded as the needs of the parish increased.

The theme of our symphony now swells in happy anticipation and fulfillment. A drive for a new Church building was started. Elaborate plans were submitted by Archbishop Vegliante of Garfield, soon approved by the Bishop. The contract was given to the Devlin Construction Company. On November 14, 1926, the people of Marion beheld the new Church of Our Lady of Mt. Carmel erected in the style of Corinthian architecture and proven to be one of the most beautiful Italian Churches in the Diocese of Newark. There it stood as a monument to the true devotion and staunch faith in their Lord and Savior Jesus Christ, on the part of the Italian-Americans of this community.

New and larger quarters meant a broader field of work for souls. Hence, the need of more laborers in Our Lord's workshops. In 1926, Bishop O'Connor sent Rev. Hercules Di Primio as first assistant to Father Moscati. And on January 17, 1927, the Sisters of St. Elizabeth under the supervision of Mother Christina Amirante as their Superior came to the parish. Mt. Carmel parish could now boast of a beautiful new Church, a Rectory, Convent and Kindergarten School. Joyful strains reechoing the happy tempo of a well organized parish, with whispered plans of a parochial school were thrown into harsh discords on April 29, 1934. Father Moscati met an untimely death at the hands of a crazed assassin . . .

AFTER the shooting of Father Moscati, nobody mentioned Dillinger for days. Before, especially among the third graders at P.S. 35, most of the arguments were about him. Dillinger was on the loose again and everybody wanted to be him when we played cops and robbers. Some boys had to be bribed to be G-men.

We knew all about murders and everything—Jersey City wasn't exactly cut off from the rest of the world. Dutch Schultz used to operate in our territory. Jersey City did its share to keep Manhattan supplied with bootleg booze and beer until repeal.

There had been plenty of *ordinary* murders. Everybody expected gangsters to get shot at one time or another. People were always killing one another over love or money or something, but nobody had ever heard of it happening to a priest. Especially not a priest you knew, from your own parish. Especially not the priest who gave you First Communion. Nobody had ever heard of a priest ending up on page one of the *Daily News*.

Grownups stopped talking about Roosevelt and La-Guardia, George Jessel and Norma Talmadge, Waxey Gordon and Al Capone, kidnappings and NRA, relief and hard times. The shooting of Father Moscati became the main topic of conversation.

There are two kinds of Italian Catholic families: those who send their women and children to church and those who don't. My father always sent us. Until we were old enough to cross West Side Avenue, my mother used to take us herself.

For a long time I never realized there was such a thing as a depression. We just thought there was something wrong with our relatives—Mother's relatives. Except for Uncle Frank, Dad's were all in Italy, where Mussolini (everybody called him Muzzy) had everything under control.

Dad had left at the end of the First World War when he was still in his teens. His first job was in Newark at a big aluminum factory. Then he went to work for Consolidated Edison as a hoisting engineer.

He was never out of work for an hour, good times or bad, and always made good money—legally. In Jersey City, during prohibition and depression, that put us in the elite of the Italian community.

Dad made wine in the cellar with equipment borrowed from a neighbor. In autumn, during the fermenting period, the whole house had a delicious smell. My job was to keep an eye on the bottles stored in the cellar to make sure they didn't explode.

The first-born son in an Italian family is always a big deal. Mother and Dad had been married in 1923, but I wasn't born until 1926. Those three years explain why my appearance and survival were something special.

When her first baby was stillborn, Mother prayed to St. Anthony to have another, just like the child in the statue. Her prayers were answered; it turned out to be a boy so they named him Anthony. But he was a blue baby and lived only three days.

"He was too beautiful to live," Mother always said. But one of her sisters already had nine healthy children and the inequity seemed too much to bear. In despair Mother turned to St. Gabriel. She made a nine month's novena at the Passionist Monastery to St. Gabriel and to St. Theresa, the Little Flower of Jesus.

So I was named Gabriel Anthony for the miracle workers. When my brother came along three years later, he was named Bernard after my father.

Then misfortune struck again. Dad came down with the flu (they called it Spanish flu that year), later complicated by a case of mumps. This was the only time I ever saw my father crying. Mother used to try to cheer him up. With two handsome sons, what did it matter if they never had any more babies? I never could figure out the connection exactly. But a few years later when Mother was pregnant again, all of us were deliriously happy. And the third Longo child—baby Catherine—became the apple of her father's eye from that day forward. Though Kay arrived without any special intercession of the saints, her birth was always considered something of a medical miracle alongside the routine longshot scored by Papa Dionne.

Dad had reluctantly voted for Franklin D. Roosevelt in 1933 as a special favor to Mayor Hague of Jersey City. But he complained bitterly and vowed never to repeat his mistake. There was little FDR could do for us in Jersey City, anyway. The Welfare State, Medicare, aid to education, all the things Congress debated for the next thirty years we already had. Jersey City was ninety percent Catholic and Hague was Catholic, so why waste money on parochial schools? I went to P. S. 23 where my mother had gone before me. Mayor Hague built the Jersey City Medical Center. It was his pride and joy and nobody ever went without hospital care whether they could pay for it or not. When the orthodox socialist agitators came over from New York, Mayor Hague turned the cops on them, sent them packing, and everybody cheered.

When I finally became conscious that a lot of people were having tough economic sledding, my father became an even more impressive figure to me. I begged him to show me where he worked, in the Bronx. In those days they unloaded tons of coal from barges anchored in the river to feed the huge generators on the shore. My father showed me the giant crane he manipulated. I was astounded at the narrow metal ladder he had to climb to get to his high cockpit—to navigate that when it was frozen in winter seemed like a daredevil feat. I wouldn't have been more impressed if he had been a highwire walker at the circus. Dad had his seniority, his job protected. He was four-square for the International Brotherhood of Electrical Workers,

5

AFL, the union. And he brought home thirty-five dollars a week, a fortune in those days. We were the lucky ones.

Of course, we always had to help Grandpa and Grandma Rose (Mother's stepmother), but that had begun before the depression and would probably go on after. In the beginning we did it the easy way—with cash. When Mother found out they were doling it out to other members of the family, we gave them groceries. We used to drive over with cases of tomatoes, spaghetti, chickens and vegetables. Mother often spent forty dollars a week to feed us and the relatives and that couldn't go on forever.

WPA helped a little. It was, according to Dad, one of Roosevelt's better ideas. But he suspected it was an American version of something Mussolini had done first and better.

My godfather worked on the WPA and one of my uncles worked with a pick and shovel paving the street right in front of our house. He was the one that always seemed to be working while most of the others just loafed around. I admired him. It wasn't long before he and my godfather got together, pooled their pennies, and borrowed some, bought a truck and started peddling fruits and vegetables door-to-door. They got off WPA and were on their own. They seemed to have the same stuff my father had.

There was nothing old country about Mother. Dad's family always called her La Mogliere Americano—the American wife.

Marching in brown veiling on parish feast days, running to church to catch all the funerals, reading "Il Progresso," listening to *Tosca*—none of this was for her.

Mother was a free soul, like Norma Shearer and Constance Bennett. She was the first one in her group to create multi-colored Jello salads in fancy copper moulds. She had been a Victory Girl singing with Ted Lewis and his orchestra at Fort Dix in 1918, and she didn't let you forget it. The one time she went to the Metropolitan Opera in New York, she and Aunt Marie laughed so loud at the screaming and the costumes—especially the pants on the tenors so tight you could, according to her, see everything (their berlock lockets)—they had been asked to leave. Dad was so mortified he never took her back. Mention a party to Mother and she had her Empress Eugenie hat on. She was a party girl. She adored Al Jolson and Jack Benny and the New York Yankees. "My Yankees" she called them and if she was dry-eyed when we came home from school that meant the Yankees had had a good day. At parties, things picked up when Julia Longo got there.

Mother would never have anything to do with parish social activities—the sodalities and the societies. But she was a religious fanatic alongside her father, Cowboy Tony. Grandpa was six foot three, weighed 240 pounds, wore a ten gallon hat and never, according to everybody, did a day's work in his life. He was a natural-born nobleman. Mother's mother had been a genuine Italian aristocrat who married this big, fascinating greenhorn, as her girlfriends called him. Grandpa lived royally off the family legacy until Grandma died giving birth to my mother. He continued to live royally for several years by judiciously hocking her jewels and furs. When that capital was exhausted, Cowboy Tony continued on sheer nerve. He married Grandma Rose on the docks at Hoboken, back in the days when you had to have a husband waiting on the shore or you were deported. With her he produced a second family, enough children so he could go into the ice cream business for a while without having to do a tap himself. The kids did all the work. Through it all he remained the gallant big spender who thought noth-

7

ing of splurging forty dollars on a dress for his bride. Once, according to legend, Grandpa had spied a New York dress merchant taking measurements of Grandma Rose where he had no business with his tape measure. Cowboy Tony promptly hung the little man upon one of his own clothes racks.

He never went near church except on the Feast of St. Luke, patron saint of his home town of Benevento. The only time he actually got inside was for his own funeral when he was 96. A real tall Marcello Mastroianni, that was Grandpa.

We never lived in what outsiders called Little Italy. We had a lovely home, very up-to-date, one of the best homes in the parish—always on the outskirts of the all-Italian section.

"They don't have to know what time we got home and what I wore," Mother would always say. "I don't want to be gossiped about."

She wouldn't have minded being written up in Ed Sullivan's gossip column in the *New York Daily News*. But neighborhood Jersey City gossip was very low-class.

Mother's real talent was for news analysis—*Daily News* analysis. She had mastered the art of reading it as if each story was a cluster of damp tea leaves in the bottom of a cup. She approached page four like an astronomer scanning television photos of the moon.

The *Daily News* was supposed to be a very racy paper, specializing as it did in rape, murder, seduction, adultery, divorce, gangsters, abortions, and all "La Dolce Vita" of the Thirties. But Mother knew that life in the raw was far juicier and more gory than the paper could ever *come right out and say*.

It took real study, real knowledge of the world, real expertise to fill in the blank spaces, to flesh out the bare bones of plot into full-blown drama. If Mother had been Anglo-Saxon genteel, she might have written some great novels. But since she was Latin, an adventurous cook and a performer to boot, her forte was oral history, served up as the final course of a Lucullan lunch.

Mother was founder and president of something that should have been called the Jersey City Historical Society. The girls of her group met three times a week, Monday at our house, Wednesday at Aunt Carrie's and Friday at Lizzie's.

Mother would brood all weekend conjuring up an eye-popping dish to dazzle the girls. While other women were busy on washday, Mother was making artistic arrangements on her silver trays. First she baked two cakes for six women and both would vanish in an afternoon. Then came cold cuts, baked beans, fancy chicken and two kinds of salad: one always a gaudy, shimmering, moulded Jello concoction. Jello wasn't fattening; besides on the radio, it sponsored Jack Benny. The cold cuts always had to be displayed artistically, with parsley, watercress and radish roses. One time she threatened never to go to Lizzie's again because Lizzie had served the proscuitto on waxed paper. Each meal was a failure unless it included at least one daring experimental dish. If the experiment was a success and someone complimented her on the creation, she might go on a kick that could last three months. When the girls finished the meal (and finishing it was a religion, for people were starving everywhere and it would be a sin to throw anything away) there were inevitably two pots of coffee. Over coffee and cake they finally got down to the agenda: who had done what to whom since Friday, the illumination of the gospels according to the *Daily News*.

No murder was too small or too gruesome to escape study. If the murder victim was a woman, her entire imagined sex life came under scrutiny. If a man shot his wife, the Monday meeting became a full-scale inquest and seminar on marriage. If a woman shot her husband, the club became a jury of her peers.

In the guise of talking about the murderers and their victims, the girls would spill out their own views of themselves and their husbands. Everything that the Papal Commission on Marriage and Birth Control got around to in 1965, Mother and her girls had thrashed out while FDR was in his first term.

On rare Mondays when my brother Bernie and I could manage to seem sick enough to be allowed to stay home from school, we used to hide under the bed and listen. You had to pay attention and exercise imagination, even undertake outside research, especially if the subject happened to be a husband who insisted on using "those things"—mysterious rubber devices to forestall the untimely proliferation of cousins during periods of economic uncertainty.

Since Father Moscati was shot on a Sunday, the murder at the rectory swept all other old business off the agenda.

I managed to get home that Monday at lunchtime to tune in on the seminar. I knew Mother's group would have more interesting sidelights on the scandal than anything I could possibly hear at P. S. 23.

For something like this, of course, the *News* wasn't the only required reading. There was the *Jersey Journal*, and for special comparative reading, one of the girls had sneaked in a copy of the *New York Times* which ordinarily had nothing at all to offer.

Here it turned out to be the exception. The *Times* had sidelights that the *Daily News* had found unfit to print. The girls explored them all.

There's only one way to discover the superiority of oral history: let something happen in your own backyard and then read the papers later.

Why had the *News* made a hero of Father Moscati while the *Times* made him the victim? Why did all the papers go to such lengths to make the poor carpenter a maniac? Besides, there was no getting away from it: moustache and all, he was very good looking. This, coupled with the certificate of good health provided by a family of six children between the ages of 5 and 20, seemed to the girls to be fundamental.

Moreover, if Father Moscati's sister-in-law really had had an argument over the price of her house by the seashore, why would she have had him around later to do repairs at the rectory?

Even if the shooting had taken place in less hallowed surroundings, the fact that the daughter of Mrs. Moscati had been sent to the hospital for hysteria the night before would certainly have rated her designation as that stock headline figure, the mystery woman.

If, as the carpenter maintained, his only animus was directed against Mrs. Moscati, and the shooting of the priest was entirely accidental, what was so crazy about that?

If the man was so sick the pastor had a nun run to his house to inquire after him, why would they let him in the rectory? Besides, a priest doesn't send nuns on errands. Not at night. And never alone. Always two at a time and then someone from the rectory always drove them. It just didn't add up. There had to be something else to it.

There was no hope that the mystery could be scrutinized in a public trial. Both as a matter of justice and a matter of political strategy, Mother's group felt this was a pity. If its purpose was to hush up a scandal, then the Irish politicians in City Hall and the Archdiocese didn't understand Italians. They were still treating them like children. They didn't trust them. They never did and they never would. What went without saying was that the feeling was mutual.

11

Father Moscati's funeral brought more pomp and circumstance to Jersey City than anything since the big NRA Parade of 1933.

The afternoon before I went with my mother to the church where the pastor's body lay in state in the main aisle right up in front of the Sanctuary. This was the first dead person I had ever seen. The picture of flickering candles, banks of flowers, old women in black bending over to kiss his hand, his stiffened body in elaborate gold vestments stayed in my mind for days. All the parades and pageantry of the funeral couldn't erase it.

There was practically no room in the church for anybody from the parish except officials of the Holy Name or the St. Agnes Societies. The place was packed with priests, monsignors and bishops. The Mayor came and all the City Commissioners. Until then I never really knew how many policemen there were in Jersey City. Most of them were there standing by, some on foot, many on horseback. I stood in the street watching the dignitaries parading in and out. Two complete church bands took turns playing funeral marches. The mounted policeman rode by, then the policemen on foot, then one band came marching in slow motion while the other band played. The caisson passed and behind it walked the Bishop and the Mayor and the City officials. Then came officials of the church societies in their uniforms. Then a whole city block of priests: monsignors with flashes of red under their capes, plain priests in their black berettas and their black cassocks and surplices. The Holy Name Society, Knights of Columbus with their gold swords and white feathered hats, the St. Agnes Society, women in black veils, the Society of St. Theresa in full mourning, the Children of Mary. A band from another parish brought up the rear, all of them marching slowly and solemnly to the cemetery.

The sidewalks were jammed. Men stared or bowed their heads. Women blessed themselves and wept. In between the sniffles were the whispers. Apparently the only surviving family was Father Moscati's sister-in-law and niece. Both of them were said to be in the Jersey City Medical Center, one with bullet wounds and one with a breakdown. Maybe they were and maybe they weren't—all anybody really knew was that there seemed to be no family. And that was, after all, the saddest thing: a magnificent funeral and no relatives to see it.

There had been guessing and speculation as to whom the Bishop would send to replace Father Moscati. Mt. Carmel had never had a pastor who didn't come from the old country. Then through the crowds the word was whispered that the Bishop had passed over old Father Di Primio and appointed a very young priest, out of the seminary just two years.

One of the young priests marching behind the coffin would be our new pastor. He was an Italian. That's all anybody seemed to know about him for sure.

The Children's Mass that next Sunday was unusually crowded. Quite a few mothers had come along to get a look at our new pastor.

He was very young but serious looking, almost stern. He was thin and wore rimless glasses and looked as though he might be kind if you got to know him. But there was something else: he looked the way a priest ought to look—holy.

When he mounted the pulpit and began a sermon in English especially for us children, that was just the beginning of the changes. Italian was never spoken at our house except when Mother and Dad wanted to say something we weren't supposed to understand. We learned all those things so quickly Mom and Dad went

13

back to English. Now church was going to be the same way. More American than Italian.

The parish women were very concerned about who was to be housekeeper at the rectory. When they heard it would be the widowed mother of our new pastor, they seemed almost disappointed. That seemed, almost by design, to eliminate the rectory as a subject of conversation. Mrs. Zita Artioli didn't seem very old, but she was as thin and serious and stern looking as her son. Almost unapproachable. Everybody seemed to think Father Artioli and his mother would be around only temporarily.

After Mass, hardly anybody mentioned the changes. They were still busy talking about what had happened to Father Moscati. Everything that went on in church reminded you of the shooting: the confessional, the choir and the candles, the altar and the pulpit, the vestments and the incense.

For days, months, even years, the parish would still talk about it. It became, like the Immaculate Conception and the Assumption, something you could never hope to understand. It could never be satisfactorily explained. The good-looking carpenter from Newark was the key to the mystery. And he was locked up somewhere, never allowed to talk. If his confessor knew the secret he wouldn't be permitted to tell it to anyone under pain of sin. The seal of the confessional covered everything. But it didn't stop people from talking. You couldn't walk past the rectory or sit in church without the whole thing coming back to you. Mt. Carmel had been Father Moscati's church as long as I could remember. For me the mystery of his death would haunt it forever.

On the occasion of Father Moscati's funeral, May 2, 1934, the present Archbishop of Newark, His Excellency Thomas Joseph Walsh presented to a surprised congregation its new administrator, the Rev. Walter P. Artioli, ordained only since May 21, 1932, and then fulfilling his first assignment as an assistant pastor at St. Lucy's Church in Newark.

When Father Artioli first came to Mt. Carmel parish the financial state of the Church was far from healthy. The enormous debt and the condition of the times that still felt the deadening impact of the depression of 1929 precluded any hopes of building a parochial school.

Under the steady, expert leadership of Father Artioli, a generous and holy priest of God, the symphony of Mt. Carmel parish resounds with a spiritual fervor and enthusiasm unparalleled. No note is passed over. No instrument lays (*sic*) idle, as the spiritual and temporal needs of all are administered to. Obstacles are met with and surmounted. The schedule of Sunday Masses is increased to satisfy the demands of a growing parish. Missions, novenas, confraternities of Christian doctrine classes are established to enhance the spiritual tone of the parish. Societies for the young and the old, for the single and married are either re-organized or introduced; external activities of the Church such as feasts, bazaars, entertainments, also receive a new impetus—all with the purpose of nurturing the social and cultural life of the parishioners. In the short space of two years, the appointment of Father Artioli as Pastor of Mt. Carmel Church on Christmas Eve, 1936, reflected the ecclesiastical approval of his energetic labors in winning souls for Christ, our Lord.

Hail Selassie full of grace
Hold Mussolini by his waist
When he hollers hold him fast
Bust a pepper in his ass

ITALO NEGRO RIOT IN JERSEY CITY
5 Injured, 12 Arrested

THE MARCH we were playing was called FACCETTA
NERA, Black Face. And "black face" is what it meant
to me—the bearded black face on a scarecrow figure
of Emperor Haile Selassie, hanging by his neck with
the feet dangling above the platform carried on the
shoulders of the Holy Name Society, the same platform on which Our Lady and the Saints were paraded
on their feast days.

I was in the front rank of the church band with my
E flat alto saxophone, my white ducks and my black
shirt and my military hat. We marched off in formation right after eleven o'clock Mass and the crowd
at the curb shouting, cheering, dancing into the streets,
hurling curses at the effigy of the Lion of Judah.

Behind us marched the Holy Name Society, gold
badges flashing, the children of the St. Theresa Society
getting extra mileage out of their expensive white First
Communion veils; the Children of Mary—teen-aged
girls in blue silk capes and blue veils; the married
women of the St. Anne's Society in their brown silk
capes and veils. Then the Honor Guard of the Knights
of Columbus, with jeweled swords swinging from their
belts. Father Artioli followed in his black cassock and
beretta, then Father Di Primio and the other assistants.
Strong young Holy Name men carrying the plat-

16

form with the effigy of Haile Selassie rocked in rhythm to the music. There was no Prussian precision in the ranks. All the bodies in the street rocked and rolled, shaking to the rhythm. The straw-stuffed Haile Selassie weaved and swung in its gibbet all through Little Italy, carefully skirting the section right off the highway where a few Negro families lived.

Members of the band committee passed through the crowds with brewery trays and people tossed money into them. Mr. Five-by-five, with his long cigar, was in charge of the fireworks. He would weave in and out of the crowd and the paraders, a little round man, lighting fuses and setting off explosive counterpoint to the rhythm of the military music.

As wild and as spontaneous as the choreography seemed, it was all an elaborate grand design. When we reached a designated point we stood firm, changed our music and broke out with the Italian National Anthem, the MARCIA REALE. Then from the maze of ropes and decorations crisscrossing the street, a basket of flowers was lowered from a third floor window toward the ranks of the committee. With elaborate ceremony the flowers were removed—and the money underneath poured into the brewery trays.

Father Artioli extended his blessing. People cheered and danced, then we moved on. Everyone in the parish was expected to donate something; money, gold, rings, diamonds, rubies and other precious stones poured into the parish coffers.

It was always either the beginning of one parish fund drive or the conclusion of another; they had a way of running together. But this one was something special, climaxed by a victory dinner in the church basement. All the merchants in Jersey City contributed to the festa; parish women did the cooking and everyone who could afford it showed up and paid ten dollars a plate.

17

After dinner that evening, the church basement was crowded for the highlight of the day—an hour film celebrating the glorious victories scored by the Italian armies in bringing the faith of our fathers to the Coptic Christian kingdom of the Black Emperor. Piles of money and jewelry were still on display in the packed basement under watchful military guard by the plumed Knights of Columbus.

Mother and Dad never took part in church affairs like this, so I was on my own. The white ducks were dirty by evening but I kept them on; my band uniform rated free entry.

When the lights went off and the MARCIA REALE came up, and Mussolini appeared on the screen the whole parish broke into cheers. I knew from Dad that Muzzy was having problems with the Pope at the time. The Pope was forever meddling in Italian politics, instead of keeping his nose out of things that were none of his affair.

We saw the soldiers bouncing on their bellies through the African dust. When a Facetta Nera got plugged, we cheered. But the great moments in the movie were those when Mussolini's nephew Count Ciano and his Flying Squadron were shown bombing and strafing. Zio Giorgio, Dad's brother, Uncle George, was in the same squadron with the Mussolini boys. I kept a sharp eye out but I didn't see anyone who looked like him. Uncle Louis, Uncle Albert and Uncle John were all in the Italian Army, too. We got letters from the family from time to time and knew most of them were in some part of Africa. Dad read the dispatches from Ethiopia in the *Daily News* and the *Jersey Journal*, trying to keep track of things.

A lot of people in the parish had relatives in the war. This was their big chance to cheer them on—and contribute to the parish at the same time.

Being a member of the church band kept me in the

middle of everything that was going on, in our parish and others. We played at all the celebrations, the feast days, bazaars, and fund drives all over Jersey. Not every parish could boast a uniformed band of seventy pieces like Mt. Carmel.

Mother hated the squeaky sound of a saxophone. As the only member of the family with any experience in show business, she could point out that Rudy Vallee never got anywhere until he put away his horn and started crooning. The processions and festas where the church band played were much too old country for her taste, the uniforms alone cost a month's rent, and then there was the cost of the horn. But you had to start somewhere and even the church band was show business of a sort. Any son of hers could be expected to have musical talent, so when I was eight I had become a full-fledged saxophonist with our Lady of Mt. Carmel Band.

Professor Edward Vicedomi came from Bayonne to Jersey City two days a week. He was our Toscanini. Every week we spent an hour with him learning a new section of an American or Italian military march.

The professor was always on the lookout for special talent and it was a great day for me when he spoke to my father. So in addition to the sessions in church, I began private lessons one hour a week at home. First, of course, I had to have my own horn.

Dad and I went to Dorn and Kirchner in Newark to look at saxophones. Wally Kirchner showed us everything they had in stock and we looked at a few catalogues. I never knew there could be so many kinds, varieties and prices of saxophones. We decided to consult the professor. In the meantime Dad remembered a friend who had an extra horn. Dad brought it home: a Great American Gretch. The case was lined with purple velvet and the horn was gold. The only disappointing feature was that it didn't have pearl buttons like the ones I had seen at Dorn and Kirchner. It was very difficult to blow and at first getting a tone out almost killed me. Dad's friend said any horn with great tonal qualities wasn't easy. All I needed was practice. But we had no basement. I had to practice in the dining room and for Mother and the neighbors, that was an ordeal.

The Confraternity of Christian Doctrine was the official name for Sunday school sessions in catechism. Our instructor was a young man, only ten years or so our senior, who taught religion in some Catholic high school in Jersey. He had once studied for the priest-hood himself but had left the seminary for unknown reasons. He still wore the seminary black suits and black ties and those thin white cotton socks. He was tall, slender and sickly looking, with very thick-lensed glasses in silver frames; his dark hair, already receding, was greased and worn pasted to his head.

Bruce Armitage was a recruit of Father Artioli who never ceased explaining how lucky the parish was to have someone of his experience and attainments to teach the Christian doctrine.

Classes were held in the big basement auditorium. Boys and girls were grouped separately in opposite corners.

My buddy, Bernie Hagerty, and I always went to Mass and Sunday school together. We sat together and sometimes talked about it afterward. There were a couple of real sharp fellows in the class, who knew how to throw those curved questions that couldn't be answered without getting into interesting territory. Our instructor always rose to the bait. Bernie and I didn't know anything about sex except what we had read in dirty comic books so we just kept quiet and listened. But it reached the point where soul kissing and sex and touching and sex and impure thoughts and sex and girls and sex began to take up the whole hour. Some of it was interesting, of course, but it all seemed a little strange in the church basement. Bernie and I would come to Sunday school fresh and clean from confession and communion, and after fifteen minutes we were in worse shape than ever—full of impure thoughts and ideas that would have to be confessed next Saturday, if not sooner.

Our instructor kept harping on one theme: we fellows had to stick together and fortify ourselves against the temptations of the girls in the opposite corner. Girls meant sex and sex meant trouble. We attributed some of this emphasis to the fact that he was Irish and he didn't understand Italians.

I thought some girls were very beautiful and I hoped I troubled them as much as they troubled me: especially Chickie Formato who sat on the opposite side of our classroom at P. S. 23. What I liked about Chickie was that she was one of the neatest girls around, neat as a pin. Her hair was rust-colored and she wore it very long. It was a spectacular frame for her skin which was several shades of luscious pink. Bernie was crazy about her sister. We decided that if we ever had to take girls to a prom, it would be the Formato sisters for us. But Chickie never caused me any real trouble. She was so shy that when I spoke to her she blushed and ran away. Whenever she used to have to leave the room at school, I would always ask to be excused immediately afterward in the hope of running into her in the hall. We went to different bathrooms simultaneously for months.

But blaming Chickie seemed carrying things a bit far. She just wasn't my idea of a dangerous occasion of sin. She was a good girl. Somewhere there were other kinds of girls. If you didn't like them you called them whores, which meant they did the comic book thing with everybody. Treating these girls the same way as Chickie didn't seem fair but I didn't want to argue with our teacher—not at first.

The first time I tried to ask a question he shut me up by suggesting I hadn't read enough of the Bible. He assured me there were several crucial Biblical passages which completely supported his point of view.

One of the other fellows told us that our instructor had had a hernia operation while he was in the seminary. From a friend who played football we discovered that hernias had something to do with sex: that was one of the things they tested you for when you got a physical exam, they examined you *down there*.

Besides being Irish, the guy had had an operation, so that explained his continual harping on sex. We didn't even know what soul kissing was until he explained it. He seemed to think that was a special trap which girls used to lead boys into sin. But neither Bernie nor I had ever kissed a girl, so we couldn't imagine worrying.

Bruce once told Bernie that he had a master plan which he would reveal later in the course to protect us from women. It was some kind of physical experience which would make it possible for us to be immune to female temptations. We spent a great deal of time wondering what this could possibly be. Bernie talked to Bruce later and told me that it involved taking your comic book thing and putting it on a porcelain table and then hitting it with a silver hammer until some black stuff oozed out of it. If this was done properly, you could never be tortured by women anymore. Someone else suggested that this was the way the Vatican Choir members continued to sing soprano after they were eighteen. But nobody was sure.

At any rate, the only anatomy lessons we got were in Sunday school. Bruce Armitage was very precise and insisted we use the proper English word for each part of the body. We used to laugh at the word penis—we thought it was Irish. Vagina sounded Italian, maybe that's why our Irish seminarian seemed so terrified. We were cautioned never to use the phrase "jerking off" in catechism class or in the confessional. The proper word was masturbation. Neither Bernie nor I understood what that was but we were too embarrassed to admit it and nothing we had yet encountered in our comic book researches seemed to fit the description.

For years the two-by-four comic books our classmates stole from their parents raised the questions, and Bruce supplied the answers. The first sexy comic book I ever saw featured Pop Eye and Olive Oyl; then Bernie got hold of one entitled RUBINOFF AND HIS ETCHINGS. (Rubinoff was the leader of the orchestra on Eddie Cantor's radio program.) It showed Rubinoff at a big society function, walking up a huge winding Hollywood staircase complete with chandelier, behind the hostess' daughter. When the hostess is suddenly called downstairs to attend to something, Rubinoff takes out the bow of his violin and gingerly lifts the daughter's dress. That was only the beginning. All these books seemed to feature girls in flimsy Jean Harlow gowns with hair showing through. The men were big and hairy too, they all looked very Italian. We used to sit on the roof of Bernie's house where we could appreciate these art works at leisure and undisturbed. Every time Eddie Cantor would mention Rubinoff on the radio I would get hot under the collar.

There was a boy in our neighborhood who was retarded mentally and overdeveloped physically. We began calling him Rubinoff and when we did he would respond to our greeting by going into some comic book poses. So we figured out all by ourselves that masturbation had something to do with being mentally retarded. We didn't want to fool around with that. No sir. Not on your life.

As we got older the books got gamier. One day Bernie turned up with one that featured a triangular orgy between Pop Eye, Olive Oyl and Wimpy. I

23

wasn't ready for that one. When I got halfway through it I got very sick to my stomach and vomited right there on the roof.

I felt so bad I went to confession the next day. I usually confessed such things by saying I had enjoyed impure thoughts. But this time I was so genuinely repentant and ashamed I confessed that I had read a dirty book. I braced myself expecting Father Di Primio at least to ask me the name. But he gave me the same old penance, three Hail Marys.

Father Hercules Di Primio remained as a relic of other days. He seemed disheveled, Artioli was neat. He mumbled Mass where Artioli sang out. His breath smelled of garlic, Father Artioli used Listerine.

But altar boys and sinners liked him; his mumbling made him easier to serve Mass for or to go to for confession. During Easter week when all the houses in the parish had to be blessed and exorcised of devils, he was generous in sharing the patronage which came his way.

I had never been an altar boy. I was much too busy working to keep my standing in the band. But one Easter week morning when I was home from school he came by the house with an altar boy carrying a candle. After he blessed the house, my mother gave him a dollar. On the way out he asked me if I would like to make the rounds with him that afternoon.

I never thought of refusing the opportunity and after lunch I went to the rectory. He wasn't quite ready so he invited me up to his room.

"I think perhaps we should do a little something about your hair, Gabriel," he said to me off-handedly, after I'd put on the cassock and white surplice.

"Yes, Father," I said, "I'm due for a hair-cut."

"No, I wouldn't say that. You have very nice hair, Gabriel. It just needs a little attending to."

He grabbed a jar of some kind of grease and rubbed my head until there was gravy trickling down past my ear. Then he got out a fine comb and tried to comb it straight back, flat, the way he wore what was left of his own hair.

"There," he said, pleased with himself. "That's better. Take a look."

While I looked at myself in the mirror, he started opening dresser drawers and pulling out rolls of bright colored silks.

"What do you make of this?" he said, unrolling a bolt of cloth.

"It's very good looking." I wondered what on earth he could possibly use it for. Then he pulled out a stack of brightly colored silk shirts, every shade in the rainbow, and tossed them on the bed.

"Wow, Father!" I said. "Those are snazzy."

"Not bad," he mused, "I can only wear them on vacation, of course. Which ones do you like best?"

I pointed to a rather tame blue one.

"Take it with you," he said. "How big is your brother?"

"Almost as big as me."

"Well, then, pick out a couple you think he might like."

I chose a green one for Bernie. Then he insisted I take another two for myself. I was sure they were too big but I didn't want him to think I didn't appreciate his taste so I came downstairs loaded.

Father Artioli did some of the more special house blessing in the parish, but Father Di Primio was left with so many stops he had to cut the Latin ritual to the bone.

When we walked up the steps, I always rang the bell. By the time the lady of the house arrived to let us in, Father Di Primio had mumbled everything necessary. He said, "Dominus vobiscum." I said, "Et cum spiritu tuo." We streaked through the rooms tossing a little holy water here and there and that was it. On

25

the way out he got the money. If the housewife handed us an envelope that usually meant a dollar. But there were five-dollar stops and ten-dollar stops, too. At a five-dollar stop he had to slow down and agree to have a cup of coffee or a glass of wine.

If he was offered coffee at a dollar stop, Father Di Primio was very gracious, expressed his regrets, explained we had to keep going. If someone handed him a fifty-cent piece on the way out, he would toss it directly to me. When things were running bad for him, they were good for me. He never bothered to keep track of the money which wasn't in envelopes.

Late that afternoon when we finished, my pockets were heavy with half-dollars. I tried to give them to Father Di Primio at the rectory.

"God bless you, Gabriel. Keep the change." Then he rubbed my head with all the grease on it.

"But Father," I protested, "I've got more than fifteen dollars here."

"Peanuts, Gabriel," he sniffed. "That's what we get, peanuts. It takes the Polish to rake it in. Some of the Polish fathers get as much as three thousand dollars for a funeral."

mcmxxxix

Many are called, but few are truly beckoned toward
The holy vineyard of our own dear Blessed Lord
We welcomed you first in baptism as one of the fold
From that moment on, your tiny soul He began to mold
(sic)
Many a chilly morn you tumbled out of bed for an
    early Mass to be the server
But it was God who guided your footsteps and warmed
    your heart with burning ferver (sic)
Your homelife was good, your pastor a source of daily
    inspiration
For sources of love and grace, there was no limit,
    no ration
You pondered, you hoped, upon your knees you did fall
When to follow a divine vocation you felt an inward call
God answered, and gave you the strength to live in this
    world, but not of it
The tears your mother shed were sadly sweet and all a
    part of it.

IF MOTHER had asked me what I wanted to be when I
grew up, I would have said a big band leader. If Dad
had asked me, I would have said a Toscanini.

There was a time—after the Morro Castle burned and
the whole family drove down to Asbury Park to see

27

them towing the charred remains of that huge ship onto the beaches—when I wanted to be like Johnny Weismuller or Buster Crabbe. Several survivors had swum eight miles to shore. I practiced swimming like crazy for a few months, Australian crawling between the breakwaters, in case the Bayonne ferry ever burned while I was on it.

During the trial of Bruno Hauptmann for the kidnapping of the Lindbergh baby, Dad kept drilling into me that his conviction in the papers didn't make it so. Dad never thought he did it, so I began thinking about being a great trial lawyer.

I had been making model airplanes ever since Italo Balbo flew from Rome to the Chicago World's Fair in 1933. Many days I dreamed of becoming an airplane pilot with one of those snazzy peaked hats. When the dirigible *Hindenburg* flew over the house I thought it might be interesting to learn how to operate one. When we heard on the radio that it had crashed and was burning I went back to thinking about being an airplane pilot again.

I definitely didn't want to be a gangster or a soldier. When I heard on "Gangbusters" that Louis Lepke had locked a man, with pockets full of cheese, in a wooden box with holes bored in the side, just big enough so the rats would eat through the man to get the cheese, I was finished playing cops-and-robbers.

When Father Artioli asked us to pray for General Franco, I prayed; any friend of Mussolini was a friend of ours. But I had seen too many newsreels, heard too many stories about Africa and Dad's brothers to want to rush down and join the Army or Navy.

I didn't change my mind until the time of the World's Fair in 1939. I got annoyed when I went with Dad and Mother because they wouldn't let me go on that terrific parachute jump. So I used to sneak out to the Fair with Bernie Hagerty and haunt the parachute jump. I decided being in the Army wouldn't be too bad if I could avoid having anything to do with the infantry.

But when the Columbia Auditorium in Jersey City began booking big-name bands—the ones we heard on the radio with the new sounds, like Benny Goodman, I went right back to wanting to be a big band leader. I was tall enough so they would sell me a stag ticket and I would hang around all night dreaming of having a radio program of my own sponsored by a cigarette company and playing at the Palladium in Los Angeles.

But Benny Goodman never asked me what I wanted to be when I grew up. He never seemed to notice me. The only person who seemed interested in my future was Father Artioli.

Father Artioli was the most important person I knew. Far more important than the Mayor, as far as I could see. On feast days, in the middle of all the broiling sausages, the cracking clam shells, the popping soda bottles, Father Artioli was always the center of everything. The politicians and the business people all kowtowed to him. Our family never had any problems; but people who did always took them to the rectory and Father Artioli always had an answer. He could get jobs; he could talk to the bank if you were behind in the payments on your house. He could keep the electricity and gas from being turned off. If you had trouble with the immigration people over some cousin who was about to be deported, or if your grandparents in Italy wanted to visit and they needed papers, this was Father Artioli's department. Politicians came and went; big business people had good times and bad. But Father Artioli seemed to get more powerful and influential every day.

Everybody admired him. The way he spoke to you on the street, at the feasts, or in the church after confession determined your social standing in the community.

Father Artioli wasn't at all like other priests; they had big bellies and red faces, they smoked cigars and drove big black Lincolns. You couldn't tell them from the politicians.

There was a certain something about Father Artioli you had to respect and admire. And if he took the trouble to be your friend, that meant you amounted to something. The first time he called me "Gabe" I felt like Jesse Owens after the Olympics.

When he asked what your plans were for the future, you knew he wasn't just making conversation. You knew he cared. And it started you thinking.

By the time I was 14 I was working nights at parish bingo games. I was a full-fledged partner in the hierarchy gambling establishment that put Our Lady of Mt. Carmel Parish on its feet.

Since bingo, like all other parish innovations, was introduced by Father Artioli, the political patronage he threw my way made him an even bigger man in my estimation. When he announced the introduction of bingo games in the church auditorium, Father Artioli asked me if I would like a job helping out. I jumped at the chance.

At the tail end of the depression, when a hot dog cost a nickel and you could buy cigarettes for ten cents a pack, I was making a hundred dollars a week manning a microphone for the overflow crowds that came from New York to play bingo. And this didn't include tips. If you had a winner, you got tips. If you had a thousand-dollar winner, a fifty-dollar tip was routine.

The Liberty Fair and Amusement Company managed most of the games in Jersey City. They handled everything, including the equipment and the personnel. The parish had a committee to work with them on details and the pastor checked the money. The professionals got forty percent of the take and the church sixty. Father Artioli introduced me to the man from Liberty who was boss of our particular sector. His name was Fred Longo. He was no relative, but before long I was calling him Uncle Fred. He got his signals from Father Artioli and what started as a one-night-a-week job in the church basement got to be a big deal. Eventually I ended up as Fred's assistant in charge of the control room where the money was shoveled in and out. I worked from 6:30 until 11:30 four nights a week on a regular schedule the year round.

We started out using only the church auditorium, but then the buses started pouring in from New York. The same crowd of ladies from Manhattan would show up regularly all over town. We packed them into school gymnasiums, classrooms, any place that could be used to rake in the money.

The ushers would peddle the single cards for a quarter or the double cards for fifty cents. A glass-enclosed blower would mix up the numbered Ping-Pong balls. The numbers on the trapped balls would be called out, and winners would be checked. The visitors were revived from faints and the losers consoled with soft drinks and pretzels and other goodies. And around eleven every night the parish priest would arrive at the control room, take his sixty percent of the take, and walk off under guard to his black Lincoln.

It was great while it lasted. And how it lasted. Hitler rose, Poland fell, France fell, and Holland and Norway and Denmark and even Singapore and Pearl Harbor, but bingo and that hundred and something a week went on for what seemed like forever.

"Gabriel, what do you want to be when you grow up?"

31

It was a Saturday night after confession and Father Artioli just happened to be there when I finished my three Hail Marys. We had been meeting accidentally for weeks, as we did at the feasts, outside Sunday school, at the band rehearsals. No matter how many people were around, he always spoke to me personally. His "Hello, Gabe" was more important than my monthly report card at school. I could explain dropping from A to C. But if Father Artioli had stopped singling me out for that special greeting, I would have been crushed.

"What do you want to be when you grow up?" was the sixty-four dollar question. I had thought about it and thought about it, I wanted to say the right thing. I wanted to be a close friend of Father Artioli. He was the only grown-up who really seemed to understand me.

"You know, Father, I think I would like to become a priest. A priest like you."

He didn't seem surprised at all. He didn't say a word. I thought at first he was saying something under his breath, like a prayer.

We walked down the church steps. It was summer vacation and not too many people were around.

"The sooner one hears the call, the sooner one can begin to prepare. It is never too soon," he said. Only then did he smile, as he began to outline the things I should study, the prayers I should learn. It began to sound very complicated. I must have frowned or looked perplexed because he immediately reassured me.

"You have nothing to worry about. If you have any worries, don't trouble your sleep about them. Bring them directly to me, either at the rectory or in confession. My door is always open. From now on one of my most important tasks as pastor here will be to be your spiritual director and regular confessor."

We walked toward the rectory. He assumed I was

32

coming inside to continue our little talk. He sat down
at his desk and I sat on the other side in a big chair.
I had a million questions. Now, with a spiritual director of my own, I didn't have to depend on Bruce
Armitage at Sunday school or Father Di Primio with
his fast three Hail Marys. I had a personal confessor
just like kings, queens and saints.

"Gabe, we could talk all night," Father Artioli finally said. "How about a nice cool glass of soda. What
kind would you like?"

I followed him across the foyer from his office to
the rectory dining room. Lots of fellows, band members, altar boys and committee members had been to
the pastor's office. But I was being invited into the
real inside of the rectory, the living part where Father
Moscati was shot. Wait until I tell Bernie Hagerty
about this, I thought.

Mrs. Zita Artioli was sitting there, with her glasses
on, reading the *Daily News*. Mother's paper. Her black
hair was streaked with grey, very plainly done up in
a bun at her neck. I had never seen her this close before. She seemed tired, but very aloof. Very different
from the women of the parish. She gave the impression of having been somebody. I had heard that her
husband once had a very famous restaurant in Greenwich Village in New York. Some said Father Artioli
had a hernia from carrying bootleg booze on the subway to his father's restaurant. His father had been
dead for a while and his mother and sister Elda lived
with him at the rectory. Elda worked for the National
Broadcasting Company at Radio City, and Frank
Scapuletti, her fiancé, the parish sacristan, drove over
to Manhattan every afternoon in his car to bring her
safely home. It was a very close family. And here I
was right in the middle of it.

"Mother, I want you to meet Gabe Longo," Father
Artioli said. I had never been introduced to her, and I

was very concerned about making the proper impression.

"Good evening, Mrs. Artioli," I said. "It's a great honor to meet you."

They looked at one another and smiled.

"The honor is ours, this evening at least, Mother," Father Artioli said. "Gabe and I have been having a very serious talk. He has decided he wants to become a priest."

His mother put down her paper, raised her eyes to heaven, and made some kind of sign.

"God is good," she said. "Who can know how happy your mother must be? Who can know?"

I wasn't sure what to say. It was a little sudden. I didn't want to tell her my mother had no idea yet of what was going on and she might be very opposed when she found out. Though I didn't expect what we talked about in the rectory to be covered by the seal of the confessional, I wasn't ready to talk to Father Artioli's mother about it before I had a chance to talk to my own. But it was too late now.

"Yes, I thought we would celebrate by having a Coca-Cola with Gabe," Father Artioli said.

"Please be seated," she said to me as she disappeared into the kitchen. (The kitchen where Father Moscati was found dead. Wait until Bernie hears about this!)

She returned in a moment with two long-stemmed wine glasses and two paper napkins. Then she brought a beautiful silver ice bucket and silver tongs.

I couldn't help admiring it. "Yes, it is a lovely piece," Mrs. Artioli said. "It was a gift to my son on his ordination. So many beautiful gifts. Wait," she smiled, "you'll see."

"Mother, you're not drinking with us?" Father Artioli said. When he insisted, she brought another glass. I was too excited to notice what they were drinking. Mine tasted something like Coca-Cola, but I was sipping so slowly there wasn't much taste to it. The idea of drinking in the rectory dining room with Father Artioli and his mother was intoxication enough.

When a door slammed in the rear of the rectory, Father Artioli called out and his new young assistant, Father Fanelli, joined us.

Then it got embarrassing. When Father Artioli had asked me before why I wanted to become a priest, I was stuck for an answer. I honestly didn't know. All I knew was that in some way I wanted to be like him. But I couldn't say that. I didn't have anything in the way of a speech which made any sense.

On the spur of the moment I had changed the subject. Father Fanelli was interested in music; when he joined the parish he had announced he was instituting a musical comedy program. I was interested in the band and in music. So I said Father Fanelli made me realize that one could reach people for Christ in all kinds of ways—even through musical comedy, which interested me greatly.

Instead of keeping this to himself, Father Artioli made it into a big bouquet for his assistant. He told him I had decided to be a priest as a result of my admiration for him.

Actually I didn't admire him at all. I thought he was sort of a lightweight and I hadn't seen any of his productions yet. But now it was too late. It was my story. They believed it and I was stuck with it.

I wanted to talk to him about the problem of my folks. How to get them to agree. But every time I brought it up, Father Artioli would smile and say:

"You just tell your parents that I'll be around to see them and explain everything."

He didn't know what a rough time he was in for. But his father had him carrying bootleg booze on the subway before he went to the seminary. From what I heard his father was one of those Italians who never went to church even on feast days. So maybe he *could* handle my parents.

But he seemed very sure of himself. "You just tell your parents I'll be around to see them one day and explain everything."

"Yes, Father," was all that I could say.

I was a little nervous when I started walking the eight blocks home from the rectory, but as I picked up speed I began to feel more assured. This was the first big decision I had ever made. I wasn't asking them if I could switch from public high school to Seton Hall. I knew Mother and Dad well enough to know they would scream and holler. But I wasn't asking them to agree with me. I was *telling* them that this was it.

It was almost nine o'clock when I got home. The kitchen was empty so I got some scissors to trim the fuzz off my chin in the mirror over the sink. But I kept thinking about the scene at the rectory instead of watching the scissors. When I saw the blood on my shirt collar I passed out cold on the floor.

When I came to, Dad had me propped up in a chair with a cold towel on my forehead. When I smiled he smiled. Then he dabbed the blood off my face with his handkerchief. I could see I had scared him half to death. At first he didn't know what had happened—he had just heard a noise and when he came into the kitchen, there I was out cold on the floor.

I decided to take advantage of the accident. Mother and Dad were sitting there watching me, a little worried. I swallowed hard and gave it to them.

"I just had a long talk with Father Artioli at the rectory," I said. "I decided I want to switch this fall from Dickinson to Seton Hall."

"Seton Hall?" Mother repeated, as if I were still unconscious or dreaming. "How can you go to Seton Hall? It costs too much money."

"How much can it cost?" Dad asked.

"Forty cents a day for two buses, maybe a little more for books and school expenses, the rest I can get on a scholarship. Father Artioli will explain everything."

I had begun bravely but I was already retreating, leaving it all to Father Artioli.

"What has to be explained?" Dad wanted to know. "It's not a question of money."

"Well, there are lots of other things involved, Dad. He'll come over any time it's convenient. You just tell me when you're free and I'll invite him."

"He's a very busy fellow," Dad said. "You ask him to tell us when *he's* free. Our door is always open."

"But Dad I think it would be nice if we could invite him to dinner."

"Why should he want to come here to dinner?" Mother asked. "He doesn't go visiting even to homes of people active in the parish. Why should he want to come here?"

"So you can get acquainted."

"Why do I need to get acquainted?" Dad wanted to know.

"Because tonight he agreed to become my spiritual advisor, Dad," I said. "I decided I want to be a priest."

"A what?" Mother laughed.

"Fine," Dad said. "Let's have the pastor to dinner, Julia. We'll tell him to his face the boy is fourteen."

"Fifteen," I corrected him.

"Fifteen years old. That's no age to decide anything. We'll have him to dinner, Julia, and tell him to his face we won't permit it."

"I've never had a priest to dinner," Mother said. Already she was planning. "I wonder what I should have?"

"For bad news, give him a good dinner," Dad said.

"I like your nerve," Mother said. "The two of you."

I said I wasn't feeling too well so I went to bed early. I could hear them talking in the kitchen for hours. It was as though I had come down with spinal meningitis.

The first time Father Artioli dropped by our house Dad was home alone, and treated him like the Fuller Brush man. He told him my mother was shopping downtown with Bernie and Kay.

When Mother got home she was all excited. "There I was in Woolworth's with your brother Bernie dripping ice cream at the counter and Kay making a mess of butter pecan on her yellow dress and who comes through the store looking for me. Your spiritual advisor! He said he came by the house. But whatever possessed your father not to talk to the man and send him searching after me, I'll never know. What happened to Joe and Willie, did they fly the coop?"

Willie and Joe were two boys from Mt. Carmel who had gone to the seminary. In the entire history of the parish, no one had ever been ordained. Italian parishes wanted Italian priests but they didn't produce them. They couldn't be imported forever.

"What did you tell him, Mother?" I wanted to know.

"What could I tell him?" She laughed. "I told him, while he was talking to me about nipping your vocation in the bud and denying God a priestly son, my other two children were getting sloppy. 'Please leave us, Father,' I told him, 'and come back another time when my children don't have ice cream dripping down their arms.'

"Imagine, right in the middle of Journal Square he's giving me a sermon. They must need priests badly, that's all I've got to say. Robbing the cradle."

"The seminaries are full, Mother, but they're mostly Irish."

"That's their problem," Mother said. "They can't afford to give their children an education, that's their problem."

Negotiations, I decided, were getting off to a bad start, so before going to bingo, I dropped by the rectory. Mrs. Artioli answered the door. Instead of asking me to step into the waiting room, she ushered me right into the dining room. I felt pretty important now. It was one thing for Father Artioli to ask me into the living part of the rectory, but now it seemed automatic.

I had my little speech all rehearsed inviting Father Artioli to dinner.

"I think if you're going to talk to my parents it ought to be real soon, Father," I began. "Otherwise there will be too much confusion."

"That's very wise, Gabe," he said. "How would it be if I came to your house for dinner on, let's say, Thursday?"

Before I could invite him he had invited himself. I wished we had a telephone so I wouldn't have to run eight blocks to let my mother know. I knew she would be furious if she didn't find out until after bingo.

Mother cooked and cleaned for two days. The house was spotless. The antipasto was arranged on the silver trays; the clear chicken soup was simmering; the baked ziti with mozzarella was in the oven; the stuffed capon was waiting to be browned; the cranberries, the peas, the sweet potatoes, and the asparagus had all been assigned to their proper dishes; the good silverware was out and the lace tablecloth; the fruit was beautifully arranged in the bowl; the special wine was ready; the nuts, the cannolli and sfogliatelli had been picked up hardly an hour before. Bernie and Kay were dressed to the nines. Mother had on a new dress under her apron. Dad had shaved again when he came home from work and I was in the window on the lookout, when Father Artioli's big black De Soto parked in front of the house.

Dad was very polite and correct but it was clear from every line of his powerful six foot body that no priest was going to tell him what his son ought to do.

Father Artioli didn't seem the slightest bit embarrassed. He knew the objections he had to overcome. He had been through this many times before. His own father hadn't gone to church either; this must have been a problem to him all his life. He knew what he was doing.

From the way Mother acted, one knew Dad was going to have to carry the ball alone. This was a party and she was a party girl. All her opposition melted as soon as the wine was poured. She was going to have something special to report when the girls came on Monday.

I knew Father Artioli was smooth, but you couldn't help admiring the way he conducted himself that night. He really had class. He was used to having dinner with mayors and bishops and rich people because he knew exactly how to behave.

He began showering compliments the way Father Di Primio scattered Holy Water. Every compliment for me he delivered directly to my parents, as if I wasn't even there. Every compliment for my Mother and Father he delivered to me, as if they weren't there.

After fifteen minutes we began to feel like the luckiest family he ever visited. When he said he was eating moulded Jello salad for the first time, Mother practically came apart.

The ugly confrontation I had expected seemed to become remote and impossible. Father Artioli was a friend of the family, interested in me. If I felt I wanted to be a priest, no one but God and possibly His Blessed Mother had the right to interfere. Certainly one could not expect a priest of God to try and discourage a brilliant boy like mé from wanting to do God's work. That I was young was beyond dispute—far too young to make a decision. But nobody was suggesting any final commitment—certainly not he.

It was merely that in case I *were* to become a priest I would need the best possible preparatory education. Seton Hall also offered the best possible education to prepare any boy for college. If in two years I changed my mind, I would have the solid grounding I needed to get admitted to the best colleges in the state. Father Artioli would see to that.

The extra cost of tuition at Seton Hall was a matter which the Parish Scholarship Fund would take care of. Since my parents were not sure they approved of this step, they should not be asked to make further sacrifices. He would insist on handling the arrangements.

After Father Artioli had finished, Mother looked at Dad and Dad looked at me. There was absolutely nothing to argue about. I had been singled out for a marvelous educational opportunity. It would be ridiculous for anyone to deny that.

It would be like having the winning card at bingo and arguing with the management over whether you should accept the prize.

mcmxlii

IN THE ORIENT they used to separate schoolboys from girls at the age of seven to intensify identification with their own sex and their interest in the opposite one.

When I made the switch in the autumn of 1942 from the free-and-easy girls-galore atmosphere of Dickinson Public High School to the sealed-off minor seminary atmosphere of Seton Hall Preparatory School, it turned out to be a big change, bigger than I bargained for.

High school was full of women teachers and neighborhood girls. I took them for granted. Seeing them all the time, I never looked at them at all.

In Seton Hall, the teachers were all men, many of them clergy. You never saw a skirt from 8:30 until 3:30 except through a window. And if you spotted a female walking past on the campus outside, it was a big moment.

I didn't have the slightest interest in sex in public high school. Once I got into special category as a divinity student at Seton Hall, suddenly the whole sealed-out world reeked of it.

There were other changes. Public grade school in Jersey City had been like an extension of the parish.

It was almost completely Italian except for a few Jewish boys and girls. Norm Zeller and Sol Bernstein were the guys you had to beat if you wanted top grades. They were completely outnumbered and they had the drive that comes from that.

At Dickinson High School was a more motley group. Still, all the boys and girls from the parish went there; it was almost half Italian. But Seton Hall had prep school students and pre-seminarians from all four New Jersey counties of the Newark Diocese: Irish, German, Polish, English. There was only one other Italian boy in my class, and he was there only because he belonged in the territorial parish. Besides, his mother was Irish.

Public high school had been a breeze as far as studies were concerned. Seton Hall was a grind. I had never had any Latin, so I had to take two years' work during my first year, to catch up. It reached the point where I never went anywhere without my Latin grammar— I even had it on my lap at night when I worked at bingo. Fortunately my Latin teacher was a former classmate of Father Artioli who had left the seminary, married, and come back to Seton Hall later as an instructor. He was a very devout man and a great teacher, who took a special interest in me because I was one of Artioli's boys.

I came to Greek cold, but so did most of the other boys.

In addition to other subjects like English, math, and history, we had at least three hours a week of spiritual direction. Lectures and talks by faculty clergy and outside priests—intensive doses of scripture, liturgy and doctrine.

I rarely had time to think about where I was headed, I was so concerned about not flunking out along the way. I couldn't flunk out. It would be too much of a disappointment to Father Artioli.

On registration day, Father Artioli had driven me

43

to Seton Hall. He had introduced me to all the instructors and the priests as one of his boys. He had made his mark there—he was still remembered for having had the highest grades in the place in his time. I couldn't let him down.

It got to be a rough schedule. I left home every morning at 6:45, took two buses or a train to get to South Orange. I was never home before four. I studied like crazy for two hours, had a quick dinner and then ran with my Latin book in hand to work bingo until after eleven. I studied until I fell asleep. Then I was up at six to make sure I didn't miss the bus. I hardly saw my parents except at breakfast and dinner; and then it was hello and goodbye.

If I had problems, I took them to the rectory. They were the kind of problems only Father Artioli knew anything about anyway. The rectory was my second home. I was excited the first time I was invited to dinner there, then it got to be a habit and I took it for granted. It was a little more elegant than home, but always a bit stiff. Besides, with only two nights off a week, and plenty of money in my pocket, I had more exciting things in mind. Like girls.

I talked to Father Artioli about it but he never took me very seriously. "Oh, Gabriel," he would say, "what am I going to do with you?" He would remind me how young I was. He talked about it as though it were something I had to get out of my system. He would talk about the power of prayer and then as my spiritual advisor he gave me blanket permission to date.

In clerical circles that was the expression: you couldn't find it in the catechism and I was never exactly sure what it meant. Dating covered that entire expanse of no-man's land between never seeing girls at all and going the whole way, whatever that was. Necking involved the head and shoulders—kissing and soul kissing and other occasions of sin like that. Petting was anything that involved you from the shoulders down. Much more serious than necking.

Most of the pre-seminary students at Seton Hall didn't have my kind of problems because they had Irish spiritual advisors who never gave blanket permission. They had to get specific permission before they could even telephone for a date. The spiritual advisor would want to know who the girl was, where they were going to meet, what movie they expected to see, where they were going for sodas afterward, and what time her mother insisted she get home. They would have to go to all that trouble beforehand, and then when they called up a girl she wouldn't be home. Or she would be busy. So they would have to start all over again with another special permission to call up another girl. No wonder most of them got discouraged and had hernias or such as our Sunday school teacher, performed other private ministrations.

Having blanket permission to date girls set me off from my classmates at Seton Hall. It was like being the first one in your block to drive a car. I didn't realize what a liberal Father Artioli was until later. About some girls, he was much more liberal than my mother.

Especially Angela.

The first time I committed a mortal sin against the sixth commandment was with Angela in Father Artioli's black De Soto. Actually—like all my sins against the sixth commandment in those years—it happened in my head.

Angela was a year older than I and she taught Sunday school as I did. But I was already shaving regularly and tall enough to pass for 17 so that didn't get in the way. She was petite and she was musical—in fact she later sang the lead in one of Father Fanelli's parish productions. She had the beat. She could dance the Lindy and the Jitterbug and the Montclair. She had dark hair and a large nose but what set her off from the other girls at the CYO dances was a certain subtlety with which she moved her behind. If there were sixty girls dancing on the floor, Angela was the one to watch.

Father Fanelli used to tease me about her. Some of the CYO boys reported that according to the grapevine Angela had the hots for me. She had heard I had been dating girls from St. Aloysius parish at dances they had given for the Seton Hall boys. This was a wild exaggeration, of course, but I wouldn't think of denying it.

I was never much of a dancer. Whenever I heard dance music I was usually too busy listening to what the E flat saxophone was doing. Angela took over and tried to be my tutor. While the married chaperones smiled in approval she put me through the paces.

It didn't take long for word of this to reach my Mother. She decided that Angela was out to seduce me. When Mother spoke to me about it I reminded her that Father Artioli had given me permission not only to go to CYO dances but to date.

"That's not what I'm worried about," Mother complained. "What worries me is that Angela has six sisters and only one about to be married. So she's got more permissions than you have, that's what I'm talking about."

Mother was so suspicious of Angela she appointed my younger brother Bernie my probation officer. She sent him to all the dances to watch me and report to her. If he saw me going off anywhere with Angela, he was supposed to follow and keep me out of trouble.

I adored Bernie but nobody likes to be chaperoned by his younger brother. I used to give him some rough times.

Naturally it was extremely flattering to be the object of so much surveillance. Whenever anybody teased Angela about me, twitted her about robbing the cradle, or tempting a young boy on his way to the priesthood, she had a very saucy answer: "I did it and I'm glad."

That got to be a running gag around the parish. Any time Father Fanelli saw me, instead of saying, "Hello, Gabe," he would say, "I did it and I'm glad," and collapse laughing at his own joke.

Everybody was laughing about it, but nothing much was happening. There was so much commotion I was practically shot-gunned into doing something to justify it.

Taking Angela home from a parish affair didn't afford much room for maneuvering. It should have made Bernie's job easy—she lived around the corner from the rectory. I walked her there and while Bernie stood out in the cold with his stop watch, I met her mother and her sisters, had a "coke," and walked home.

But later on I got bolder and asked Angela if she had ever had a ride in Father Artioli's black De Soto, which he had given me permission to drive when I couldn't get Dad's car. That did it. Before I knew what was happening, she had her coat on. I made her wait in the checkroom while I got the keys. Then she walked home alone and I picked her up there in five minutes. This way we gave Bernie the slip.

After I finished showing off the car, I was stuck for an encore. I knew she expected me to attempt some kind of sin against the sixth commandment but I wasn't sure how to begin.

One of the gaps in my education was that I never made the transition from dirty comic books to Legion of Decency movies. I never could stand the movies. The result was anything Clark Gable or Robert Taylor or even poor awkward Jimmy Stewart had to teach me, I missed.

So I was on my own. I suggested we stop somewhere for a sandwich and a soda. I took care to park the big De Soto in a dark lot. While we were eating I tried to figure out how to start necking. I knew what to do in theory: I had learned all about what *not* to do in Sunday school. But now that I had a chance, I didn't know how to get started.

When we got back into the car, as I was starting the motor, I reached over to Angela's side to make sure the door was locked. She grabbed me and I could feel greasy lipstick all over my mouth. It tasted horrible, like some kind of cough medicine.

I was so surprised I reached for the emergency brake.

"There," Angela said, "I did it and I'm glad."

"I'm glad too, Angela," I said bravely.

"You'd never know it," she said.

She had challenged my Italian manhood so I grabbed her and started saying Hail Marys at the same time. It occurred to me that in all the seminars about soul kissing, nobody had had much to say about the lipstick you might run into, which seemed to me to be the main thing.

We necked and necked until I was tempted to start petting. I think she was tempted too. I put my arms around her and began gently rubbing her back and shoulders. She leaned forward invitingly. But I had never petted and I didn't know where to begin. Everything I was doing I could have done on the dance floor at the CYO and the chaperones would have smiled—except for the kissing of course. But I was busy trying to figure whether I was getting a petting kind of pleasure out of it.

Was rubbing her neck intended to produce sensual pleasure? If it wasn't, I could relax. If it produced only as much pleasure as I thought I was licensed by my spiritual advisor, I was okay. If it produced more, I

48

was in dangerous waters and better start the Hail Marys.

All this concentration got to be exhausting. Fortunately a police car pulled into the parking lot and flashed its lights on us. I straightened up and looked at myself in the rear view mirror. Angela didn't wear very much make-up. Nobody did in those days. But I seemed to be covered with it.

She grabbed the handkerchief out of my pocket and handed it to me.

I started wiping my brow.

"Not there, silly," she giggled. Then she grabbed the handkerchief and began daubing at my jowls.

I took her home to her mother, had another soda, returned the car to Father Artioli, threw away the handkerchief and began making mental notes for my next confession.

It was really my first big sin against the sixth commandment and I looked forward to confessing it in some detail. Especially about rubbing her shoulders and back and whether the sensual pleasure induced by that had been too long extended or not.

I tried to clear up the whole thing the next time I went to confession to Father Artioli. But I had never done any petting and apparently neither had he. We went round and round. I was trying to build up the incident into a *thing* and he kept trying to cut it down to fit the catechism. Finally he said, "Oh, Gabriel, what am I going to do with you?" As a penance for my sins he gave me some Hail Marys and ordered me to chauffer him to Jersey City Medical Center where he had to make a sick call. While I was waiting, I was supposed to study my Latin. And that was the end of that.

I was halfway through my penance before I remembered that I had forgotten to tell him the whole thing happened in his black De Soto.

Angela and I tortured each other and our respective spiritual advisors for years. Finally, after she had become the soubrette of the parish musical comedy theatre group and a successful secretary in Jersey City, and I was pretty well along in my studies, Angela looked me square in the eye and said: "Gabe, when are you going to throw in the towel?"

I wasn't sure what she meant.

My spiritual fortitude compounded of fear of hellfire, fast Hail Marys, and fear of doing some dumb thing, was a threat to any girl's most precious notion about herself that she is irresistible. Either she meant I was not her idea of a would-be priest, or I was not her idea of a would-be boyfriend.

My blanket permission to date, at Seton Hall, helped to keep me out of the hermit's life lived by so many minor seminarians. Since part of the student body at Seton Hall follows a regular Catholic college course, they are subject to fewer restrictions and encouraged to pick up some of the social graces.

In my second year at college, I was elected secretary of the student governing body. In that capacity, I was up to my ears in many intercollegiate activities—one of them being social director and fixer in charge of boy-meets-girl; I picked up know-how little by little (all of it theoretical) on manners and morals among Catholic girls. I handled the delicate negotiations for delivery of male bodies to the boring tea dansants given by the nuns at nearby girls' Catholic colleges.

Divinity students were usually never invited. But here again I was the exception—along with members of the Schola Cantorum, the Seton Hall group which occasionally went along to sing at intermission.

By the time the entertainment ended and the mixing and dancing began, the young Catholic ladies had usually figured out from the way we huddled together which of us were marked for the priesthood. The girls would gossip and titter and finally a couple of brazen ones would insist that we dance with them. The future priests seemed always to attract the liveliest and best-looking girls. They wouldn't leave us alone. I began to understand what our Sunday school teacher had been talking about. It wasn't just his Irish and his hernia that had caused him to feel threatened.

Dancing with an ordinary boy who's too short for you, who can't dance to begin with—what could be more boring? But holding hands and rubbing tummies with a future priest is something else. Since thinking about it can leave you in as much peril of hellfire as doing it, whatever "it" was, the presence of a few seminarians could turn any boring dansant into a jungle of temptation. For a few moments at least, it gave any plain Jane a chance to play Sadie Thompson.

When a friend was working in a political campaign and wanted to attract girls for some shindig, he wanted to promise them men would be there. Since Seton Hall was a veritable warehouse of male bodies, he telephoned me.

Nurses, especially Catholic nurses, were supposed to be very hot numbers. So I called Orange Memorial Hospital and spoke to the Director of Social Affairs. I promised her that Seton Hall boys would show up at the political doings, and within fifteen minutes we didn't have enough cars to pick up the girls. When I told the non-Divinity students at school, they were thrilled. As anyone who ever spent time in the locker room of a Catholic football team can tell you, nurses are guaranteed to give you something to confess.

That night after the shindig, I took one of the nurses to a drive-in. She was a beautiful girl, sweet and angelic. But as soon as I parked, she grabbed my hand

and stuffed it inside her blouse. I was shocked. I yanked out my hand so fast that her blouse tore right down the front.

"Oh, I'm so sorry," I said. She just sat there. I started to say that I was studying for the priesthood but then I decided not to bother.

When I began to look in the glove compartment, she said, "What are you after?"

"I think there might be a safety pin in here somewhere."

"Oh," she said. "How exciting."

I was trying to back off without hurting her feelings.

"Look," I explained. "I don't really want to get involved. You're such a nice girl."

"That's what you think," she said. "If I was, I'm giving it up for tonight."

I was finally compelled to take refuge in my vocation. I explained what it meant to me. That only got me in deeper. It seemed to drive her crazy with excitement. She began pawing me and I started the Hail Marys.

After I got out of that situation, I began to think maybe the blanket permission to date wasn't such a good idea. It was more a torture than a privilege. I decided to speak to Father Artioli when we had plenty of time.

Maybe we should work out a system like the other guys had, where they had to clear each date beforehand. I could warn him about how dangerous the nurses were and ask him to prohibit me from seeing them.

I let it go until summer vacation. When he invited me to spend some time with him at his cottage at Seaside Heights, right on the ocean, I decided that was the place to discuss it.

We were going to have an entire week to ourselves, Father Artioli told me. His mother wasn't coming out until later. Willie and Joe would be on vacation from the seminary and they would join us. We would be bachelors, doing our own cooking and cleaning.

The invitation to spend a vacation with our pastor was exciting enough, but to be a foursome with Willie and Joe, guys in their twenties who had been through the seminary ropes that were ahead of me—this gave me a feeling of really being in.

It was a beautiful spot, between the ocean and Barnegat Bay. The cottage had a nice living room, a porch, two bedrooms and a dorm in the attic with a pulldown stairway.

But we spent most of our time on the beach.

This was the first time I had ever seen a priest in bathing trunks. I was surprised that he looked no different from anybody else. He could have been my older brother. Joe and Willie, too, were regular guys. They enjoyed sports and swimming and we had a great time. Joe considered himself a ladies' man. Everyone talked about the girls in the parish he left with broken hearts when he went to the seminary.

I felt so grown-up, so flattered to be taken seriously by these fellows six years or more older than I. I even started smoking. I didn't want to be left out of anything.

Every morning we drove with Father Artioli to the church at Seaside Park where he said Mass. We all assisted and all received Communion from him. This was my first experience at receiving Communion every day. Everything was built-in. If I had gotten into trouble or had any impure thoughts I could confess in the car on the way to Mass in the morning. But all the things that had been bothering me in the city seemed to vanish in the ocean air. The nurses, Angela, the college girls, the dances, the necking, the petting, it all seemed too far away; it seemed ridiculous to think of bringing it up.

I had often gone to the beach on vacation with my family. But this was something different. Father Artioli made it very clear I could spend as much time there in the summer as I wanted to. I hated to spoil things by bringing up any of my silly problems with girls, or asking him to change the rules to protect me from myself.

One day when I was discouraged in general and over my geometry marks in particular, Father Artioli said, "Oh, Gabriel, what am I going to do with you?"

It was usually a question without an answer. But that day he tossed me the keys to the car and said, "I know what we'll do. It's time I showed you around."

"Around where?" I wanted to know.

"It's a beautiful day. Let's take a drive to Darlington."

Darling was the name of the original owners of the castle and 1400-acre estate that stretched across two rolling green mountains of the Ramapo chain. Later the estate passed to the Macmillan publishing family for a number of years, and eventually was sold to a syndicate which turned it into an exclusive country club.

Then, Father Artioli told me, it fell on bad days just as the Archdiocese was scouting for a major secluded seminary plant. The entire seminary system from the high school freshman level to the priesthood had until then been housed at Seton Hall, which was bursting at the seams. After Bishop McLaughlin was shown the Macmillan estate, he buried a statue of St. Joseph on the premises and started everyone praying that the diocese would be able to buy it. Their prayers were answered and the estate became the Immaculate Conception Seminary. The mansion, complete with a giant pipe organ, had been turned into luxurious classrooms, libraries and recreation rooms. Dormitories and chapel were built separately in an expanse separated from the main estate by fabulous formal gardens that had been nurtured and tended since the good old days.

The place was a world in itself, completely surrounded by mountains and woods, crystal streams, the Ramapo River with a private beach of its own, football fields, baseball diamonds, and great expanses of wild untouched wooded country.

The opulence and elegance of another day had survived, and liturgical frosting added. The dormitory buildings mocked the designation. Each seminarian had his private quarters, with a bath between each two apartments shared by the "chateau-mates."

Bishops and archbishops, whatever their strength in areas of the spirit, are usually men of advanced years and prone to certain physical weaknesses—especially fatigue of the kidneys. So in the Newark diocese at least, all temporal premises which enjoyed the patronage of the bishop tended to a certain lavishness in the number of toilets.

Not the least of these was the seminary. Everywhere you turned, indoors or out, there was another toilet.

I couldn't have been more impressed. The luxury, the style, the aura of the place topped anything I had seen anywhere. It was a place where the rich and famous had walked and played.

Father Artioli's presence opened every door. It must have taken him two hours to show me everything and introduce me to everybody.

As soon as he was spotted on the premises, his boys (the two seminarians Willie and Joe from our parish) were sprung from their daily chores and joined us on the grand tour. It was the first time I had seen them in their black cassocks and their Roman collars. The severity and the elegance of their outfits seemed to go with the surroundings. I felt out of place in my baggy tweeds and my heavy brown shoes that seemed to make such a racket on the shiny inlaid parquet floors.

"Well, Gabe," Father Artioli said after a while, "you haven't had much of anything to say. What do you think of it?"

I stuttered and stammered. I was speechless and couldn't explain it. "God is good," he said. "Here you will spend some of the happiest days of your life."

"I don't doubt it, Father," I said. And I didn't, not one bit.

Calling it "the Rock," as the guys at Seton Hall sometimes did, suddenly seemed like a sacrilege.

When I got home that night I couldn't get the seminary out of my mind. Already guys I knew were enlisting, or being drafted into the army. I had gotten my vocation before the draft ever came. Otherwise I might have felt guilty. If either of my two older brothers had lived, they would have been old enough for the draft. The worst that could possibly happen to me was, if the war went on forever, I might have to do duty as a chaplain.

Suddenly the most significant aspect of our family confabs was the thing that was never mentioned. Dad never made any more speeches opposing my continuing toward the priesthood.

In the early forties there were worse places for me to be than the seminary—far worse. That went without saying.

"Are you still dating girls?" the Bishop asked.

It was D-day for thirty prospective seminarians at Seton Hall College. We waited in line in the administration building while Bishop Boland, the rector of the seminary, pored over our files and then interviewed each of us privately. Alphabetically I was in the middle of the line. I knew that would be one of the questions so I was not surprised.

"Yes, Your Excellency," I replied. "But I'm sure the

file will show that I have permission from my spiritual advisor and. . . ."

He cut me off. "When was your last date?" he said bluntly.

"Last evening, Your Reverence. I took Marilyn to a basketball game and. . . ."

He cut me off again. "Do you intend to continue dating girls while you pursue your seminary studies?" Before I could answer he re-phrased the question. "Or to put it another way, how long do you intend to continue dating girls?"

"Well, Your Reverence, until my spiritual advisor offers objections I imagine, Your Reverence," I said. "But I certainly know I can't date once I'm in Major Seminary." The Bishop dropped the subject at that point. And there were no other questions. The way he received me and dismissed me, I got the feeling I might never be admitted.

When I walked out of the office, the guys at the tail end of the line asked, "Any trick questions? What does he want to know about?"

"Girls," I told them. They looked at me as if I were joking.

I went down to the deserted locker room in the basement to pick up some dirty gym clothes. The Bishop had made me feel like a reprobate. Not because of anything he said—it was the way he stared at me, with a kind of sniff. Our talk hadn't been man-to-man at all. It hadn't been relaxed and pleasant or warm like my meeting with Father Artioli. I was used to talking to priests on my own level. With Father Artioli you got the feeling that he was really your spiritual father. He treated you like his son. There was some kind of love there.

The Bishop had acted more like an Irish judge. He treated me as if I had been arrested as a sex maniac.

I opened my locker and grabbed my dirty laundry.

The door of the locker was scrawled with hundreds of names of former Seton Hall boys dating to before 1900. I never bothered to look at them closely until now. After I did, I took out my pen, picked a spot between John Barrymore and Will Durant—two famous names Seton Hall never boasted about—and I squeezed in my signature.

mcmxlvi

The cycle of vocations continues as proof of our pastor's zealous efforts to foster vocations to the priesthood among Italian-American boys. The latest "recruit" to serve in the Army of God for the salvation of souls is Gabriel Longo of Pavonia Avenue, who left Monday, July 8th, for the Immaculate Conception Seminary in Darlington, New Jersey, to study for the Holy Priesthood. Gabriel will begin his seminary career as he enters the Junior Philosophy class, finishing his first two years of college training at Seton Hall, South Orange, N. J.

Gabriel has well manifested taste for matters pertaining to the Church in his enthusiastic participation in parochial affairs, particularly in the Sunday School, choral and athletic departments.

The Parish is one in wishing him the choicest of God's blessings and favors. May he be a credit to Mt. Carmel as his two predecessors of late.

FROM the very first day, from the archbishop on down to the lowest member of the junior philosophy class, rectors, faculty and students alike, the entire population of "the Rock" was divided into flits and non-flits. The flits may have had other names for us, I don't know. But to us this division was natural, obvious, taken for granted, and it colored every phase of seminary life.

Flits walked a certain way, talked a certain way, wore their piety on their sleeves, never took part in athletics except maybe as second team subs. They suffered in silence, aspired to be masterful monks, rated the designation as "prudent companions," and in most cases survived the six-year ordeal.

Non-flits walked like men, talked like men, took to sports as a great outlet, were in periodic conflict with rules and regulations, suffered visibly from girl problems, and often left or were driven back to civilian life by the inexorable, insufferable pressure of their glands.

The troubles which led to expulsion or departure were invariably caused by non-flits. The only kind of scandals the flits ever got into occurred inside the seminary and those were hushed up. Only once, and then before my time, had there been an open scandal involving two flits, one young and one older. It was referred to obliquely always, to underline the seriousness of the rule that no seminarian was ever allowed to step over the threshold of another seminarian's room. Any violation of that rule meant automatic expulsion. Most violations of the rule meant merely that you were *liable* to expulsion, which was something else.

The flits had developed or inherited the ability to think, to act, to feel, without ever involving their balls, so the seminary, like the army or navy or jail, was their natural element. I can't remember a single flit who left the seminary during my six years there. At the beginning there were 35 guys in my class. At the end there were 19. Of the 16 who left, all of them had balls of one kind or another. A few were fellows you couldn't imagine being of any help or example in anybody's priesthood, but most were wonderful guys who had been my friends. It wasn't very dramatic at the beginning; but later on when I was in a big tangle of doubt and confusion myself, it was always a shock to come to class and find that empty seat.

The empty seat would haunt the classroom for days. You always wanted to know why. If you knew the guy well enough, he told you before he left and you chatted with him and wished him well. But sometimes you got the story third hand, from his chateau-mate via someone else. If someone left from another class, you missed him at meals or in the locker room.

The more mysterious the departure, the more certain you could be that some girl was involved. Then the gossip would inevitably center about "I wonder what she's like. How could it be worth it?" We would all swear to do nothing that foolish. We would privately renew our determination. But the next empty seat usually belonged to the guy who had been most vehement in vowing it would never happen to him.

Our first course in basic training was intensive instruction in obedience to The Rule. We were drilled and examined and drilled some more, so any recourse to ignorance as an excuse for later violations might be extinguished right off the bat.

Our day was divided into periods of silence and periods when we could speak. The first casualty in our class was John, a wonderful guy, a real dead-end kid of marvelous vitality. The silent life drove him out of his mind. He couldn't sleep without the sound of trolley cars and automobiles, and after a year he threw in the towel.

Talking in the corridors was not permitted. We were not allowed to use the telephone without permission and then our reason had to be important. After the midday meal, the Dean of Discipline would go to his office to receive and process all requests for telephone calls, permission to see a doctor, anything at all.

There were some Holy Joes who took everything literally, but I was never one of those.

My Latin temperament showed from the very first day, so they paired me off with a Holy Joe as my first chateau-mate, a boy who was very trustworthy on The Rule. He was supposed to tone me down but he didn't even last through the first year.

I still feel sorry for the guys who left during those years. They clung to an ideal image of what a priest should be. They took that injunction about being "Another Christ" seriously; they honestly felt themselves wanting. In many cases, I felt, they were far worthier —and much more brutally honest—than those of us who stuck it out. They faced the contradictions. We went through the motions of prayer and meditation and relied on the promise of our spiritual advisors and confessors that one fine day we would achieve a kind of faith which could resolve all contradictions and all doubts.

When you enter the seminary, you are required to take out an insurance policy of $5,000 with the Archdiocese as the beneficiary. If you die, the Diocese gets back the money invested in you. Some guys who left were so conscientious they attempted to pay back at least part of the money spent on their education.

The day began at five-thirty with a buzzer that sounded like the honk of the Queen Mary. We had twenty minutes to get up, shave, say private prayers and pull ourselves together before we were due in the Chapel at five fifty-five. Anytime we stepped out of our rooms we were to be wearing our long black cassock and collar, unless we were on the athletic field or in the shower.

Morning prayer was a communal affair. The first prefect read prayers and we answered. Then there was a period for silent meditation and preparation for

Mass. Faculty priests alternated in celebrating Mass at the main altar. The rest took turns at side altars. Students alternated in serving Mass. We were expected to receive Communion every day except in case of serious illness.

After Mass there was a brief period for thanksgiving, first in public then in private. Then we returned in silence to our rooms for 15 minutes in which we were to make our beds and straighten up the room. Each group of ten or twelve bedrooms became a camerate (camera is Latin for bedroom) which was supervised by a prefect (a member of the deacon class: those in the last year before priesthood).

Electric bells signalled the silent procession to the refectory for breakfast. The prefect system continued at meals, where each deacon shepherded a table of eight. It was his job to enforce the rule of silence against whispering, to supervise table manners, referee disputes over leftover food and keep the gluttons from overdoing it.

Seminarians took turns waiting on tables. Food was served family-style at each table. The kitchen was staffed by married couples of middle age, usually displaced persons from Eastern Europe, Slovaks, Lithuanians and Poles. One wonderful lady, Mrs. Frannish, made me her favorite and was forever sneaking me special treats when I waited tables.

There was a big head-table at which the Dean of Discipline sat with the Spiritual Director of the seminary and the priest on duty, the equivalent of the army Officer of the Day. At breakfast the three sat in solitary splendor. At lunch and dinner they ate in private dining rooms catered by another kitchen where superior fare was prepared.

Each month we had a new place assigned at table. When we arrived for breakfast we remained standing until the priest on duty, who had been celebrant of the main Mass, said grace. When he finished his prayer, we answered "Deo Gratias." This was the signal that the *magnum silentium* was over. We could talk.

Magnum silentium had been in force since seven the night before. Since we had endured that for the good of our souls, it might have been wiser had the silence been extended through the meal for the good of our bodies. But no, we tried to talk and eat at the same time, wolfing down boring institutional food we didn't really like—bowls of stewed prunes for our bowels, hot cereal, pitchers of milk and coffee. If you saw hard boiled eggs and warm fresh rolls on the table, you knew it was Sunday.

Breakfast began at seven-thirty. There were no real rules governing the *manner* of our eating and drinking, like the strict ones Buddhists have for silence and chewing properly. One could leave when he was finished, simply by saying a silent thanksgiving and walking off. Since morning free time was at a premium, it was long on prayer and short on exercises for proper digestion. Nobody ever considered that the two could be combined or that the meal itself might be taken as a sacramental rite. Food was for the body. Prayer for the soul. The spiritual and the physical were one in reality but two in theory. And in the seminary, theory carried the day.

Classes began at eight-fifteen in the mansion building 250 yards away. Each class was an hour long and after each two-hour period we had a 15-minute breather during which smoking was permitted in specific areas reserved for this indulgence. One Polish seminarian made himself famous for managing to have a cigar going at all times in all the forbidden places. When he reported to the Dean of Discipline for reprimands, he would arrive smoking his stogie, leave it on the ledge of the transom overlooking the Dean's office, then retrieve it still warm, and go back to his room to smoke some more.

The angelus bell rang at noon and that meant the last morning class was over. We returned to our rooms for a moment and then to the chapel for spiritual reading and back to the refectory, standing until grace was said. Then came a reading from the martyrology performed by a lector or reader, usually a member of an advanced class which had already received minor orders. Each man took his turn. Some were real Charles Laughtons, extracting the last ounce of blood and gore out of vivid descriptions of tortured lives and deaths of the saints. The saints selected for our edification seemed to have been born of noble parents, taken the vow of virginity at the age of two, and died devoured by Roman animals or in some other gory way.

Then, if we were lucky, they brought on the rare roast beef or the meat loaf or roast pork, in thin transparent slices. Or, if it was Friday, sewer trout or whale tail, which nobody ever touched. We waited until it returned at supper time disguised as fish cakes which could be eaten if drowned in ketchup. Mashed potatoes, peas and succotash arrived with gruesome regularity. Ditto beets. About four meals a week were really edible. For the rest we had to improvise in between. We got baked noodles occasionally, and rice. What they called spaghetti and meatballs was so foreign to me, if they had called it "cous cous" I might have believed them. For dessert we usually got little slices of cake. Ice cream came on rare occasions. And then the inevitable pitchers of milk and coffee.

At the end of lunch or dinner, there were more readings and prayers, then a procession during the Benedicite, a long prayer blessing everything God made from *sol et luna*, the sun and moon, to *omnia quae moventur in aquis*, everything that moves in the

65

water, chanted in unison as we filed into our assigned places in Chapel.

The services concluded with prayers of thanksgiving; after, we were given a few moments for smoking in the first and third floor recreation halls. Nonsmokers had the second and fourth floor rec rooms with Ping-Pong tables, pool tables and radios.

Then afternoon classes began again for those who had them. For others there were assigned spiritual readings, examination of conscience, or private study in your room. All this until two-fifty.

Then came a compulsory hour outdoors. Nothing except the most inclement weather was an excuse for being caught under a roof during that hour. Wednesdays and Saturdays the compulsory outdoor period was a long one, from one-thirty until four-thirty.

Every day we had an optional extra hour to stay out, or to use for indoor activity. The outdoor periods became my solace.

There were leagues in all sports. We had our own beach on the Ramapo River, where a fieldstone wall had been built by some of the guys, sand filled in behind it with bathhouses and diving boards—the works. We carried our towels and could swim and dive for an hour.

Indoor sports were limited. The recreation rooms stocked only the most boring juvenile official Catholic publications. No daily newspaper. None of the magazines.

Since I was the seminarian most likely to succeed each day in getting permission to leave for the outside world on some real or imaginary errand, at lunch time or during the Benedicite, I was constantly taking orders —in Latin—for contraband from the outside world of Suffern, New York.

If Fat Tony leaned over the table at lunch and whispered "*Tempus*," that meant I was to bring him a copy of *Time* magazine. Someone would whisper as they passed me at prayers, "*Vita*," which meant *Life*, and "*Verum*" which was *True*. *Panis Angelicus* was angel food cake. *Bovum sin ossibus* was minute steaks for clandestine cooking in the woods; *Panis et canis* was hot dogs and rolls.

I never came back from one of my jaunts without three or four layer cakes, hot dogs and rolls to burn, plenty of bloody red meat and a pile of magazines. The trick was to arrive when everyone was in chapel. Mr. Winters, the regular cab driver, knew the seminary schedule like a railroad timetable. He would arrange my arrival right on the dot so I could sneak in with the contraband and stash it in my room. The customers would know the stuff was at hand when they saw me. They would turn up in the hallways outside my room to pick and pay.

The recreation period ended at four-thirty. We had a few minutes to clean up and return to the chapel for private spiritual readings and examination of conscience to prepare us for the actual ritual of confession later in the week. From there we went directly to supper, which was a carbon copy of dinner, except with a lighter menu. It began with grace while standing; when we were seated the lector read further selections from the lives of the saints. After supper, we had a final 15-minute smoking period—our last chance to talk before the *magnum silentium* which began at seven o'clock, when we ordinarily returned to our rooms to study until nine. Night prayers continued until nine-fifteen and then it was lights out.

Several spiritual advisors and members of the faculty and staff were available for hearing confessions every evening. As far as I was concerned it was a good thing, or I never would have been able to make Communion in the morning. Most nights I thought I had something to confess.

There was nothing hit-or-miss or haphazard about the examination of conscience we were trained to give ourselves. It had a regular format, as long and full of fine print as a government form. A schedule of virtues against which you were to measure your sins of omission. A schedule of vices against which you were to pose your day's deeds. Actions were one thing, but thoughts spoke louder than words in our sinning scale. And, of course, violations of the rule were matters for confession. So there I always had something to report.

I was constantly testing the rules, stretching them, breaking them and then becoming overcome with remorse at my own willfulness and sense of pride. Uncharitable thoughts about the Irish nationalist members of the faculty were always a running motif. Humility was always in short supply. I always had to admit to being unduly critical of my superiors. Whether I was attempting to be the best priest possible was my matter of concern. Obedience wasn't enough; it had to be cheerful; one had to want to obey one's superiors and to identify their orders with the will of God. Patience, prudence and charity didn't give me too much trouble. But the way I played fast-and-loose with the rule of obedience kept me in the confessional for inordinate amounts of time.

During retreats and special spiritual exercises, I made a concentrated effort to work out these problems. Perhaps the other seminarians *thought* they were sinning too or invented sins as I had done as a kid. And in that context, my cheerful obedience never stood out too conspicuously. I was always expecting, anticipating, almost begging for someone to lower the boom and tell me I was a hopeless reprobate. But it never happened. Instead I always got pious reassurance, which seemed to be rather empty and *pro forma*. I was seriously disturbed about my progress, but my advisors and confessors assured me that by constant prayer and work all my problems would dissolve in faith and grace.

The image of Christ was held before me constantly as something I would grow into. One day I would try it on like a new cassock and with the grace of God it would fit me. At that point I was supposed to be able to say, as Paul said, "It is no longer I who live, but Christ who lives in me."

One trouble was that the members of the faculty had all supposedly succeeded where I felt I was failing. They had apparently become Christs to somebody's satisfaction, perhaps their own. But I just couldn't see it. They seemed like a pretty wishy-washy bunch to me.

We were expected to grow under their auspices and influence, physically, intellectually and spiritually. Yet, at the same time, we were told that growth could best be accomplished by perfect conformity to the Rule. For me it was going to be a struggle.

At the conclusion of our first two years, we were to receive a B.A. degree. Then came four years of graduate study in the catechism, designed to prove the infallible authority of the Church upon which all doctrine and dogma rest.

The most brilliant man among my teachers never talked like a priest at all. He was our professor of logic and church history. He seemed to be a giant among the robots. His classes were so vivid, his insights and asides so memorable you didn't need notes to remember them. His acid contempt for exaggeration and sentimentality burned through layers of what Renan called "the rust of religion." The sentimental holy-picture-Sunday-school version of church history was stripped down to essentials; the idea of there being five thousand customers on hand for the miracle of the loaves and the fishes was to him too ridiculous for comment. The hordes of martyrs who theoretically died in early

69

Church days, he regarded as a lot of libel against the Roman lions and tigers. Only basic doctrine escaped his sand blasting. But then, that was not his field.

It soon became clear that the only foundation for the dogma of the Church was the same one which was supposed to turn up one day to fortify and validate my priestly career: faith. So I was to spend four years searching for an acceptable understanding of that five-letter word. It would take time for me to discover that faith could not be pursued frontally or searched for actively, that it was, like happiness and beauty and poetry, very will o' the wisp. Faith was a gift, a by-product of something else. But in order to achieve it I would, at the very least, have to have faith that it was attainable.

I knew, if I were going to find faith anywhere, it wouldn't be in chapel but in the open air, in the wilds and the woods that I loved. Most of the seminary guys were Irish city boys and afraid of the wild wild West around Darlington. That made it even more alluring to me. I could explore secret places, stake them out and then go in search of more without running into any familiar reminders of where I was. I wore my recreation greys and hiking boots and I was on my own.

One day I was deep in a new part of the woods, with nothing but the setting sun and the shadows to give me direction, when I suddenly spotted what I assumed was a mirage. On second thought, I was sure it couldn't be, because I would surely have dreamed up a girl in white tulle draping, not a strange little man like this one with a white pillow case in his hand.

"Greetings," I said at first. I thought he was probably some new faculty member I hadn't met. When I looked at his outfit I thought better of it. He was an experienced woodsman of some kind, I could tell from the mesh-lined, snake-proof boots that he wore. Only Gokey makes boots like that.

When he saw me looking at the boots he hauled out his credentials: a professional collector for the serpentarium of the Bronx Zoo. The famous municipal snake pit. And he had been out there in the woods every day for two weeks looking for specimens to replenish the collection.

"What kind are you looking for?" I asked him. He was in the market for hognoses, black racers, copperheads and timber rattlers.

"Well, then," I suggested, "I'll take you over to the ledge on the side of the orchard section, behind the reservoir where the snake dens are." He was grateful for the tip. He had been tracking without a map, snagging them the hard way. I showed him how to trap them by the dozens.

That's how I got into the serpent business. Collecting and wholesaling snakes from the sacred, holy and anointed seminary grounds was certainly a symbolic cosmic joke, but it never occurred to me at the time.

It was as profitable as mink farming. I made a deal with the Bronx Zoo representative. We selected a tree on the edge of the grounds. I would trap snakes according to his orders, slip them in a pillow case, tie the top and then nail them to the appointed tree. He would arrive regularly to pick up the merchandise, leaving my fee from the municipality in the bag: three to four dollars a head for the little fellows depending on their size and rarity. It was a handshake deal and the Bronx Zoo was as good as its word. Later, when I was in the hospital, I had to take on a partner to handle my end of the bargain.

Even stranger than this story—which I told no one except my confessor and my partner—were the legends that I picked up from senior seminarians. According to them, there was a motley tribe of uncivilized souls living just beyond the place called Tobacco Grove, our permissible outdoor smoking area. These people were called Jackson Whites, the official designation given them by sociologists and anthropologists who had attempted to study them.

History had passed them by; they lived in the Ramapo Mountains, descendants of criminals and convicts, refugees from the Revolutionary War, Hessian deserters from their British masters, slaves and Indians—a self-contained rural version of Skid Row. According to the stories, some of them ventured into the small towns from time to time to do odd jobs and minor chores, and then vanished again into their settlements. They lived as wild as the deer which shared their mountain retreat. The hatred of the Jackson Whites for deer hunters caused them to figure in many a woodsman's story. Hunters had been known to wander into their domain and remain missing for years. A Protestant minister was said to have driven into their territory with a loudspeaker spouting the biblical message of salvation, never to be heard from again. It was reported that my confessor, Father Dougherty, in his seminary days, had entered their domain in hopes of converting them. But when I asked him, he merely laughed. I suppose the shakier one's own faith has become, the more insistent is the urge to convert somebody else. That was the excuse I gave myself for striking out in search of them.

One afternoon I scaled Mountain Number Two in Hillburn and approached the area overlooking Pidgeon Rock near Suffern. As I came through the underbrush I heard a strange noise and I froze. A horse wandered along the path in front of me dragging a tripod made of young saplings. Tied to it was a human corpse. I was transported. It was an Indian funeral unchanged from hundreds of years ago.

Another day I got bolder and found a family, or at least a group of people together. They could have been man and wife or mother and son, there was no way of telling. Their language was barely understandable. The signs, their emotions were all we had in common. Many of them were strangely misshapen, with hydrocephalic heads, no eyes, and when they did have eyes there was no expression in them. They lived in little huts and lean-tos.

I always had my pockets full of contraband food. I gave them some hot dogs and rolls and a copy of *Time* magazine. They seemed very pleased. They knew I was a seminarian; that made the groundwork easy. I went back often and took them more food. I felt I was getting along great with them. One family practically adopted me. They called me by name and welcomed me like a relative.

I kept returning to their lost village whenever I was deeply troubled. If I wanted to save souls, I saw no need of going to Peru or the wilds of Brazil. There were enough souls in need of saving within a stone's throw of the seminary—including my own.

The seminary was self-contained in many ways. We had our own barber shop and it was decided that the seminarians could learn to cut one another's hair for a quarter, instead of paying a dollar to a union member. The barber shop looked to me like a likely center of life, so I volunteered. I took my turn on Tuesday afternoon, and learned how to please customers while staying within the rule that the trim had to be neat and tight without being extreme. I was giving Madison Avenue haircuts before they got that name.

Guys who needed haircuts had to sign up on a list in the recreation room, made out by the day. The Tuesday list got so long I became the clear favorite. Soon it was "by appointment only." Then the word got out and I began to get twenty-five cent customers among the faculty. They had to tip and we were allowed to keep the money. At the end of the term, guys who had worked in the barber shop were given leather bound breviaries—four books of the Holy Office, one for each season. That was a forty-five dollar tip right there.

Barbering, like photography, which I took up with a vengeance, became a welcome way of getting out of my room during the afternoon study period and seeing what was going on in the rest of the world— even if it was only the limited insular world of the Rock.

Jolly Jack Castle was our mentor and professor of homiletics. He was the example of what we were attempting to achieve when we mounted the pulpit. He had the only television set in the place. His ideal in turn was Monsignor Fulton Sheen—or Uncle Fultie— as we called him, after Miltie (Berle). When Fultie held forth every Sunday on the Catholic Hour on radio, his programs were piped all over the seminary on the P.A. system, like "big brother." Most of the seminarians adored him. He was the man our mothers expected us all to be.

Father Castle had that jolly Irish-priest manner right out of the movies. I couldn't stand it when Frank Mc-Hugh and Bing Crosby tried it and I found it no more attractive live.

Jolly Jack was not only a movie priest; he was the man who had to approve the movies that played the seminary circuit. No better clue to his taste could be imagined than the films we were shown. With the exception of "Gone With The Wind" and movies which starred Jeanne Crain or Joan Bennett—for whom I had a special "thing"—I was not much of a fan. But Jolly Jack's choices were a joke even before I got to the seminary.

The only worthwhile film I saw there was "How Green Was My Valley." The rest were either jolly-priest pictures or weepy epics in which June Allyson was looking for someone to take care of the orphaned Margaret O'Brien.

We had such a dose of these juvenile weepers that movie night became a ritual of release. The whole audience would wait on the edge of its seat for the first tear. When it came, pandemonium would break out: applause, stomping and cheering and cries for "More!" The poor projectionist, who spent his life on the private institution circuit, always claimed that inmates of mental institutions had saner reactions than ours.

I didn't realize how much Latin-Italian I had soaked up at home, and through my family, until I began to study Latin formally. With most of the guys it was a dead language which they learned by rote; I could tell from the way most Irishmen and Anglo-Saxons read and spoke Latin that they didn't understand or feel anything; it was as if they were speaking in Morse code. The proper accents, the nuances of emphasis, the shades of meaning were all absent. With me, Latin was a living language full of feeling and emotion and shadings.

Soon I discovered myself thinking in Latin. It came to me as naturally as breathing. I had very little difficulty reading the Latin textbooks.

But even this ability proved troublesome, because the literal sense of the Latin texts registered directly on the thinking part of my brain. In many cases the meaning was absurd. Other guys had the advantage; they were so busy extracting the meaning, through translating word by word, that the absurdity never hit them until later, if at all.

It soon became a problem for me to repeat something in English which I had first come to learn in Latin. English became my second language.

There was only one other Italian in my class; we

75

used to talk about this mutual problem and compare notes. Mario had come to Darlington after doing his preparatory studies with an order of priests who took showers in bathing suits so as not to be subject to temptations of the flesh. To him the seminary seemed like a Unitarian summer camp.

But even if he took baths in a trench coat, Mario couldn't extinguish his Latin blood. He was the wrong sort of confidant—he had more women problems than I did. He had a girl he had been kissing too long and too frequently on vacations. He dreamed about her and prayed to stop dreaming about her, talked to his confessor about her, and was in torture most of the time over whether or not to see her on his next vacation. Mario went through torment for years and ended up volunteering to go to Peru as a missionary. Another non-flit bit the Darlington dust.

During my first few years in the seminary, I was always flexing my theological muscles, trying to convert everyone I met. One of my first victims was Wally Kirchner. I was trying to organize some seminary buddies into an orchestra to play at special occasions, so I hit on Wally to loan me some instruments from his store for the guys to practice. I was very fond of him. Wally was Jewish, but he had married a Catholic girl and had signed all those agreements binding him to rear the children in the Catholic faith. Now there were three kids, and Wally was living up to the letter of the agreement, even teaching the kids their catechism and prayers by the book. He was always ready to meet me halfway and discuss Catholic doctrine, always ready to give me an audition. One night, at his home, we got going on religious history. Wally insisted his religious education was practically nil and he wouldn't put up with the technical lingo I had picked up in the seminary.

"Look, Gabe," he said, "remember you're talking

76

to a guy who doesn't know the score. So let's not get hung up on any ecclesiastical tongue-twisters. You just tell me who are the good guys and who are the bad guys."

There was no disagreement between us about Lord God Jehovah until it became necessary for me to single out Christ and his followers as "good guys," and the Jewish High Priests and the Sanhedrin as the "bad guys."

Wally asked: "Is this just the Catholic way of looking at it—or is it taught this way by the Jewish teachers, too?"

That threw me. It never occurred to me there was any other way of looking at Christ except as a "good guy." In order to make sure, I started proving that Christ was God before He became man. When I made the good guy out to be God, I was flustered because we had agreed on this in the first place. So I explained that God, the good guy, had a son who was called Jesus, who was out doing His Father's work. He traveled around this little area of Galilee and Judea teaching people to live the way His Father wanted them to live. To help Him with His Father's business, He picked twelve other good guys. Then Wally wanted to know: "Were the sides even?"

"I don't know how many men there were in the Sanhedrin."

"No, I don't mean that," Wally said. "What I mean is, wasn't the other set-up on the side of God, too?"

"Yes, I suppose so," I said. "That was a theocracy but. . . ."

"Hey, I said no seminary lingo."

"All right. That was also God's set-up."

"Then I don't get it," Wally said. "You mean to tell me God was playing a private little game of his own?"

We went round and round well into the night without resolving Wally's question. I was a zealous know-it-all when I began, but I left Wally's house deeply troubled. There were so many questions I hadn't been able to answer. And so many of his questions forced me to look at the Gospel as history. The idea that the early Christian era had merely been the story of a dispute among two groups of Jews had never occurred to me. Neither had the idea that the High Priests were acting rightly according to their own laws, the way the Popes acted later during the Inquisition and the Reformation. The High Priests were the religious professionals; they opposed a group of fishermen, an internal revenue man, a loafer and some of their younger brothers, all led by the son of a carpenter. One day I would be a professional, a member of an establishment more similar to the Sanhedrin than to the other gang.

But another of Wally's questions haunted me even more. Wally wanted to know how Catholic bishops and priests had reacted to Joseph Smith and Brigham Young and other Mormon leaders in this country, and more about the Spanish Inquisition and other sorry episodes in Catholic history. I started wondering about Catholic doctrine and ended with great grey areas of doubt. When I examined my conscience these were matters for my confessor.

But my confessors refused to take my problems seriously. These are not doubts but "difficulties," I was told. Eventually, I was promised, I would see the light. They treated me as if I were twelve. Illumination would come to me if I continued to pray for faith.

Again and again I resolved to find faith, but the more I prayed the more I doubted. I began underlining passages in my texts that troubled me, and would write in the margin: "Lord, help my unbelief." In order to be a good priest I would have to have faith. And I knew I didn't have it. The next move, I decided, was no one's but mine.

At Christmas, when my parents came to see me, I decided it was only fair to begin to let them down easy. When it was time for them to leave, my Mother had tears in her eyes.

"Don't carry on like that, Mom," I told her. "Don't be surprised if I show up at home with all my suitcases one of these days."

Mom looked at Dad. Dad looked at me and simply said, "You know what you're doing."

When I got back to my room, I wondered how they would feel if I threw in the towel. How many years could I spend trying to make my parents proud of me and hating myself all the time?

The next time Father Artioli visited me, I wondered if they had talked to him, or if he had guessed. He kept reminiscing about his own problems and discouragements and pointing up the fact that it took two or three years in the seminary before he was sure the priesthood was really for him.

I asked Father to hear my confession. I told him how my doubts had deepened and widened to cover almost every area of doctrine and history. I told him flatly I had decided that whatever faith was, I didn't have it. Without it, even thinking of a career in the priesthood was dishonest.

"Oh, Gabriel," he began, "what am I going to do with you? You don't understand how strong you are. Because you are one of the strong ones, you must expect temptations of Satan almost beyond endurance. Perhaps you are not aware of your own potentialities as a priest of God, as another Christ. But the Devil himself sometimes knows us better than we know ourselves. Why do you think you have been singled out for these torments? Because Satan sees you as an adversary capable of phenomenal strength in the contest for souls. Your temptations have only begun, my son. You will be tested almost beyond endurance. God knows that and does not stand by idly. Offer your torment as a constant prayer and he will never forsake you."

Before he was through he made me feel like a sissy for wanting to back out as soon as the going got rough. He convinced me that everyone there was going through the same kind of temptation, that Darlington was a fortress which Satan was storming day and night.

By the time I made the Act of Contrition, I was almost in tears, wondering how I could have even confessed being a quitter. I thanked God for giving me a friend and advisor as wise as Father Artioli, who understood what I was going through, and was able to fill me in on the strategies of Satan. I was simply going to have to live with the Devil as my imprudent companion. If he was after me, I would give him a good fight.

One Christmas my Mother brought me enough turkey, ravioli, special cakes, pastries and candies to feed an army, so the seminary's Rule One went crashing. It was the custom, if you were lucky enough to get more than one portion of anything edible, to share it with your buddies.

Plenty of guys risked automatic expulsion to step over my threshold for ravioli and dolci. If a guy could step into your room to eat, why couldn't he be trusted for any other reason? Were the flits really so terrified of tempting one another that they had to cling to this kind of Berlin Wall physical discipline?

There was nothing in my room but a bed, a desk, a closet with a built-in dresser and sink. No radio, nothing but clothing and personal effects and books.

But enforcement of the rule was left in most cases

to underlings with one-track minds. During my time at Darlington, one of the doctrinal dangers they were worried about was a heresy called Hugoism. Father Hugo of Philadelphia had eventually been silenced by the Bishop of Philadelphia for over-emphasis on priestly poverty, self-denial and mortification. Father Hugo was very close to the Catholic Worker movement and its founder, Dorothy Day. A few seminarians had become over-zealous followers of Father Hugo. One guy had practiced self-mortification until he cracked up and was committed to a mental institution, from which he escaped and was never heard from again. After Father Hugo's literature and the Catholic Worker were banned, the rule enforcers' job was easy. Forbidden literature was something tangible they could search for. Monsignor Tierney, the Dean of Discipline, became a regular FBI man on the prowl for this dangerous material.

One afternoon Father Tierney tip-toed down the hallway and pounced into my room in a pre-supper raid. There I was with my feet up on my desk, a copy of *Life* with a beautiful girl on the cover, and a cigarette in my face.

Smoking in your room was expressly forbidden. There was no point in dousing the cigarette now—the place was blue with smoke. I reconciled myself to the reprimand.

But Father Tierney, with his one-track mind, coughing and sputtering from the fumes, merely said:

"Oh, *you*. *You* wouldn't have any Hugo literature. I'd be wasting my time searching *you*."

One heresy at a time. If I had been mortifying myself with that cigarette in violation of the rule, I was safe as long as it hadn't been recommended by Father Hugo.

One day the rector of the seminary sent for me.

Something was up. I got the notification in Moral Theology class, so I had no time to worry about it. I walked down to his office and when he asked me in, Bishop Ahr was waiting with a letter in his hand.

"Gabriel," he said, handing me the letter, "what's this all about?"

It was blue writing paper with crinkled edges and it smelled of perfume, so it had to be some kind of girl trouble. I wanted to turn the letter over and look at the signature, but I thought I had better not. I took a deep breath and started reading.

"Dear Reverend Father," it started. "We think the world of Gabriel and he is the only boy we have ever met whom Marilyn could love as Christ loves and is loved by His Church."

Marilyn! That was putting it on a bit thick. Marilyn's mother was trying to get me thrown out of the seminary! I swallowed hard and read on.

"If you could see them together, Reverend Father, you could not help share our prayers that God may vouchsafe to grant that they might spend their life together in Holy Matrimony, nourishing many beautiful children, His tenderest branches, until the splendor of Christ's love, mirrored in them, would draw their sons and daughters to the religious life to spend and consume themselves for souls. Gabriel would make such a wonderful understanding Catholic father." With a small *f*.

Wow! This didn't sound like Marilyn's mother. She was a real politician, trying to get the rector on her side.

"Marilyn is an excellent Catholic girl. I cannot believe that God and His Blessed Mother would not bless her union with Gabriel with many beautiful children. If God sees fit to call these children to the holiness of marriage, the Holiness of Holy Orders would not be losing one priest for Christ, it might be gaining many more."

Wow! She wants me. Her mother wants me. Does *she* want *me!*

I wanted to look at Bishop Ahr but I didn't dare.

"We are confident Gabriel shares our feelings. But he will need the prayerful understanding of his superiors to help him make the right decision. We feel his superiors should know what he is going through at the present time.

"I think if you could meet Marilyn you would understand and approve their holy union. Gabriel was very young when he began to study for the priesthood. I feel if he had known Marilyn then, he might have taken an entirely different course. Before it is too late, I hope his superiors and his confessor can help him to make the difficult decision to leave one of God's vineyards and go into another."

A vineyard with Marilyn! There was more to the letter but I had read enough to get the pitch. The rector looked at me and I started to stammer.

"Sit down, Gabriel," he said. "All I want to know is if there's anything to this. Let's hear your side."

"Well, Father," I began. "Marilyn is a very beautiful girl—almost like Hedy Lamarr. I met her again at a basketball game about six months ago. Prior to that I had not seen her for three years."

"You've been dating her?"

"I had permission from my spiritual advisor prior to seminary, Father, and I dated her a couple of times when I was at Seton Hall."

"You seem to have made quite an impression."

"Well, Father, her mother is a widow, or anyway she has no husband. At least I've never seen one or heard him mentioned. Marilyn is an only child and. . . ."

83

"She's a very beautiful girl."

"Yes, Father, her mother is always inviting me to visit them in Bayonne during vacation."

"And you go?"

"Once or twice. I couldn't get out of it. She feels that Marilyn and I would be a marvelous influence on the community."

"Yes, I gather that."

"Father, I think her mother finds it impossible to believe anyone could prefer anything to her daughter."

"I think that's quite evident. But how about you?"

"Oh, Father, this is a surprise to me, this thing, this letter. I had no idea it would go this far."

"Well, exactly how far has it gone, as far as you are concerned, Gabriel?"

"Father, nowhere. She seems to be crazy about me but I haven't been dating her. . . ."

"You stopped. You're sure."

"Yes, Father."

"So you don't give it another thought."

"That's right. I never really think about her."

"Well, then, let's not worry about it."

"Thank you, Father."

I was certainly lucky this happened when Bishop Ahr was rector: he was the only one who didn't treat us like babies. Ahr was German. The Irish rectors would have made a whole big thing of it.

"You just leave it to me, Gabriel. Don't worry about it."

I didn't worry about it, exactly. But it did start me thinking. I began to wonder what it would be like, a holy union with Marilyn to make priests for God. Then I had to stop thinking about it because my thoughts always got hung up on the one thing: that picture of me and Marilyn in the other vineyard.

I always felt Marilyn would have done anything I asked. She was Irish—or at least, with an Irish name

84

like Hogan, her father was Irish. But he was out of the picture. I wondered what her mother was. Whatever she was, she was a very practical lady. She watched Marilyn like a hawk, but when I was at their house she always left us alone. If I had gotten Marilyn into trouble, I'm sure her mother would have welcomed it as a miracle. She was probably praying to Our Blessed Mother for something like that to happen.

I wondered what it would be like to be in bed with Marilyn.

That blue letter with the perfume on it started a whole train of thought.

In theology class, when we studied marriage as a sacrament, it would remind me of Marilyn. The encyclical of the Pope on marriage reminded me of Marilyn. The conjugal society *in fieri* and *in facto esseo*, a permanent union of one man and one woman, the *Encyclical Casti Connubi*, *Bonum Prolis*, *Bonum Fidei*, *Bonum Sacramenti*, the benefits of marriage, the attacks on marriage, everything reminded me of Marilyn. She wanted me!

Ben Franklin was the eighth of ten children, Lord Nelson was the sixth of eleven, Napoleon the fourth of ten, Jefferson the third of ten, Coleridge the tenth of ten, Washington Irving the eleventh of eleven, Tennyson the fourth of twelve, St. Ignatius Loyola the thirteenth of thirteen, General Putnam of Bunker Hill the eleventh of twelve. Some of the most famous men and women of history were members of large families, from Rembrandt, who was one of six children, and Washington, who was one of ten, to Caruso, who was one of twenty-one and Catherine of Sienna, one of twenty-five.

All this was supposed to be an argument against Margaret Sanger and the two-hundred-fifty-million dollar contraceptive industry. All these great men would not have been born and their contributions would have been lost to humanity if their parents had been followers of Mrs. Sanger!

But all these great men would not have been born, either, if their fathers had gone to Immaculate Conception Seminary and left their mothers living with *their* mothers in a small apartment in Bayonne.

Later that year I got a new chateau-mate, Joe Bagley. He came from Bayonne, where he had known Marilyn and her mother for many years. When he found out I knew them too, he used to talk about Marilyn a lot. Each time I got around to forgetting about her, Joe would bring her up.

Just the mention of her name was enough to start me thinking and dreaming.

I was always alone in bed. It was usually early afternoon before Marilyn woke me up with a big kiss and a big hot cup of coffee. The children were always in school. The house was quiet. Marilyn always wore a transparent white negligee made of first-communion veiling. While I finished my coffee, she would be turning on the shower. I would come out of the shower naked and dripping and there she stood in all that white veiling, handing me a white towel with a cross on it. Her hair hung down to her shoulders like Hedy Lamarr. I would look at the clock and she would say: "What time are you due at the Paramount?"

"I have a rehearsal but Phil can cover for me." I would say it with a smile. Marilyn would smile at me. And then I would grab her and lift her up in all that white veiling. And we would jump into a big, cool, clean, white, beautiful bed to create clean, white, beautiful babies who would all grow up to be clean, white, handsome priests for God.

Daydreams weren't my only sex problems. There were also those unconscious and semi-conscious nocturnal sessions. You went to bed warm and dry and awoke in a cold sweat which turned out to be not a sweat at all, but something else. The criss-crossed pads between the sheet and the mattress were called score sheets.

Whether our soiled laundry was entered in our records I never knew. But many of my classmates had big annual scores. Since this was a solitary problem-pleasure it became the topic of much theoretical discussion. Had one assented to the pleasure consciously or unconsciously?

Having never had a conscious orgasm in my life, and only three non-dry dreams in my entire seminary career, I had no standard to compare things with. I was in a never-never land. One of my buddies once explained that this problem was largely confined to flits anyway; the rest of us, according to him, worked it out during our recreational period exertions. It came out of our pores and follicles and went down the shower drain.

For better or worse, the entire seminary laundry set-up reeked of suggestions of sex. The first batch was practically a puberty rite for incoming seminarians. Our minutely-marked laundry was forwarded to the Sisters of the Good Shepherd Home for wayward girls in Morristown. The nuns there watched their charges like hawks: still the girls managed to make memorable long distance contact with the seminary through the only method of communication open to them.

Underwear would come back with the fly carefully sewn up, or the crotch removed by a delicate pinking shears operation. T-shirts would have brassiere cups sewn into them. Lewd little love notes—"Nicotine can't be removed," or "You can smoke down there, should see what I can do"—would be inked into strategic spots. Jock straps were starched rigid; pajama legs sewn, or with lipstick marks in private places. The Holy Joes kept these private incidents to themselves. But the non-flits shared them with one another until the Dean of Discipline moved in and lectured to us about turning the weekly laundry rite into an occasion of sin.

But cleanliness—at least in the underwear department —never smacked of godliness to us. It was difficult to change your drawers without being reminded of some lewd little poem once written across a strategic inseam.

The more tangled up I got mentally, the more I needed to let go physically. Long walks, private explorations, jaunts into town on imaginary errands— none of these were enough. I spent every free minute trying to exhaust myself on the athletic field. In football where you could really let yourself go, I pushed hard.

One day when I was out for a long pass, I rammed into a hefty fullback. He made a wild grab for the ball and jammed his extended fingers into my face. I felt a wild stabbing pain in my head. The sky darkened, the trees turned black and then I was absolutely blind.

I could hear and feel everyone clamoring around me, running for blankets. Some of the fellows started lifting me. Then there were shouts and orders to keep me motionless. I wallowed in intense pain, swimming in it, hoping to pass over the line into unconsciousness. Instead I hung there on the edge. I could move my legs, I could move my arms—but I was afraid to touch my face. One eyeball seemed to be somewhere in my throat, choking me. The other felt as though it was coming out of my left ear.

They rushed me to Good Samaritan Hospital in Suffern, where an eye specialist was waiting. I felt as helpless as a new-born baby. I could feel strange hands pulling and hauling at my clothes to get them off; strange hands washed me with warm water, then little spots of cool alcohol were applied and then the needles.

And then came the bandages, layers of them.

The specialist ordered me to stay motionless. As soon as the pain began to subside and give way to the half-drugged dopey state, that was easy.

They were trying to slow down my circulation with massive doses of Vitamin K. I should have been scared but I wasn't, not a bit. All my real fears, real problems, real pain, were left in the seminary. I welcomed this helplessness. I began to understand why some people could wallow in invalidism for years. It was a way out.

All my problems belonged to the doctors and the priests. The buck had been passed.

That first night in the hospital I felt as though I had escaped to the other side of the moon. I had only my ears to tell me what was happening. Soon I could sort out the different voices and match them with the distinctive smells. The nuns were all Lifebuoy soap and starch in their wimples; doctors, tobacco and shaving cream and a musty mixture of fresh laundry and old pill bottles. The nurses were like a parade of perfumes; they reminded me of different girls I'd known.

Each nurse had her distinctive way of approaching me with that needle. Each had her own way of holding my head when she changed the bloody bandages on my eyes.

The whole hospital atmosphere seemed to change after midnight. In the afternoon and early evening everyone called me Gabe and treated me like a big sickly baby. At midnight I heard a new pair of heels padding down the corridor and smelled a new perfume. I almost suffocated with it as the night nurse reached behind my head for the bandage clip.

She unrolled that bandage as if she were stripping me down to the skin.

They had been talking about corneal replantation

and coagulants to stop the bleeding, so I asked her what she thought.

"It's dark in here. Doctor's orders. I can't see a thing."

When she got the bandages off, she daubed at my face and eyes with great tenderness.

"Can you see anything now?" I asked her.

"A little," she answered. "Why do so many good looking guys have to become priests?"

"I'll bet you tell that to all the seminarians."

"Oh," she said. "Shut up and turn your head this way." I complied with her order. She wound the bandage smoothly around my head. I could feel the stiff neckline of her uniform under my nose as she reached behind my head to fasten the clip.

"Anything else I can do for you?" she asked. "Pineapple juice, ice cream, cold rice pudding? Let's see, what have we got here you boys have to get along without at the seminary?"

It sounded like a leading question. I opened my mouth to say thank you and she was all over me. She pounced on my mouth with her lips. Suddenly all the soul-kissing sins from my checkered past became venial. She had her tongue halfway down my throat. This was the road to perdition.

When I reached out to grab her, she pushed my hand away and held both my arms fast. She seemed very powerful so I just relaxed and became the invalid.

"Didn't the doctors explain to you you're not supposed to move?"

"Uh-huh."

"Well, then, keep still. If you want anything just ask for it."

"Okay, please put your head down here again."

When she moved closer to me I just waited, then I gave her back every trick she had just taught me.

"How long do you think I'm going to be here?" I wanted to know.

"A while."

I had begun to think about Dad and Mother. I didn't want anyone from the seminary or the hospital calling them and scaring them to death. There was no need to tell them anything. I didn't even want them notified until the bandages were off. I spoke to her about it and asked her what she could do.

"Relax," she said. "You can't do anything about it. The doctors will do all the deciding. If they have to do a replantation, your parents will have to be notified."

"Why?"

"If you won't keep quiet, I'm going to have to give you a couple of pills."

So I took the pineapple juice and the pills and forgot about everything. I lay there half asleep, half awake, waiting for those footsteps. As long as she came to me I was the helpless victim. I couldn't do anything about it. But if I pressed the buzzer, even if my night nurse was kissing someone else at the other end of the corridor and one of the starched Lifebuoy nuns came in her place, I felt I had already committed a mortal sin.

It had been so long since I had anything interesting to confess that I went to sleep imagining all the fascinating possibilities for violation of the Sixth Commandment that I had at my beck and call.

That night I caught myself thanking God and his Blessed Mother for arranging for me to have this accident. Wow, I thought later, that's blasphemy. The occasions of sin in my new situation began to seem almost limitless.

With gauze sealing out all light, night and day didn't mean anything. Life began at midnight with the arrival of my night nurse. We would talk and neck, joke and neck, play games and neck some more. When she took her regular day off, she warned me the night before and we tried to pack two nights of fooling around into one.

I lost all interest in my own recovery. I was bored by each report of progress. On the seventh or eighth day when the bleeding stopped, and they promised the bandages could be removed—if all went well—in another seven days, I began to wonder what it would be like to be able to see her.

Then I began to wonder how I could get back to see her after they discharged me from the hospital. It wasn't going to be easy. She knew everything about me and I knew almost nothing about her. Whenever I asked a leading question she would order me to be quiet. I didn't know if she was single or married, tall or short. I knew she had a great shape and she smelled lovely and her hair was cut short, and her voice was low and her speech slangy, but that was about it.

We shared a weird kind of intimacy. I was the passive victim, completely irresponsible, there by accident; she cared for me like a combination Mama and geisha girl. Meanwhile the nuns hovered around with warm concern, continually asking me if everything was being done to make me comfortable. It was a dream sequence from beginning to end.

All visitors had been barred, but on Sunday Dad and Mother arrived unannounced. I didn't want them to see me all bandaged up but there was nothing I could do about it. The doctors had briefed them to be cool and not start my circulation racing. But Mother got excited as soon as she saw the bandages. She wanted my promise to cut out the football. If I needed exercise, what was the matter with baseball? I was pale. I had lost weight. I might never see again.

"Don't worry, Mother. Now that the bleeding has

stopped, I'll be okay. In another week they'll remove the bandages."

"The bleeding stopped? When did it stop?"

"This morning when they changed the bandages, no blood. It had just stopped, that's all."

"Benny," Mother said to Dad, "did you hear that? It stopped bleeding this morning. Tell me what time. I want to know exactly."

"Ask the nuns on the floor, Mother. I can't see my wristwatch or anything, remember?"

"Oh, my poor boy," she moaned. Then I could hear her hightailing it off in search of the nuns. I could tell from the Lifebuoy smell that she brought one of the sisters back with her.

"Sister just showed me your chart, Gabriel," she said solemnly. "You know when you stopped bleeding? Right after Father Artioli asked all the children at Mt. Carmel to pray for your recovery at nine o'clock Mass." Of course my rear end was sore from getting shots of Vitamin K for a week, but I didn't want to bring that up.

"How do you know what happened at nine o'clock Mass?" I asked, kidding her. Mother's staunch Latin faith in miracles was nothing new. After all, I had been a miracle child myself. But Mother and Dad going to Mass regularly—this I would have to see with my own eyes to believe! Bernie kept telling me that everything had gradually changed at home since I had left for the seminary. As the mother and father of a prospective priest, Mother and Dad began getting social invitations they had never received before; they were treated like VIPs in the parish. Father Artioli invited them personally to the banquets and the feasts. They got preferential seating at the parish operettas. Small honors and attentions became very difficult to ignore. Gradually they began showing up at Mass on Sunday.

At the celebration of the First Mass of Willie and

Joe, they had been given honorary seating. There they could catch a glimpse of what might be in store for them in a few years. The First Mass and Father Artioli's sermon were practically a canonization of the parents of the newly ordained priest. Every moment Father Artioli was recruiting for the Army of the Lord. He knew his main opposition was not the Devil himself, but the Italian parents. So he never left anything to chance. He spelled it out clear as day; having a priest in your family was an ironclad guarantee against damnation. No matter how big a sinner you had been before, your place in heaven was insured.

There in the hospital, with nothing to look at, I began to feel the changes. My parents' opposition to my being a priest had gradually melted away. The more I began to have doubts about my own future, the more they took it for granted.

What would they think, I wondered, if they knew what a ball I had been having every night with my nurse in this very room, while they were praying and making novenas and dressing to attend nine o'clock Mass on Sunday, sitting there while all the little children were told to get down on their knees and pray out loud for the recovery of their son so he could go on to be another Christ?

I felt like a hypocrite. While everyone was wearing his knees out praying for me to get out of the hospital, I was hoping to stay there until Christmas or longer. I tried to make a joke out of it after midnight that night with Miss Nightingale. But she was a real tough apple. She wouldn't have any part of it. Whenever I started talking seriously, she would slide her hand under the top of my pajamas, twiddle my nipples with the palm of her hand, and kiss me flat into my pillow until I could barely breathe.

Then she would back off and sneer: "What do you want, all this and heaven too?"

The next seven days weren't as exciting as the first week. Everything got to be routine, the necking as regular as my nightly backrub. I got tired of being treated like a baby or a piece of forbidden flesh. I began wondering where I could go when they let me out of the hospital. Somewhere where I could go incognito. Somewhere where I could pretend to be something I had never had a chance to be: just a plain ordinary six foot three dark-haired stupid healthy Italian-American jerk from Jersey City.

No such luck. When they took the bandages off at the end of the week they presented me with a special pair of dark wrap-around sun glasses. They fitted snugly around my temples and the lenses were completely covered with tape except for a tiny pinhole. I could see about three feet ahead of me and that was it.

The doctor laid down the law: no studying, no gallivanting, no going outside alone. My father would pick me up and I could spend a couple of weeks at home with my parents. They were pledged to see that I took it easy.

It wasn't easy to take it easy. Soon I was holding more audiences every day than the Pope. It was approaching holiday time and all Mother's non-religious relatives kept arriving bearing special gifts for me. With those dark glasses and the peepholes and my black and white uniform, everything changed. I wasn't cousin Gabe anymore. I began to feel like some sort of plaster statue with burning candles around it. Nobody—not even Aunt Carrie and Lizzie—acted natural. Nobody told any funny stories. Everybody was on his best behavior. It got to be a big strain.

My brother Bernie kidded me about it, but it was serious.

"You used to be my older brother," Bernie would say. "Now you're the Holy Trinity all in one."

Everyone would arrive with cartons of Camel cigarettes and envelopes full of money. A five or a ten from every member of Mother's club. They would beg me to come and visit them. I knew they wanted me to come in my seminary outfit—the clothes were half the thrill—so I would always put it off.

But now they treated me as though I had been wounded fighting in the Third Crusade.

"If we put you in a shrine and had you carried through Wales Avenue, they would worship you," Bernie would say. "Aren't you going to visit Lizzie? If you decide to give her the honor, she'll need a couple of days notice to go to Macy's and get a red carpet."

Though Bernie had kept telling me things had changed it wasn't until I spent those five weeks convalescing, on exhibit every moment, that I understood what he was talking about.

Having your own family and friends treat you as if you were a relic of the true cross is pretty strong stuff. It can go to your head in a minute. It's a good thing I had those blinders on.

When I got back to the seminary on a regular schedule, I had a lot of catching up to do. Still I had to check in with the doctor every week or so and was on orders not to overwork my eyes, so I didn't. I just coasted.

It was winter and too cold for hiking. When the old urge for physical exertion returned I started playing basketball with the same fury that had gotten me into trouble on the football field.

One day when the whistle blew and I took my first jump, I felt a grinding pain in my lower abdomen. But I ignored it and kept going. At the half I felt a little feverish and thought of knocking off. But our team was only one point ahead and my compulsion for winning was stronger than the pain in my guts. So I kept going, keeping my eye on the scoreboard and the clock. After we finally won I headed for the infirmary. By the time I got up the gym stairs I was doubled up with pain; I could barely stand.

Sister Alice Benedict took one look at me and said: "I'll get someone to pack your bag." Then she went to the telephone and called Good Samaritan Hospital.

As soon as I heard the name Good Samaritan I thought of Florence Nightingale. I wondered if she was still on the midnight shift. I looked around the infirmary for bandages. When I was snug and safe in the hospital bed in my pajamas I would wrap the gauze around my eyes as a gag so she would remember me. She might not recognize me with eyebrows.

The cramps in my stomach were killing me but after a few shots of the needle that would clear away and I could just lie in the darkness of a narcotic haze and wait for those perfumed wrestling bouts.

Sister Alice Benedict dragooned one of the professors into driving me to the hospital in his car. I walked up to the second floor where a nurse sat at a desk. Before trying to persuade her to give me my old room, I wanted to know who was on the lobster shift.

"What do you think you're doing, standing around bothering our nurses?" someone shouted from the end of the corridor. It was Sister Connie, Sister Alice Benedict's buddy and protege. She took my little bag, made me take off my clothes and stood on guard until I piled into bed. Before I could turn over, the orderly was there with the tray and razor. They gave me a blood count and five minutes later they had me wheeling toward the operating room.

Johnny Petrone, the regular doctor who made calls at the seminary, was a surgeon and a good one. He had been alerted and before they gave me the spinal anaesthetic he walked in in his green outfit, all ready. After we shook hands and I wished him luck, Sister Connie slipped a gauze pad over my eyes. When Petrone started slicing my abdomen, I could feel pressure without pain. I felt like a piece of lousy processed American cheese. I tried to inhale so I could dislodge the gauze bandage and catch a glimpse of what was going on, but when I got the blinder off, Sister Connie would slap it back in place. Within twenty minutes they had my appendix in one place and me in another.

I was sitting in a silver-chrome wheel chair wearing a purple corduroy bathrobe over lavender silk pajamas. Underneath I was a mass of bandages from my chest right down to my knees. My face was pale, my hands thin and bony. I was looking out the hospital window, waiting for the bad news.

D-Day was finally at hand. After three fantastically delicate operations, Doctor Frangepani, the famous specialist from Johns Hopkins, had come up from Baltimore for a consultation with my father and my surgeon. All morning they had been poring over the records, looking at the X-rays.

When Dr. Frangepani entered in his white coat he was so jolly he scared me to death.

"Doctor, please," I pleaded. "Give it to me straight. No beating around the bush. I'm prepared for the worst."

"Okay, Gabriel," he said to me, tapping his finger on the brown envelope full of X-rays. "That's the way you want it, that's the way I'll give it to you. I've seen some tough ones, but yours is one of the most unusual cases I've ever encountered. Unusual in the delicate complications it presents, the delicate choices which have to be made."

"Doctor," I pleaded. "Will I ever walk again?"

"Gabe," he said soberly, "the only way I can answer so direct a question is to say that *depends*."

"I'm not afraid of more operations. Not afraid at all," I protested.

"You've been a very brave lad," said Frangepani. "Very brave. The hospital staff here keep remarking on that. *But* you have your heart set on continuing toward the priesthood. That is a complication. A rigorous vocation."

"Yes, I know. That's why I thought I felt only a Catholic surgeon could understand my problem."

"Quite right.

"Gabe, I want you to understand I am talking to you in the strictest confidence. This is something that may have to be taken up with the College of Surgeons of the Archdiocese of Newark. Of course, I will prepare the special report and then sometime later you may have to appear *pro forma* to answer a few questions. Then and only then, could we proceed. After we had received clearance from Rome."

"For another operation?"

"In a manner of speaking. Your surgeons and I have studied your metabolism and your hormone quotient with a view of determining the possible impingement of the present malfunction which has thus far resisted alleviation."

"Yes."

"You know there are some very interesting new things being learned in physical therapy nowadays. Doctor Horowitz in Melbourne has had very interesting results in a case involving an Episcopal bishop who had spent some years with the Bantu.

"First of course, I would need *your* permission to proceed. But I do urge you to consider it. In any case I brought the papers along. I want you to think about it seriously before affixing your signature."

He took a legal document in triplicate from the brown envelope and tossed it on my hospital bed.

"One of the nurses here in the hospital happens to have the same blood type as you, and is in all other respects a healthy person. She has courageously volunteered to participate in this therapeutic experiment as a silent partner, so to speak. In fact she has already given written consent. Since she is mature enough and unmarried, no other permission seems necessary. And since she is not a member of the Newark Diocese; her clerical clearance will be processed through separate ecclesiastical channels."

"If it's going to be a bone graft, Doctor Frangepani, wouldn't it be more logical to ask someone like my brother Bernie or one of the other seminarians? Not a girl."

"Gabe, I'm afraid you don't understand the seriousness of your own situation. A bone graft would be simple alongside this."

"But why from a girl?"

"It is much more complicated than that, Gabriel. If your physical recovery could be facilitated in any other way, God knows I would not want to risk this one. But yours is a case of *summa extremis*. If you consent we will proceed, with the permission of your superiors, the Archbishop and the properly designated representatives of His Holiness and the College of Surgeons, as soon as possible. After proper rest and some special preparational therapy, and under clinical hospital conditions, then you shall have regular daily sexual intercourse, *copula*, with Miss Hotpants of Ward Seven until with God's help you may walk again in the fullness of your strength to do God's work on earth as it is in heaven."

Dr. Frangepani was so busy talking he didn't make a move to keep my wheel chair from tipping over as I lunged to sign the paper.

The fall knocked me back to consciousness. Once I was awake I went crazy trying to find the paper.

But it was only a dream. The whole damn thing was a dream. My private tailor-made clerical fantasy.

At the behest of my body, my mind was forever

trying to wangle some special dreamy dispensation for me to get raped.

I had never been sick in my life before my seminary days. Now it seemed I spent half my time as an invalid, real or imaginary. And I wasn't the only one. The Rock was a set-up for epidemics. If one guy had a runny nose, it would spread through the entire place. The older guys still talked about a hepatitis epidemic as the year of the jaundice. Ninety percent of the guys had been infected and with some of them the lingering effects were still visible. The flu and the grippe were just like a change in the Rule—they hit everybody. Then half the guys had their own individual private physical disorders.

The infirmary was always busier than the library.

God's army was in no better shape than Caesar's.

No matter how you slice it, institutional food is institutional food. A lot of the fellows couldn't take it, including me.

Father Charles Damianovitch, who was in charge of the kitchen, was a strange duck. In his fifties, he talked through his teeth and to the young students just coming in; he could ruin a meal simply by walking past your table and hissing, "I hope you enjoy your dinner." His real claim to fame was his dead sister, Sister Miriam Theresa, who was in the process of being canonized. One day, if he lived that long, Charley D. would be the brother of a saint and a big man. In the meantime, the word was out: if you wanted to get relics in advance of that great day—a piece of her hair or something—the man to see was Charley D. However, this promise of future glory didn't produce any miracles in the kitchen.

When I developed tiny white warts on my arms and hands, I was scared to death. Every time I went to a doctor's office I prayed he would keep me waiting so

I could case the medical books. Then I discovered that syphilis and gonorrhea were bracketed with skin diseases and I panicked. I was sure I had picked up something from my necking sessions with Florence Nightingale. After all, if she necked and soul-kissed with all the guys in the wards the way she did with me, she was a regular Typhoid Mary. Maybe that's why she had disappeared from the hospital and everybody was so vague when I asked her whereabouts.

But according to the medical texts I skimmed, I should have had a sore on my lip before the leprosy broke out in other places.

If I found a tender spot on my lip while shaving in the morning, it would drive me crazy all day. Finally, when the syphilitic sore didn't appear, I decided it was time to go see a doctor. I checked into the infirmary and got permission to see a specialist in New York. He gave me a routine examination and then he applied some thick white stuff like cake frosting all over my arms. I waited about fifteen minutes for it to dry. Then he scraped it off and the little warts came off with it.

When I tried to pin him down as to what *caused* the things, I couldn't get any answer. Just conversation. I asked him if he was a dermatologist. According to the medical books I had read so sneakily, all dermatologists treated syphilis. No, he was a specialist in allergies. He felt I was allergic to something. If the warts returned, I was to come back to see him.

That answer wasn't good enough for me. I was worried about breaking out with syphilitic lesions and he was talking about allergies.

When the warts reappeared, I tried another doctor in Suffern. He was a big help too. He gave me injections. Another doctor scraped them off with a knife. I tried another specialist in New York and he burned them off with a needle.

I asked them if they didn't think I ought to have

blood tests or something. I looked up the addresses of those public health clinics in New York and thought of going and taking the test. Then I heard they take your name and investigate you, and ask you for the names of anybody and everybody you had made love to in the past six months. So I gave up that idea.

Then I remembered Dr. Lane in Jersey City, and got permission to take a day off to see him. At least he acted a little interested. He asked me all sorts of questions about the seminary, how I liked it, what kind of routine we had, whether I had been working too hard, whether I liked the food or not. He wasn't a Catholic himself so he seemed interested in what went on at Darlington. When I complained about the food, he asked me what I was eating at the seminary that I never ate before at home.

"I never ate food like that anywhere if I could help it," I told him.

"Well, what are you eating now that you don't like?" he asked me.

I guess it was hate-Monsignor-Powers-week for me. He had just come in as new rector of the seminary and brought with him all the trappings of Irish nationalism at its ugliest. He was as bigoted as possible, full of nasty digs at Italians. Since I was one of the older Italians in the place now, it really used to rile me to have him speak about Father Artioli as "that Dago priest." He made a point of never being able to remember the name of my spiritual advisor. The fact that Father Artioli had given me blanket permission to date girls during Seton Hall, where Powers was Director of the Minor Seminarians, struck him as a kind of incipient Roman heresy that might infect his precious Irish Church. I had never heard a priest use words like "guinea" and "wop" until Powers came on the scene.

So when Dr. Lane gave me the opportunity, I opened

up on the new regime and told him that we seemed to be getting Irish potatoes morning, noon and night.

"You don't like potatoes?"

"Of course not," I said. "We never had them at home. And I never eat them out unless it's an occasional French fry slipped on the side of a hamburger."

"Well then," said Dr. Lane, "cut down on the potatoes and see what happens. Especially cut down on boiled and baked potatoes."

Allergic as I was to the Irish clergy, it stood to reason my system felt the same way about Irish potatoes. So I started experimenting on my own body and watching the results. For two weeks I didn't touch any kind of potatoes. I went hungry but I never touched them. The warts just faded away.

So then I experimented in reverse. For lunch I ate three boiled potatoes. In two days I had a cluster of warts on my arms again. Eureka, I had found it! I felt like Euclid and Pasteur rolled into one. I had the nerve to assume my body wasn't *that* much different from other people. No wonder the Irish were so full of warts and wens, inside and outside; so constipated, so terrified of women, so bigoted, plagued with hernias and rimless glasses, such a bunch of flits. They were full of potatoes.

I kept my scientific secret to myself and decided I would share it only with my Latin blood brothers—at least only non-flits.

I knocked off potatoes for good and the warts completely disappeared. Then I realized they were my automatic passport to the outside world. Any time I felt like a jaunt to the city, all I had to do was eat two or three boiled or baked potatoes a couple of days in advance and I had my visa to see the dermatologist.

Father Charley D.'s lack of menu imagination never let me down. The boiled potatoes, like the Tree of the Knowledge of Good and Evil in the Garden of Eden, were always there. Plates of them.

Two weeks after I got the warts under control, I broke into a cold sweat in front of my shaving mirror one morning. I had awakened with very wet pajamas, and now there was a big pink sore on my lower lip. This time I was sure it was VD. No doubt about it. Like a movie the scenes of an incident that happened at Seton Hall several years back flashed through my mind.

I had gone to one of those tea dances given for the college girls at Notre Dame College on Staten Island. I arranged to date a girl from Brooklyn I had met. While we were dancing I went into a cold sweat. I had such a tremendous physical urge I had to stop dancing close to her. I backed away and she tried to snuggle next to me. I turned aside and then I was afraid other people would see. Between my waist and my knees my whole body was rigid. I thought I had appendicitis of the penis. It hurt so much that I asked to be excused.

The bathroom at this girls' college was a tiny one-seater and occupied. Obviously the Archbishop didn't visit very often, or they would have had better facilities. I was dying to open my fly and take a look. I was sure I probably had broken out with warts and sores or something down there. When I got into the booth, I was sweating and shaking so that I could barely undo my zipper. I was scared to look but I had to. It hurt when I touched it. It was as swollen and as distended as a baseball bat and the head was as red as a strawberry. The foreskin was stretched tight beneath the head like I had never seen it before.

I started saying Hail Marys and sweating but nothing happened. It seemed as if the head was choked by the foreskin and the whole apparatus was swollen for keeps.

It would take some kind of surgery, I was positive, to get out of this predicament. I didn't know what to do. I couldn't stand, I was feeling faint. I was afraid to sit down. I couldn't rearrange myself. If even my shorts touched, a jabbing pain went right through me. I just stood there saying Hail Marys with some guy knocking on the door begging to get in. That probably spun me out of it because finally, to the accompaniment of another pain like a swift kick in the groin, things down there returned to a kind of normal. Everything was still sore. But I could walk. I threw cold water on my face and went outside, leaving my date wondering what happened.

Now there was this sore. I had to find some doctor right away. I checked over the list of physicians I had consulted for my warts.

Then I decided I better try some different guys. First I'd have to arrange my visa. I would have eaten potatoes for breakfast if they had served them. But I had to wait for lunch. Sure enough my precious warts returned by the next evening. The following morning I checked into the infirmary and got permission to go to New York to see the dermatologist.

First I went to the public library. I knew where they kept the medical books, the medical dictionaries. I had read them all before, but I read them again, copying down the key parts, memorizing the others. Then I went to see the dermatologist. I showed my warts and the sore on my lip. He took one fast look and reached for his needle. I tried to ask him leading questions but he didn't pay any attention to them.

He treated me just like any sickly seminarian—in oher words, like a ten-year-old. He just *assumed* because of the clothes I wore that it couldn't be anything serious. I wanted to tell him, "Look, fellow, I practically lived with a nurse for two weeks. She was down my throat at least ten times a night. Just give me credit for some balls. Treat me like you would an ordinary healthy 22-year-old stud. Give me the benefit of the doubt. Take a blood test, for God's sake. A Wassermann and a Kahn. Give me some of those Jewish diagnoses I read about in the library."

No, I decided. He probably reports everything to the rector. I'll go see *my* doctor, Doctor Lane in Jersey City. He's not a Catholic. Maybe he'll at least ask me to open my pants and take a look at my penis instead of treating me like some dried-up 65-year-old nun.

So I kept quiet. I took down my shorts and he gave me a shot in the rump. While I had my back to him I got very brave and said:

"What kind of shot is that, Doctor? Sister Alice Benedict is going to ask me."

"Compound of bismuth," he replied offhand.

Bismuth. That's what the medical dictionary prescribed for syphilis. I was hooked. Now I knew I had to see Dr. Lane.

It took ten days before I could get to Jersey City to see him. By that time the sore on my lip was just a memory. He had to take my word for it. He asked me if I had been eating potatoes. I couldn't lie. I admitted it. He asked me if cutting out potatoes did any good and I said I was too busy to notice. I wanted to pin him down on the bismuth thing but I was too embarrassed. I told him this dermatologist in New York had given me bismuth shots.

"Is that the usual treatment for cold sores and fever sores?" I wanted to know.

"Well, yes, that's part of the family of drugs sometimes prescribed for skin lesions."

Skin lesions. Lesion was another word out of the medical texts. There was no time to lose.

"Doctor, one of the guys at the Seminary has been seeing this girl, and he had trouble with his, you know, his penis," I began. "He's a nice guy but he's shy and you know how it is, when you're a seminarian everybody just assumes you wouldn't even if you had the chance, you know what I mean?"

He laughed. "If he's worried about anything, Gabe, why don't you bring him in? I'll look at him, give him a test. We're supposed to report these things if they're positive but it's common practice to look the other way."

Doctor Lane was so nice he had me trapped.

"Okay. I'll bring him in. I wanted him to come today but he's very shy. I don't know him too well myself."

"Well, tell him you talked to me and I gave you my assurance of complete confidence."

"Does positive mean yes you've got VD?" I asked.

"Yes. Negative means good news. It's sort of reverse in medicine. Positive is bad. Negative is good."

"Another thing I wanted to ask you was about this drinking water business. We eat most of our meals in the seminary but every once in a while I've used a strange glass in a strange diner or restaurant or bathroom. I sometimes get a bite in a diner near Suffern. The place is filthy. Is it possible, can you. . . . I mean, what do the specialists say?"

"It's always a good idea to use a paper cup. But I never saw a case of syphilis or gonorrhea yet where there hadn't been some kind of contact. If you've had the contact, then there's a chance. If not, well, you've nothing to worry about."

"You mean kissing and the other."

"Oh yes, the mouth can be as great a source of infection as the vagina. Certainly. Why?"

"That's what I figured."

I left his office in a daze. I didn't know where to turn. I was positive the sore, the swelling, was the beginning of the end. I remembered all the horrible stories guys told who had been in the army. Those films they showed the GIs. And the way the pharmacist's mates and the medics were such sadists with their injections.

All my serious ailments, like the eye injury, the appendicitis emergency, I had welcomed with great relief. They gave me a break from routine.

If I lost the sight of one eye, or couldn't walk again and had to leave the seminary, everybody would understand that and feel sorry. But if I got caught with VD, what would happen when Monsignor Powers and the Irish nationalists found out? They hated Father Artioli anyway, and I was one of his boys. I was the only Italian from the Archdiocese in my class in the seminary. It could become a big political thing.

I tried to think it through but it was too horrible. All I could think of were the stories one was always hearing in the seminary about this one or that one who got into trouble. There was Father Barry who was always sneaking out in the afternoons to go see the doctor in New York and he was spotted by someone sitting in the balcony all afternoon listening to Helen O'Connell singing "Green Eyes" with the Dorsey Band. There was practically a court-martial over that. And a few years later poor Father Barry died of cancer of the testicles or the penis or somewhere down there. Why hadn't I thought of it before? Maybe the pains and swelling in my penis weren't VD after all but the beginning of cancer. But cancer was better than VD as far as I knew. Cancer was at least respectable. You didn't catch it from soul-kissing. Or did you?

My worries began to interfere with my sleep. There was nobody around I could talk to. I couldn't get to Father Artioli for confession. Besides, it had gone too far for that. The sins were all forgiven, washed away. But maybe I was being punished because I had taken the whole thing too lightly. Every time I got my sins washed away I ached to get back somewhere to repeat the process.

I reached the point where I had regular nightmares. All the seminarians would be lined up in formation on the football field. They were all in their black cassocks with their little white collars. Then Monsignor Powers arrived with the Bishop and they marched out of chapel and stood there in the center of the football field. Then two Sub-deacons marched toward the single line of seminarians. They stopped in front of me. I stepped out of rank and marched off between them until the three of us stood in front of the Bishop. All their faces were frozen. Nobody said a word. A bell tolled and then the two Sub-deacons backed away.

Then Monsignor Powers said something in Latin. His Latin was always lousy, he had such a thick Irish accent. Then he reached out toward me and I felt a pain in the back of my neck. He yanked the crucifix hanging around my neck so fiercely that the chain broke and fell into the grass. Then the Sub-deacons ripped my cassock off. I was being cashiered out of the seminary, like poor innocent Alfred Dreyfus being bounced out of the French Army in that movie with Paul Muni. Then all the seminarians just walked away whispering about syphilis. And I stood there in my tattered football uniform with a number eight on my black jersey. A single tear dropped from my eye, trickled down my cheek. The salty liquid burned when it reached the mass of sores around my lip.

The seminary gave us three vacation periods every year: three weeks in June, two weeks in September, and one week in February. During those weeks we got our first taste of the deferential treatment the clergy receives from the world outside. This, combined with the fact that most of our contacts with old friends became distant and more tenuous, caused us to spend our vacations in groups.

We were enjoined to travel about in twos much

like the nuns, always with a "prudent companion." So we ended up week-ending at one another's homes. Our families got to know one another; they had something in common and quickly became friends.

Mother, still the party girl, soon became the Perle Mesta of the clerical set. Every vacation she threw a big dinner for all my friends from the seminary, plus Father Artioli and his mother and the other priests from the parish. There were never less than twenty at the table and Mother always cooked for three days in advance. Her cooking was already famous from the holiday catering she used to tote out to Darlington. But the sparkling burgundy, the champagne, the linen and the silverware and the expensive Italian pastries gave her dinners that final touch that made them conversation pieces for weeks back at the Rock.

By some kind of automatic process, my family had been transformed into the very model of what a Catholic family ought to be. Both Bernie and Kay had now transferred from public to parochial school. It cost money to be the family of a priest; Kay had been enrolled at a very expensive private girls' school for the elite—the very snob daughters of mayors and congressmen and politicians were her friends at St. Dominick's. And when she played hooky for twenty-nine days straight to go to the Paramount Theatre to hear Frankie Laine, she wasn't expelled. As the sister of a future priest, she got special dispensation. She was made to come in early for three months and clean windows as penance for disobedience, but she wasn't expelled.

Bernie had it tougher. He was deputized my watchdog and guardian angel during vacations. When nice Catholic girls would stop me on the street, Bernie was always around to throw himself into the breach and head them off. When girls telephoned, Bernie gave them the brush. When girls invited me to dinner or to

111

parties at their homes, Bernie made it discouragingly clear that he was coming along and if they thought they were going to corner me alone, they had another think coming.

It got to be a game. One summer when we went to a dude ranch together for a few days, I gave Bernie the slip. After square dancing—out of uniform—for fifteen minutes I found the girl I was dancing with was a nurse. From then on it was automatic. I sneaked off with her into the parking lot and we necked and petted for a half hour while Bernie was running around in the darkness, frantic.

"Gabe! *Gabe!* Gabe!" he kept hollering.

"Isn't that your name?" the nurse asked me between smooches.

"A lot of guys were named after St. Gabriel," I explained.

"What is he worried about?" she wanted to know.

"I'm studying for the priesthood and I'm not supposed to be doing this sort of thing. But I'm on vacation."

"I'll say you are," she said.

At my next confession I had sinful necking and petting, genuine mortal sins to check in with instead of just an elusive bunch of thoughts and some petty infractions of the Rule.

Father Artioli always appreciated my problems. He knew how silly it could be for seminarians to go to the seashore together. Healthy athletic guys swimming and sunning all by themselves, avoiding the girls like the plague, get taken for flits.

Father Artioli understood this without any discussion. So one of the first things he did was to extend the open invitation I always had to spend as much time as I could manage at his cottage at Seaside Heights.

"If you want to invite any of your seminary friends,

just tell them how to get there," he told me. "We don't need any advance notice. We have the car. We'll manage the cooking. If the weather is good and they want to sleep over, that's fine."

This became the perfect solution to summer vacations. I would invite from two to three boys down for a weekend. Some of them were anxious to get away from their families and they would stay even longer.

It was like old home week for Father Artioli, a small seminary without any boring rules. We didn't need them. We all went swimming together, we played beach ball until we were exhausted. Then we did the shopping and the cooking and the cleaning.

There was only one threshold in the place. Nobody had a private room. When we had three guests I had to bunk in the attic or in a double bed with Father Artioli. I decided that rule about not stepping over the threshold of another seminarian's room had to be made to order for the flits anyway.

Father Artioli was more than a spiritual advisor. I could turn to him with any of my problems. Anybody could. During the war I had never seen anyone work harder than he. He used to answer every letter he got from a serviceman. That ran into thousands. He worried about families left behind; when their allotment checks didn't arrive on time, he loaned them money. When boys were in the hospital, he went miles to visit them. He burned himself out worrying about other people's problems. And with all that, he still had time for me.

He would have been a perfect rector at the seminary. He had everything. If his name had only been McCarthy or Clancy he would surely have been rector and gone on from there to being a Bishop. But the Irish had a strangle hold on the American heirarchy right from the beginning and they knew how to keep themselves in power. The Italians were moving into city politics and taking over some of the city machines. But the Irish hung on to the Church machines, and wouldn't let go. One worry I wouldn't have. I'd never get to be a Bishop.

I told Father Artioli about the girls on vacations; I told him about Marilyn. I told him about the nurses—all of them. And I told him about the dreams and the nightmares—down to the last detail. Sometimes we would discuss it far into the night.

"Temptation is everywhere, Gabriel," he said, turning to me. "You're an honest boy. I know you're telling me the truth because lying is not your nature."

I could lie to others maybe, but not to him. He knew that.

"Of course you were tempted. We are all tempted. But the truth is you did not yield, did you?"

"No, Father," I said. "I guess I didn't. At least I never went all the way, as they say."

"And why not?"

"I don't really know. Something always held me back."

"Because you're strong, Gabriel, strong. That's what I like about you, your strength. I know you enjoy the company of women so I think it foolish to prohibit it. I trust you."

One day when I had permission to visit the doctor in Jersey City, I decided to pop in at home and surprise the family. When I walked in I thought Bernie was acting strangely.

"Oh," he said, "it's Father Longo."

"Yeah," I said, "what did I do now? Where's Mom?"

"She's at Aunt Carrie's."

"Oh, a meeting of the club?"

"No, she went alone to have a good cry."

"A good cry? About what?"

"She's been crying for a week. Ever since she got that letter from the seminary."

"What letter?"

"The letter, about you."

Why hadn't they told me they were writing my parents? "What kind of letter?"

"Oh, it was a beautiful letter. Gorgeous."

"Did you see it?"

"Mother cried so much I finally made her show it to me."

"She cried because it was so beautiful?"

"You've been accepted for Ordination. We are no longer your family. The Church militant is your family. Mother is no longer your mother. You belong to God and the Virgin Mary now."

"Oh, Bernie, cut it out."

"I'm quoting exactly. No wonder she sat down and cried for a week. 'But I gave birth to him,' she said. 'I gave birth to him.' "

"They send these things to all the families, I guess."

"Well, you explain it to her."

"Bernie, I haven't got the time. I just came in to see the doctor."

"What's the matter now?"

"Nothing."

"Oh, just goofing off again."

"Yeah."

"And another thing Mother asked me about. I need the straight dope. Some Lithuanian woman she met when we were visiting at the seminary got Mother all hopped up. She told her at your Ordination they anoint your hands with holy oils and wipe them with a special pure linen cloth. Then they put the cloth in a big velvet case with a glass top. The nuns paint something inside and this gets presented to Mother. Mother is supposed to keep it forever—or at least until she dies.

After her death they wrap her hands in it and then place it in her coffin. That way everyone knows she's the mother of a priest and she gets that express flight to heaven."

"Yes, and what is your question?"

"Is this the straight dope?"

"Why, did that upset Mother too?"

"No. Not at all. She thinks it's marvelous. She can't wait. She talked to your buddy John the Greek about it and he thought it would be a wonderful privilege."

"I'm sure that's the way it's intended, Bernie. I'll inquire about it, though. Any other questions?"

"Yes. What about my coffin, and Kay's and Dad's?"

"I'll see what I can do."

"How about seats for your June Ordination to the Sub-deaconate? Everybody's been after us. We only get ten seats. There are four of us. Six invitations and all Mother's family—there's going to be trouble."

"Bernie," I told him, "whatever happens, I'm sure you can handle it. Just tell them invitations are limited. Or talk to Father Artioli about it. Let him explain it to them."

In five seminary years, I had packed to leave at least three times. Another half dozen times, I had seriously slammed my suitcases on the bed, but somebody was always able to talk me out of it.

This time, I decided, I would just plain leave. Nobody could convince me any more that my doubts weren't real. I would postpone all of the talking until later. The Ordination to Sub-deaconate would be in a month. It was now or never.

Half my class had left for one reason or another. Why should I let anyone tell me I was one of the chosen ones, that God permits the Devil to design a special obstacle course for me more rigorous than the one designed for ordinary Holy Joes? Brainwashing was brainwashing, whether the Communists did it or we did it to ourselves.

Father Artioli had come up to Darlington for a day of Recollection. It was a special ritual in which former seminarians, now priests, came back to spend time amid the seminary surroundings in search of religious refreshment. When he came on surprise visits, every two months or so, I sometimes had him mostly to myself. We took long walks and had a very relaxed time. But today he had a whole entourage with him.

A visiting priest was a walking holiday in the seminary. If you knew him, and he knew you, his presence there was automatic permission for suspension of the rules. You could leave your room anytime, cut study time—you could even cut rituals and prayers if he permitted you to bull with him in his suite.

On Sunday night when Father Artioli was leaving, I was lost in the mob. Father shook hands all around, gave everybody his blessing. When he said his usual "Goodbye, Gabe" to me, there were twenty guys around, laughing and joking.

"I'll see you in a couple of days, Father," I said.

Nobody seemed to notice that Father Artioli was startled. But he didn't say a word. I figured it was just as well. Everything he could possibly have to say, I had already heard. I watched him drive off, then I went up to my room to continue packing. When I got the empty suitcases on the bed, my eyes started getting misty. Before I got my closet half cleaned out, I was almost crying. I went to the bathroom and threw some cold water on my face.

Then I thought I heard a knock at my door. I left the water running and dashed across the room to slide my packed suitcases under the bed.

Father Artioli was standing at the door. Why was I surprised? I had practically begged him to come back with that "I'll see you in a couple of days" remark.

117

I had taken the vow to leave first and talk afterwards. Why couldn't I stick with it? Why did I have to fish for his attention? What was I trying to do?

But I had to tell him. He had to be the first to know as a matter of fact. He had guessed I was about to leave a few times before. In the seminary, our whole conditioning teaches us to substitute someone else's feelings for our own, someone else's thinking for our own. You learned to bend to the rule. By the time it became habit, your own feelings and resentments were buried so deep they barely showed. You barely felt them yourself. But Father Artioli had known me for too many years.

I could feel the tears starting to come when he looked at me, so I turned away.

"I decided to spend the night and say Mass here in the morning," he said. "You'll serve, won't you?"

"I'd like to very much, Father," I said, "except I. . . ."

I wouldn't make a clever criminal. I had shoved the packed suitcases under the bed, but I'd left the closet door wide open. He took a look at it and closed the hall door.

"You don't want to talk to an old friend?" Father said.

"Father Artioli, may I ask you something?" I began.

"My goodness Gabriel, what a *question!*"

"Are you proud of me?"

He smiled. He beamed. He nodded his head.

"Father, may I be so bold as to ask why?"

"Why?" he said. "You mean that what you call your doubts, your difficulties, now include your old friends?" It took a few seconds but finally I nodded my head. Then I knew I was going to cry so I excused myself, ducked into the bathroom.

Father Artioli came to the bathroom door.

"My parents are proud of me too, why? The people

in the parish are proud of me too. Why? What do they know? Don't they know pride is sin? Tell them to get ready. They can stop being proud. I don't want anybody to feel proud of crazy Gabe any longer."

"Gabriel, the very first day you expressed your desire to become a priest, I thanked God and I prayed that you would persevere until the end. I knew the difficulties, the trials and the tribulations you would encounter along the way. I knew them as well as I know my own weaknesses and failings. I still pray for you every morning. I will continue to pray for you, no matter what happens. You have spent five years under severe strain, cut off from the pleasures and ambitions of the world. You have worked hard. God has endowed you with talents, gifted you with—oh, Gabriel, you have so many gifts. We must accept the bitterness. We must learn to accept despair and suffering. You are young. You have been through so much—your accident, your operations. Give yourself a chance. The boys were telling me only today how you brought life and music and laughter back to Darlington when you returned from the hospital. It wasn't the same place without you. This is a gift from the Lord Almighty, Gabriel. A precious gift. Many poor souls have come to the seminary and suffered and abandoned their vocation and left. And when they go, in our hearts we can only say: 'Thy will be done.' Even though the harvest is great and the laborers are few, we say: 'God's will shall be done.' Not everyone has the strength and the power and the fortitude for the difficult life that lies ahead—rescuing tormented souls from the enemies of Christ and His Church. Here at Darlington, attracted by your personality, your good humor, your music, your gift for laughter, many boys have been touched by your sanctity and your sincerity. This is not pride on their part. This is love, Gabriel.

"We are all searching for light. But without the

119

darkness of temptation, we can never know or appreciate the Light of Divine Guidance. God guides us through darkness so we may know its powers. God allows Satan to tempt us, so we may know His powers. Unless we know His powers, how are we to feel mercy, mercy for the lost ones of this world? God allowed His only begotten Son—of whom He was so proud—to become man so He could experience, so He could feel and suffer as you are suffering. For unless we know the powers of Satan, we shall never know this world in which we must labor, in which we must contest everlastingly with the Devil to rescue souls from the enemies of the Church.

"To become *man*, Gabriel, means to suffer as you are suffering. To become *man*, Gabriel, means to have known each of the Devil's lures and wiles and stratagems. Otherwise how are we to help others if we do not know sin?

"As a priest, Gabriel, you will know all men. Before you can know all men, you must know yourself.

"The chosen ones are tempted beyond endurance so they may be able to extend the fullness of God's mercy for other sinners.

"To become man is to know mercy. To become man is to know Satan. To become man is to go to the brink of despair where Almighty God waits with the gift of grace.

"Tomorrow morning I will say Mass and you will serve. It will be a Mass of Thanksgiving to God for having brought you through the deepest despair to the fullness of His Grace.

"It will be a Mass like any other Mass. Nobody will know our secret intentions, our secret joy, except you and me and Almighty God, God bless you, Gabriel."

I was crying. I felt awful. One thing was true. I was not merciful. I felt no mercy really for my superiors. Maybe they had troubles worse than mine, but they were not quitting. Maybe when I had been through what they had been through, I would feel a little more generous and human and merciful. Father was right. I was an awful prig. I had always had it too easy. My parents were always so great to me, I didn't know what hell a family could make for one another.

Some guys I knew didn't have anyone they could turn to. I had my own father, and Father Artioli who was on my team all the way. I didn't have any worries except about myself. Maybe that's it. Maybe that's what he meant. Maybe that's why I was having my share. I needed to have a rough time to take the starch out of me, to make me a little more generous and merciful and not such a damn prig.

Who was I to accuse other people of pride? Whose pride was I worried about? Wasn't it my own? A little less pride and a little more mercy for my fellow man. Think about other people for a change.

Father Artioli had a genius for putting his finger on things. If I hadn't packed, we wouldn't have had this time together.

I was still crying when he left. Then I rushed down to the chapel to thank God for sending Father Artioli back to help me. What would I do without him? Whenever I needed him, he always seemed to be there.

My seminary career had begun with Father Artioli explaining things to the family and that was the way it would end, apparently. The details and the minutiae began to mount. Once a candidate has been accepted, he begins to receive what are called Minor Orders. I became a Cleric when my hair was clipped symbolically in five places with appropriate prayers. (In Europe, Clerics wear the ancient tonsure in the form of a circular shaven spot on the top of the head, but in the United States the custom has disappeared.) I was ordained a Porter and given a symbolic key to open and close the church. As a Lector, I was authorized to read the scriptures in church to a congregation, or to read the martyrology in the refectory before and after dinner. As Exorcist I was empowered to drive out evil spirits—but this was symbolic too. It was an investment of power which could not be used without special permission. Finally as an Acolyte I received the right to assist the Sub-deacon in serving at Mass—a function relegated in practice to altar boys—something I alone, among my class, had never been.

The Minor Orders are symbolic of positions that were active and important in the earlier days of the church and may be revived again. Next came Ordination to Major Orders. When we became Sub-deacons, we would incur all the obligations of priesthood with none of its privileges. We would be allowed to wear our Roman collars in the street, and my official title was to be Reverend Mr. Longo.

This was the ceremony coming up next. It is the next most solemn occasion to priesthood ordination itself. All the parents and friends were invited—to the limit the small chapel would hold.

I had the ten invitations in my room. Giving those pieces of paper to my parents would become my final commitment. After that there would be no turning back.

During these last few weeks, stories of defections from the priesthood spread through the seminary; all of the renegades had been a year or two ahead of our class. One ran off with a married woman. His classmates formed a posse, rescued him and brought him back. Then he fled again. They dragged him back a second time. Then he left again and when last heard from was working as a night clerk in a Florida hotel.

Another great guy ran off with a nurse from Newark. They got married and he became a minister in a Protestant church in Jersey. This one unrolled too fast for his classmates to perform any rescue operations. Once he married there was no turning back. Anything but that. Anything, but anything. "As long as you don't get married," was the by-word of all priestly scandals. Even becoming a Protestant minister was a forgivable aberration, but marriage was final.

Another non-flit priest who had graduated two years before suffered through two years as an assistant to the worst priest imaginable in a terrible parish, threw in the towel and moved to Philadelphia, where he took a job in one of the few things for which he was qualified: semi-pro basketball.

We talked about these guys endlessly. We recalled their ordinations; how we had served at their First Masses. We tried to imagine the humiliation of their families. We got out the special prayers for spoiled and wayward priests.

We felt our prayers had been answered when we received news that one of the unfortunates had been finally admitted to Via Coeli, an institution located in the New Mexican desert, dedicated to the rehabilitation of priests who had fallen from grace through drinking, through loss of faith, or through temptations of the flesh.

"There but for the grace of God, go I," was always in our thoughts. We knew these men as well as we knew ourselves. If it could happen to them, it could happen to anybody. But for the grace of God.

I began to feel that perhaps my greatest temptations were behind me. Maybe Father Artioli was right; maybe I was strong. Maybe surviving all these temptations had helped to make me stronger. Maybe that's why he had given me permission to date all through minor seminary at Seton Hall. To test me, to let me try my wings, to see if I would survive. Well, I obviously had. I had no more faith than I had when I began at the seminary. But I had no less either.

123

Maybe the thing to do was keep on praying and hoping and one day I would be worthy. So I prayed. Those words became as natural as breathing: "Oh, Lord, help my unbelief."

You are cordially invited to the
Ordination to the Sacred Order
of Sub-deacon
to be conferred by
the Most Rev. James A. McNulty, D. D.
Auxiliary Bishop of Newark
at Christ the King Church
Immaculate Conception Seminary, Darlington, N. J.
Saturday, May 19, 1951 at 9 A.M.

Mother and Dad were both very superstitious. Over-planning meant an invitation for something to go awry. So it wasn't until those invitations for my Ordination as Sub-deacon were actually in hand that the whole thing seemed real. Until that time, I had an "out" to leave like so many others. After Sunday, I would be committed. Dad was a very proud man, yet always a complete realist. When he saw the invitations he had said: "I don't think I am worthy to have a son a priest."

Bernie was going to be in charge of all the arrangements, costumes and choreography for the Ordination and my First Mass. He went shopping with Mother to decide what she would wear. It turned out to be royal blue lace.

Our last few months in the seminary were devoted to the external side of the priesthood. Long lectures on how to handle our own finances and those of our parish. Rehearsals in the celebration of the Mass. How to counsel parishioners; how to administer the sacraments validly and licitly, with special attention to the Last Rites; and how to cope with the questions of women in the confessional, especially as they concerned matters involving sex.

124

Then there were almost daily letters from the family about arrangements for celebration of First Mass at my home parish, the inevitable banquet, the invitation lists, the gifts, the schedule, what everybody ought to wear. In between these details, the main speculation among the Deacons involved: who was going to get stuck with the impossible pastors in the Diocese. Next came the big decision of what kind of automobile we would use our gift money to buy.

Individuality could only really register in two places, our automobiles and our chalices. According to custom, the chalice is a living memorial to one's family. Every time Mass is celebrated, the family receives special divine favors and indulgences. At Easter time, when most of our parents came to visit, the seminary had—in cooperation with various official archdiocesan jewelers— arranged an exhibit of the latest models, varying in style from the simple to the most ornate.

The custom-made chalice of one of my Irish classmates was arranged as the feature of the display. It had a huge cross of diamonds at the base and looked like something out of a museum.

I had chosen a rather simple streamlined model but when Mother saw those diamonds it must have started her thinking: "We've got to do something for Gabe." She never said anything to me, but immediately set about making an inventory of our family jewels. Her diamond engagement ring, all our baby rings, her diamond earrings—all these were thrown into the hopper to be melted down and transformed into something spectacular.

Mother's wedding ring was not melted down, but attached intact in the hollow at the base of the chalice, so that every time it was elevated in consecration, my fingers would always be touching that precious plain gold band.

125

mcmli

The whole Catholic world is on bended knee in fervent prayer for the young men on retreat this week to be ordained priests on Trinity Saturday. Amongst them is one of our own boys, born and raised in our parish, who studied at Seton Hall and Darlington Seminary, approved by his superiors to become another Christ among men. Rev. Gabriel Longo, son of Mr. & Mrs. Bernard Longo and brother to Bernard and Kay Longo. He will be ordained a priest forever at St. Patrick's Cathedral in Newark on Saturday at 9:00 by his Excellency Archbishop Thomas J. Walsh. He will say his First Solemn High Mass in our Church next Sunday at 11:00 with the pastor as Archpriest and preacher, Rev. Robert Garner, Deacon, Rev. Mr. George Macho, Subdeacon, Rev. Salvatore Citarella, Master of Ceremonies, Mr. Benny Militello, Ass't. Master of Ceremonies, sung by our Adult Choir with Mrs. Gilda Muller at the organ, under the direction of Rev. Vincent Garoffolo assisted by Rev. Eugene Fanelli. Please note that next Sunday Father Longo's First Mass will be the last Mass in Church. For the benefit of those who cannot attend the First Solemn High Mass there are two Low Masses in the Church Hall at 11:00 and noon.

After the First Solemn High Mass, Father Longo will give only his General Blessing because there will be a dinner in his honor with the priests, sisters, family, relatives and close friends at Ilvento's at 1:00. He will be celebrant of the Solemn Vespers sung at 4 P.M. in Church with panegyric by Rev. Dr. Bertrando Pandolfo of the Dominican Order, after which he will also give his general blessing. A reception open to the public, with refreshments, will be tendered him from 5:00 to 8:00 P.M. in the Church Hall, where everyone may receive, individually, his first priestly blessing gaining a 50 day indulgence by kissing his freshly anointed hands. There will be on display on the stage all the gifts that a priest can well use, donated by his family and the Societies of the Parish. We ask individuals or families to give money which a young priest can well use to buy the things he personally needs in beginning his holy ministry.

> "I LIVE NOW, NOT I,
> BUT CHRIST LIVES IN ME."
> *St. Paul to Galatians 2/20*

"This, indeed, is the day which the Lord has made. Let us rejoice and be glad. A young man returns home to his own parish, welcomed by his devoted Pastor, embraced by his beloved parents, brother and sister, and greeted by priests and sisters, relatives and friends with great joy and sincere congratulations.

"He comes back to his home town, not as some would expect, a leader of a big name band, a player in the major leagues, or a star in the Show of Shows. In fact, he returns not merely as a student who has honorably completed his course or mastered a profession, nor as an explorer or an adventurer after heroic and daring achievements, nor as a brave soldier who has fought and bled for his country. He comes back to his loved ones with something more respected than membership on the Hit Parade, or in the Hall of Fame, or for an Oscar award; something more honorable than a mere profession; something more praiseworthy than discovery or exploit; something more glorious than a soldier's victory.

"Today, he returns a priest, 'Taken from among men, ordained for men in things that appertain to God that he may offer gifts and sacrifices for sins.' Behold him, anointed with the oils of ordination, clothed in the robes of the Holy Priesthood, vested with the authority and powers of Christ Himself. Behold, him, an Ambassador,

127

aye, more than an Ambassador. Behold Him, another Christ!"

THE SANCTUARY was stacked with so many flowers that from where I sat, up against the wall, I could barely be seen. Monsignor Artioli was in the pulpit delivering his sermon. I didn't want to listen. The sermon wasn't for me anyway. It was for Mom and Dad and all the mothers and dads who might be telling their sons they were too young to be thinking about entering the priesthood.

In the stillness of the sanctuary, Monsignor Artioli's dramatic vocal delivery was like a sleeping pill. It seemed the first chance I'd had to relax in days. My right arm was already sore from delivering blessings to everyone who asked. In the street. On the sidewalk. When I came out of the bathroom there was someone kneeling waiting to get that precious indulgence.

Mother and Dad were in the front pew. Then Bernie and Kay; Uncle Frank and Aunt Marie; Aunt Carrie and Uncle Nick; then the Branco family, Dad's buddy and my godfather; Uncle George, Mother's brother; Aunt Tessie from Connecticut, and all my cousins. Then everybody who was anybody in the parish, arranged in the strictest order of protocol. The heads of the societies and their officers. The ushers, the families of my assistants. An entire hierarchy just as complicated as the one at the Cathedral Ordination the day before, Saturday. Today was Sunday: Trinity Sunday. I had to remind myself.

Last Sunday we had begun a week of fasting and retreat. No meat. Seminary fish was always inedible. No wonder some of the guys were faint when they got off the bus at the Cathedral Saturday, linen down to the ground, arms full of vestments, like a bunch of supers at the Metropolitan Opera, weak from fasting and all the emotional strain of a first night. And poring over the manual of Ordination. I was neither the first in line nor the last. I was in the great middle in the order of seniority. We dressed at the rectory and then gathered in the street to walk into the Cathedral and down the main aisle. Then the music and the bells began. I tried to keep my eyes straight ahead of me in the procession. Then I saw Mrs. Artioli and her daughter standing in the street. I wasn't expecting to see anybody and just seeing them threw me off. I remembered that first glass of Coca-Cola at the rectory and the ice bucket. "Many beautiful gifts. Wait, you'll see," she had said. I felt a lump in my throat. I tried to fix my mind on something steady, some kind of control. The music was beginning to get to me and I didn't want to do anything silly and have to reach for a handkerchief later.

Once we got inside there was safety in numbers. Our class was augmented by some Passionist Fathers and some Benedictines, so the sacristy was a mob scene, with barely room to move.

The Ordination ceremony includes a Mass said *en masse* with all the newly ordained priests pronouncing the words in unison with the Bishop. Father Artioli was in the sanctuary somewhere, but I couldn't find his face. When we turned to bless the congregation I tried to catch sight of my family but all I could see was Mother's navy blue hat. It stood out all right, like Bernie said it would.

The Bishop had his hands on me and I could hear the Latin prayers. Intention. It was a matter of intention. Giving and receiving Holy Orders. Our Gabe is a priest at last.

"Another Christ! That is why the dignity of the Catholic priesthood is so sublime. That is why we pay him such reverence and respect. It is because now and forever Christ lives in him. 'I live, now, not I, but Christ lives in me.'

"My dear friends, if we wish to realize and appreciate the dignity to which our Gabe has been raised today, if we wish to enter the spirit of this joyful occasion, let us consider how the priest is another Christ. In order to draw all men to Himself, Christ chose fellow-workers, apostles, priests to spread His teachings and to bring the benefits of His Cross and Passion for all times to the ends of the earth.

"*His mission therefore, is not over,* for He said to His priests, as was said to Father Longo yesterday by one of the successors of the apostles: 'As the Father has sent me, I also send you. Go into the whole world and preach the Gospel to every creature, teaching them to observe all things whatsoever I have commanded you.'

"*His power is not extinct,* for it is vested in His priests. 'All power is given to me in heaven and on earth. Whatsoever you shall bind upon earth, shall be bound in heaven; and whatsoever you shall loose on earth, shall be loosed in heaven.'

"*Nor is His mercy exhausted,* for the sinner can still obtain pardon from the priest to whom was said, 'Receive ye the Holy Ghost, whose sins you shall forgive, they are forgiven them and whose sins you shall retain, they are retained.'

"*Not even has the Sacrifice of the Cross ceased to be.* From morning until night in some part of the world, the tragedy of Calvary is reenacted in the Sacrifice of the Mass. At the Last Supper, Christ changed bread and wine into His Body and Blood, instituting the Mass as a renewal of His Passion and Death. And, turning to the Apostles, His priests, He said, 'Do this in commemoration of Me.' In the words of St. Paul, 'As often as you shall eat of this bread, or drink of this Chalice, you shall show the death of the Lord until He come.'

"Christ, therefore, still lives in His priests today. Through them, His mission, His power, His mercy, His redemption, are spread throughout the world. Wherever there is a priest, there is also another Christ.

"Hence, when the Priest breathes upon the infant in baptism, that breath is the breath of Christ. When he gives instructions for the reception of the Sacraments, it is again Christ teaching the people and suffering the children to come unto Him. When, in preaching, he warns and threatens unbelievers and hardened sinners, when he condemns modern errors and vices, that warning threat and condemnation are those of Jesus Christ, Himself. When he blesses persons, places or articles, there is Christ imparting His blessings. When he marries bridal couples, it is as though Christ, Himself, were present as He was at the marriage feast of Cana. When he anoints and prays over the sick and dying, that anointing and prayer are those of Christ.

"To whom does a poor sinner go, bowed down with shame and remorse, yearning for pardon and encouragement? He goes to a priest as to Christ, Himself. He kneels at his feet and, in sorrow and repentance, tells him secrets known to God alone. The priest raises his hand and says to him, 'I absolve you from your sins.' Note, he does not say, 'Christ absolves you,' but '*I* absolve you.' It is Christ in the priest who forgives the poor sinner and sends him away healed, consoled and encouraged.

"And when the priest ascends the altar to offer the Sacrifice of the Mass, as Father Longo does the first time for us today, who is it, but Christ renewing the Sacrifice of Calvary. On that first Good Friday, Christ was nailed and raised on the Cross to suffer and bleed to death for the sins of men. What happens now, in the Mass? The priest takes a piece of bread and says, 'This is my Body,' and instantly, the Sacred Body of Christ is on the altar. He takes the Chalice of wine and says, 'This is My Blood.' Scarcely are the words uttered, and the Precious Blood of Christ is there in the Chalice. Note again, that the priest does not say, 'This is Christ's Body—This is Christ's Blood,' but 'This is My Body—This is My Blood.' It is Christ, again, who offers Himself to the Father for us. Christ adores, Christ begs graces; Christ gives thanks; Christ pleads for pardon and makes satisfaction for our sins. Here, in the Mass, Christ and the priest are one. 'O exalted power of the priest in whose hands, as in the womb of the Virgin Mary, the Son of God is made flesh.' "

After the Cathedral ordination ceremony we had all moved to give our first blessing to the Ordaining Bishop, then to our classmates, and then we moved to the altar rail and turned around to bless our relatives and parents. The families had all been instructed to walk up reverently to the rail and stand still there.

Everything went fine at the rehearsal when none of the parents were there but now in a flash half the women in the Cathedral became a pushing, sniffing mob of stage mothers, elbowing their way to get to that area of the railing where their little boy was holding up his hands.

That's when they should have turned off the music and sent the choir home. The choir and the organ had overdone it and sparked a real emotional orgy. Some of the new priests were bawling, some started passing out. But the veteran priests were ready for that too. They just waited for one to keel over and then carted him off to the wings.

Mother didn't have to push and squeeze. She stood out like the star of the show. I raised my arms in the direction of her blue hat and vaulted my blessing over the others like a sneaky forward pass. Then I had to bless my way out of the Cathedral, bless my way through the crowd. Everywhere I turned people were falling on their knees. Rudolph Valentino's funeral must have been something like this. Then Mother was hugging me and kissing me. Dad held me so tight I felt like a weakling in his arms. My father was as hard and tight and as strong as the last time he had hugged me, which must have been years before. Mother was weeping and talking at the same time, until Bernie barked at her:

"Julia, your mascara! Enough already."

Bernie could always whip out a joke and pull Mother out of anything.

Then Monsignor Artioli found us and took over. And somehow we all ended up at Bruno's in Jersey City. The proud mother wore the blue hat and the head waiter got the message. The whole place broke out in smiles and Mother basked in it. This was her debut as mother of a priest and she was ready. A little man with a flash camera began turning up everytime I turned around. The flash of the camera replaced the music. I asked him who he was. Monsignor had arranged everything. The recruiting poster with the pointed finger. God Wants You.

"No wonder then, that the priest has always been regarded with the deepest veneration and profoundest respect. Not because he is tall, dark and handsome, nor because he has a dynamic personality, or is a star ballplayer, or a grand singer, or plays an instrument, not even because he may be an eloquent orator or a convert maker. But, rather, as St. Francis of Assisi so well explained: 'If I should happen to meet on the way an Angel and a priest walking together, I would salute the priest and then the Angel.' Why? 'I would salute the priest first because he represents Christ Himself, whereas the Angel, great as he is, is only God's servant.'

"Now, do we realize better the sublime dignity conferred upon Father Longo? In this, his First Solemn High Mass, as in all his future works of the priesthood, this young priest stands in the place of Christ. He personates Christ. He is an instrument in the hands of Christ; Christ using him, acting through him, so that his hands are the Hands of Christ; his voice, the Voice of Christ; his heart, the Heart of Christ. From now on, he, also, can say with St. Paul: 'I live, now, not I, but Christ lives in me.'"

Mother and her friends had been scouting dinners and receptions after celebrations of First Masses and she had a list of mistakes to be avoided. Nothing would be left to chance. Ours was going to be without flaw.

The preparations had gone on for two years. It took three solid days just to write the invitations: 404 people to dinner and more than a thousand for the reception. It took weeks to decide on the lists.

Bernie had a good job working as a salesman for a national men's clothing manufacturer in the Pittsburgh area. The long-distance wires hummed with Mother and her friends worrying him. Bernie took over completely. He issued a series of decrees.

The basic one was that black dresses were out. Black was Italian Old Country. If your husband died in the meantime, you either came in navy blue or you stayed away. He wasn't having anything jar the festiveness of the occasion.

The second communique decreed that Mother had priority in terms of color. After she had selected what she would wear, her friends could pick and choose from what was left of the palette. The dress-buying began in February. Bernie would come in from Pittsburgh almost every Saturday to escort Mother, or the aunts, or the friends to New York on their shopping trips. He was the arbiter and they listened to him and loved being told what to do and what not to do.

It was decided that Mother would wear grey. Getting the special hat to match the special grey of the special dress became a big production. Her regular milliner from Jersey had to take her into New York to see Madame Titania of Saks.

Two years before, Dior had made his big splash in Paris, so Bernie took Kay to Lord and Taylor and covered her with one of Dior's creations in romance pink organza. A special hat had to be made to go with that.

When Bernie finished outfitting the ladies, he laid down the law for the members of the Holy Name Society who were being given the privilege of acting as ushers. Navy blue suits for all of them and nothing else. Ditto for uncles and cousins. When that was settled he and Dad rented morning coats, complete with striped trousers and vests. He went to Fifth

Avenue for the gloves and the shirts and the handker-
chiefs and the fittings. He wanted the family to stand
out. The distinction was to be complete.

"My dear friends, we can well be proud of Father
Gabriel Anthony Longo, who, from Our Lady of Mt.
Carmel Parish, follows the footsteps of Father Cestaro
and Father Dell'Orto, in the Holy Priesthood. May his
sacred vocation be imitated in the lives of many other
boys of our parish. Through his spirit of sacrifice, in-
spiration and encouragement, may other girls follow the
example of Sister Agnes De Pasquale and Sister John
Mary Scopelletti in the Sisterhood.

"You may ask, what attracted Father Longo to the
priesthood? Vocations to the religious life come in so
many various ways, and at different times, that it is difficult to decide how or when I got my vocation. Perhaps,
through the prayers of pious parents, or the example or
encouragement of a priest or sister or the preaching of a
missionary or the reading of the lives of the Saints. For
Gabe, it was the priestly zeal of Father Fanelli who uses
his pleasing personality and varied talents so well in draw-
ing people to God and His Church. He is not only the
king of the kids, or the little clown, as some call him, nor
is he only the blessed friend of the youth, but rather, he
knows how to bring Christ within himself out from the
Church, into the home, the school, on the street and at
play. In a word, as another Christ he is all to all men for
the glory of God and the salvation of souls.

"Father Longo then accepted wholeheartedly the guidance and counsel of his Pastor and professors. Overcom-
ing obstacles and doubts, he completed his course of
studies at Seton Hall Prep and University with praise
from his superiors. In the seminary, he used his natural
talents well to enliven the life of the seminarians, was a
source of edification in his own personal spiritual life, and
proven worthy to receive the character and powers of the
Sacrament of Holy Orders, conferred yesterday at St.
Patrick's Cathedral in Newark by his Excellency, Bishop
McNulty."

Crazy Gabe they called me. Monsignor Artioli
wouldn't let me forget that.

Saturday had been such a beautiful day, but Sunday

topped it. Everyone looked at the sunshine as some kind of a sign.

Monsignor Artioli got out of mothballs all the splendrous gold vestments for special occasions. When we vested together in the rectory it was like vacation at Seaside Heights. Everyone who assisted me was a personal choice. Of course there were Willie and Joe, who were the first priests ordained from the parish. I was number three. Now Benny Militello, another boy from the parish, had gone to the seminary, so he got the important job of assistant master of ceremonies. Continuity. Monsignor Artioli's boys.

As each one came into the rectory he shook my hand, knelt before me while holding my hand and said: "May I have your blessing, Father?" and I blessed him. It was one thing to bless people on the sidewalk, in the crowded street—but to bless other priests! Then the music began to boom through the whole neighborhood. The choir had rehearsed for months to learn a special Mass. Then they began chanting the processional and it was time to move.

Thou Art a Priest. *Tu es Sacerdos*. The cross bearer left first, flanked by two acolytes in cassock and surplices bearing huge candles. They were joined by the little girls of the St. Theresa Society, two-by-two in their white dresses and white shoes, carrying baskets of rose petals which they scattered in the street. Then came the little boys in their blue suits and white satin armbands with the flowered rosettes dangling from them.

Then the parish troops of boy scouts and girl scouts, in their uniforms. The Children of Mary, unmarried girls in blue veils. All the officers and members of the parish societies who had been standing in the schoolyard in formation. The cross bearer had already entered the church and the schoolyard was still full of people waiting to take their place in the procession.

Guest clergy, friends of Monsignor Artioli (there must have been at least a dozen of them) marched two-by-two in their cassocks and surplices and berettas. Then the acolytes, the Sub-deacon, the Deacon. Father Monsignor Artioli was a few steps ahead of me, and after him Benny Militello, who carried a huge bucket filled with holy water. I carried the sprinkler. The music was timed so its most triumphant passages had been saved for the moment I stepped outside. My flowing gold cape hung heavy over my arms as I dipped into the holy water and sprinkled right and left. Familiar faces blessed themselves as I passed slowly down the street toward the entrance to the church. We passed the spot where I had stood on tiptoe with my Mother twenty years before, watching the funeral procession for Father Moscati. I looked at the kids standing where I had stood. Looking bug-eyed at me the way I had looked bug-eyed at the Bishop years ago. I quickly turned the other way, afraid of breaking up.

Then we were moving slowly up the main aisle, and everyone in church turned to look at me. The music mounted to its mightiest pitch. Behind me crowds of people from the street pushed and pleaded with the ushers to get the last few remaining seats.

And then my First Mass began. I had gotten through the Introit, the Oration and the Gloria. Now the spotlight was on Monsignor Artioli as he preached from the pulpit and I had a few more moments alone behind the flowers.

> "Your hosts of relatives and friends, from far and near, from every walk of life, of every nationality, race or creed, can well rejoice that Gabe is now God's chosen priest. You remember well when he left Dickinson to go to Seton Hall, some thinking he was crazy. When you realized he was sincere, determined to succeed, and persevered in the long journey to the altar of God, you were thankful that your prayers were heard. Now, you can glory in his sacerdotal success.

"I hardly know of any other family more close to each other than the Longos; father, mother, brother and sister. They pray, work and play together. They always share in one another's joys and sorrows, failures and successes, pleasures and pains, disappointments and hopes, and even their secrets. Gabriel, Bernard and Catherine see in their mother and father models of upright, industrious and pious living. Mr. and Mrs. Longo saw their children grow in age, wisdom and grace, before God and men, giving them the opportunity of a Catholic education. They accepted, without fear, the holy vocation of their eldest child and saw in him a single honor for their family and a mark of the special love and providence of Our Lord. In all of these years of preparation, the thoughts, words and actions of Benny and Julia, Bernie and Kay, have been centered about Gabe, their son and brother, who, today, is a priest.

"What can I say to you, Mr. and Mrs. Longo, on this, the happiest day of your entire lives, which you wanted to share with the whole world even in having your folks in Italy celebrate this Day of Days? Surely, a dream come true. Imagine, yours is the privilege of being the father and mother of a priest. You remember well when your son first revealed his intentions. You accepted it as God's will and kept all things in your heart as did Joseph and Mary at the Temple, when Our Lord said that He must be about His Father's business. You would not hold him back, as so many other mothers and fathers do, who think it is too much of a sacrifice for themselves as well as their son or daughter. Your faith told you that God had the first claim. You practiced that faith all these years, and to the edification of all, joined willingly and wholeheartedly your prayers and sacrifices with his, so that you may glory in his triumph. True it is, that God took your boy from you, but today, as a reward for your generous sacrifice, coupled with sickness, He presents him to you, a priest forever—Another Christ!"

The canonization of Benny and Julia, that's what Bernie called it. There was more truth than poetry in that. Everyone in church was rubbernecking to get a glimpse of them. Every parent in the parish was being invited to become a saint by giving their son a chance to be another Christ. I had never seen Dad cry since that time he had the mumps. Now that he had a thousand people staring at him, his eyes were dry.

Dad is strong. He enjoys the company of women. He *is* strong. Maybe that's why I like him. Maybe I'm strong like he is, like Monsignor Artioli says I am. Maybe when I am as old as Dad was when he had the mumps, maybe then I'll be strong. I'll need to be. I'll hope to be.

"Gabe, now Father Longo, in the name of your fellow priests, I welcome you into the ranks of the Catholic priesthood. The very first day you expressed your desire to become a priest, I thanked God for another vocation and prayed that you would persevere to the end. You have spent six years under severe seminary discipline, cut off from the pleasures and ambitions of the world. You have devoted long hours to fervent and hard study, interrupted by joyful and consoling, refreshing and restful moments in the choir, sports, the band or in the recreation room, the barber shop and dark room. You have wrestled with weariness, discouragement and even disappointments and overcome them in the hope that the priesthood would be yours.

"Before you lies a vast and varied field. The harvest is great, but the laborers are few. Innumerable souls are searching for light, hungry for the Word of God, thirsting for inspirations and longing for mercy and pardon. God has endowed you with talents, gifted you with a congenial personality, vested you with the powers of the Sacred Priesthood so that as man and priest you might rescue these souls from the enemies of Christ and His Church.

"May showers of blessings and graces flood your life. May Mary, the Mother of Christ and His Priests, take you under Her protection. May your Patron Saint guide and inspire you. May thousands of souls hear the eloquence of your voice, be attracted by your personality, touched by your sanctity and sincerity. May Jesus Christ, the Eternal Priest with Whom you are now identified, rejoice one day in the abundant harvest you will reap in the glorious field of immortal souls. Amen."

The organ let loose a triumphant blast of sound as

the Monsignor came down from the pulpit, holding the rolled typewritten text of his prepared address in his hands. Then I mounted the altar again and intoned the Credo.

When I finished the Mass, at another signal from the organ and choir, the Recessional began. The photographer was busy every step of the way as we walked slowly back to the rectory. When I removed the heavy gold cape and began to take off my vestments, I discovered myself lathered with perspiration. I went upstairs to Monsignor Artioli's bedroom. Alone in the shower, I could be Crazy Gabe again for a few minutes before facing the rest of the day.

The family waited in the rectory until we got the signal from the head waiter at Ilvento's in Jersey City that most of the 404 dinner guests were seated.

When we entered and walked to the dais, the whole group stood up and applauded. Then I noticed the flowers, banks of pink and white roses on every table and tons of them on the dais. I knew Dad was paying for the dinner but I wondered who sold him all these posies. When Mother decided she was going to top every ordination she had ever seen, she wasn't kidding. In front of the dais, two red upholstered *prie dieus* had been set up for the ceremony of the first blessing, and these were banked with flowers.

When the six-course banquet ended with ice cream cake and espresso, Monsignor Artioli took over as M.C. and toastmaster. Everyone on the dais had to be introduced or to say a few words. Everybody took his favorite mush section from Monsignor Artioli's sermon and repeated it until I began to hate the sound of my own name.

Then Monsignor Artioli announced that the ceremony of the first blessing would begin. The guests walked up and knelt at the two *prie dieus*—blessing two at a time would speed things and also cut down the wear and tear on my sore right arm. The waiters, the priests, all pitched in to keep the crowd moving and orderly. Bernie stood right beside me and after they kissed my hand, they handed him white envelopes with money inside. While I was blessing the next couple, Bernie would stuff the paper offerings in the zippered black bag at his feet. There were precautions, needless to say. The front door and kitchen entrance were manned by dependables, who kept an eye out for crashers and strangers.

Despite all the efficiency of the speed-up production line, I blessed people until the four o'clock deadline, to when they rushed me back to the rectory to dress for the celebration of Vespers. Then back to the rectory to change again for the reception in the auditorium in the basement of the church.

The ordeal of blessing four hundred at the dinner was just a warm-up. At the reception there seemed to be thousands of people. They led me past buffet tables loaded with food to the head of the reception line on stage. Old ladies mobbed me; while one was kissing my right hand, another would be pressing money into my left. But Bernie was always there with his little satchel.

This went on and on until Bernie's zip bags were filled, my right shirt sleeve was soaked with perspiration and one arm seemed six inches longer than the other.

Behind the reception line on the stage of the auditorium there was a huge five-tiered display that looked like a Christmas window at Gimbel's. Lamps, radios, tables, wallets and other gifts were piled, labeled with the names of their donors; official gifts from the treasuries of all the church groups, carefully screened in advance by a joint committee to avoid duplication.

While Bernie kept an eagle eye on the bags full of

money, Dad kept an eye on the rest of the crowd. We had had one Manhattan cocktail and wine at dinner, and no booze at all at the reception, but Dad knew what might happen if you put a couple of thousand people together, so pepped up by the emotionalism of the day. He wasn't going to have any incidents or scuffles mar the occasion. The men acquitted themselves admirably. The only time he had to signal the ushers to blow the whistle was when he spotted some of the parish ladies descending on the buffet tables and shoveling salami into their handbags.

The festivities went on into the wee hours of the morning but around midnight Bernie hustled me home to bed.

For two hours I had dreamed of taking another warm shower, or maybe soaking my right arm in the tub for an hour. But when I saw the bed, I had trouble finding the energy to take my jacket off. I was sure I wouldn't wake up for a week.

The next morning, Bernie and Kay and Mother had a production line going on the dining room table. Kay was opening envelopes, Bernie was putting the bills into piles and making entries in a huge ledger. Mother was keeping careful track of the whole operation. Every name, every amount was recorded. For every dollar I received, the family incurred an obligation. Practically every donor had a son or daughter with an upcoming wedding, a graduation, something. My priestly dowry was like a Liberty Loan from the parish that would have to be paid back in almost weekly installments of gifts over the next twenty years.

For the next weeks I had a commitment to say a special First Mass at the parish convent, and at St. Elizabeth's Hospital in Elizabeth, New Jersey, where Sister Connie was now stationed. The next Sunday I was expected to celebrate the Children's Mass at 9

A.M. at Mt. Carmel. The nuns had been rehearsing a "This Is Your Life, Gabriel Longo" pageant that was going to be presented afterward in the church auditorium.

Bernie and Mother and I had planned to take a few days holiday somewhere as soon as my last ordination personal appearance had been made. Bernie had already arranged to take his regular vacation from work to be on hand for all the backstage duty. Now we all needed a clean break.

We didn't want anyone to know where we were going. We just got in a car and headed in the direction of New England.

Mulberry Street, in front of the grey concrete office building at Number 31, was black with shiny new automobiles. Vacation time was over. It was old home week at the Newark Diocesan Chancery office on June 28, as we gathered together to receive our parish assignments.

The Irish priests were still guessing and wondering where they would be assigned. For me there was very little suspense. St. Rocco's was the oldest Italian parish in Newark. At one time or another, every Italian priest from the seminary ended up as an assistant to Father Joseph De Sanctis. Most of them didn't last very long. He had a reputation for being impossible. So there was always an opening. Since I was the only Italian in my class, I was sure that's where I would end up.

Bishop McNulty walked into the conference room in his street clothes and gave us a little send-off speech. His aide distributed the envelopes. Mine was addressed to Father Joseph.

There was much looking at each other's new black chariots as we wished each other luck and parted company. There were black Fords, black Chevrolets, black

143

Buicks, black Pontiacs, black Oldsmobiles, but only one black Hudson—mine. I had studied the catalogues and brochures for a year before making my decision. I got into it and drove off to begin my days as a working priest.

St. Rocco's rectory didn't look like a rectory at all. It was just like every other house in the street, an old converted two-family, two doors away from the church. Diagonally across the street, in another converted two-family house, three Maestre Pie Fillippini nuns ran a small nursery school. That, plus a modest church, was it.

A big, dark-haired, plain, buxom woman met me at the door.

The way she said: "Oh, you must be the new priest," gave me the feeling there might have been two or three others that week. "Just a minute," she added and disappeared.

She brought back a torn piece of paper with some handwriting on it.

It said: TO THE NEW PRIEST. SAY ROSARY PAOLERCIO FUNERAL HOME TONIGHT AT 8:30.

"Thank you," I said. "Thanks very much. My name is Father Longo. Father Gabriel Longo. And you're ——"

"I'm Father De Sanctis' housekeeper. I come in every day but I don't live here. I live in the parish."

"Oh," I said. "Well, I'm happy to meet you."

"Likewise."

"If you live in the parish you could probably direct me to the funeral home."

She took my measure carefully, and left without saying a word. I heard her pick up the telephone in the next room. "Hello," she said. "This is Angie." I made a note of that. "The new priest showed up after all," she said. "You come. You pick him up."

Then she was back and said, "They come. They pick you up in the limousine. They tell you what to do."

I felt like telling her that some young priests were allowed to ride the streetcars all by themselves, especially after they had been ordained.

Angie seemed to behave as if it might be foolish to waste any time on me. New priests were a dime a dozen, here today and gone tomorrow.

I didn't know whether to invite myself to sit down, or to go in the car and wait until the undertaker arrived to instruct me in saying the Rosary.

Finally Angie stepped aside and said, "Make yourself at home." Then she was gone.

The big black limousine arrived on the dot. The smooth young assistant funeral director, doubling as chauffeur for the night, looked me over as if he were hiring an assistant. Apparently he felt I passed muster.

"Busy night," he said. "Tamburo's got one and we got two." He couldn't be talking about anything but funerals. I took that to mean that they were one up on their rival. "Which one you draw for tomorrow?" he asked.

"I haven't met Father De Sanctis yet," I explained. "I just arrived."

"Oh," he said. "You're the new priest. Well," he started, then he gave me a full briefing. St. Rocco's was a gold mine for funerals. All the old Italian people for miles around insisted on being buried from St. Rocco's. The church averaged one funeral a day. Often there were two. Three—as there would be tomorrow—was not unusual. The parish was always short of priests to do the honors at the funeral home, the church, and the cemetery. The funeral directors virtually ran a shuttle service on busy days.

"You speak Italian, Father?"

"I think I can get by."

When we arrived, he explained the choreography in

145

detail. He would walk in first, quiet the mourners and prepare for my entrance. Then I would change into my surplice, enter and take my position kneeling at the bier. The deceased was an old man and his widow Vincenza was the tiny woman sitting at the foot of the coffin. Her face was covered with dark black veiling which hung to her shoulders.

When I walked in, all the mourners dropped to their knees and I felt very solemn and unnecessarily tall. I began the Rosary in Latin. The responses welled up behind me.

When we finished the Rosary, I walked over to the widow and took her hand. She seemed so frail and so tiny. I was searching in my mind for a sentence, a phrase, something from the seminary manuals that might be appropriate for this sorrowful occasion. But all I could say was "I'm sorry for you in your trouble."

She looked at her husband in the coffin and then turned her huge dark dry eyes upward and looked straight at me. She squeezed my hand. Then from deep in the veiling came this bell-like contralto voice:

"Eh, Padre, e meglio esso che me!" ("Ah, Father, better him than me!")

The bloodless one-dimensional never-never landscape, the cardboard Catholics of the seminary seemed to vanish out of sight, memory and mind. After a decade I was back in the real world.

mcmlii

FROM THE instant Father Joseph De Sanctis greeted me and showed me to my room in the rectory, the entire second-hand picture of him I had received from the seminary underground began to collapse. He appeared to be mean, crusty and unapproachable; he had the reputation for wearing out at least one assistant a year. But he was really a warm and wonderful gentleman of the old school.

He had come to the priesthood late in life, after almost fifteen years as a medical officer in the Italian Army. His old country seminary training may have been sketchy, but his worldly experience more than made up for that. He had a sure instinct for putting first things first and keeping petty regulations and insignificant rules in their proper places.

He was available, day and night, to countless numbers of priests who sought him out as a confessor. His rectory was a haven for the poor and the needy. His peasant wisdom, his feeling of brotherhood for all men, his capacity for mercy and understanding, his sure instinct for the magnificent gesture, the right word at the right time—qualities which the entire world was to discover later in the sainted Pope John XXIII—Father Joseph had in good measure.

Father Joseph ministered to two congregations: one visible, the other not of this world. "Father Joseph's friends," the parishioners called them. They showed up at odd hours at the rectory—as they had for years—and Father Joseph always ministered to them personally, deciding whether they needed a good meal, a drink, or a dollar. Gypsies, derelicts, hoboes, or bums, others might call them. To Father Joseph, they were separated brethren. He loathed the institutional approach of charities, for he felt that the social workers, with their forms, their questions, their investigations, robbed these unfortunates of the one thing they needed most: a sense of dignity, a sense of belonging.

"A man needs more than charity," he would always say. "The thing he looks for in his trouble is not money. It is a friend." No man needed to be friendless if he knew where Father Joseph lived. The unexpected arrival of some of his special friends turned an ordinary day into an occasion. Feasts were ordered from the housekeeper. The guest of honor would regale us with wonderful stories of his months of wanderings. Only later would I get the fill-in on their pedigrees from Father. One was a former rabbi, another a scientist; there were musicians, ex-priests, all manner of lost souls.

Each time a guest resumed his wanderings Father Joseph asked from him only one resolve: to stay away from cheap whiskey and buy instead, with the money slipped into his pocket, a glass or two of decent wine.

The days of a curate, or assistant in a church, only begin with Mass in the morning. There are babies to be baptized, weddings to perform, sick calls and last rites for the dying (we were on call at three hospitals), a regular schedule of confessions, instructions for new converts, preparatory instruction for young people contemplating marriage, meetings, sermons, meetings, guidance, encouragement, more meetings, and at all times—priestly example.

Each curate guides some of the groups that are the nuclei of the parish. Father Joseph assigned me to handle the Catholic Youth Organization, or CYO, with its various cultural, athletic, social and spiritual subdivisions. Soon I was deeply involved in pleading cases in Juvenile Court, breaking up gang wars in empty lots, chaperoning teen-age dances. All this was aimed at recruiting youth for the religious classes we held.

As soon as Father Joseph saw my saxophone, he insisted that I play for him. It took no pleading at all for him to give me permission to organize a CYO band, and later a drum and bugle corps. It was a big leap from gang warfare to catechism classes. Sometimes the gap could be bridged or at least baited with music. The stenciled T-shirts and leather jackets of rival gangs could be put aside for fancy uniforms in which to strut and parade. After all, I had begun with the parish band. Things weren't that different twenty years ago. Father Joseph encouraged me, and looking in on rehearsals—especially dress rehearsals—became a great joy for him.

Word of our work soon got to the bishop, and it wasn't long before I was appointed chaplain to the County Parental School to superintend work with delinquent Catholic youngsters. Later I was appointed assistant director of the CYO for the county, which made me an official of the Diocese. Father Joseph was extremely proud because I was one of the youngest priests ever to get such an appointment. He was even prouder when subsequently I was named to the President's Committee on Juvenile Delinquency.

Our band wouldn't have been possible without my

149

good friend Wally. I could always borrow anything in his store. We bought the drums and bugles and he always made sure that we got bargains.

I had never resolved the question about the "good guys" and the "bad guys" of the early Christian era. We hardly discussed it anymore, but each time I saw him I discussed it with myself. Though I did as much as I could for the people of the parish, throughout this time I was continually plagued by the matter of my own belief. The old doubts were there and some new ones; I was still waiting for the faith I had been promised.

I now heard confessions almost daily. My own difficulties got more complicated with each confession I heard.

My first penitent had been a boy not more than seven, quivering with guilt, who claimed in his baby voice that he had committed adultery. I asked what he had done.

"Father," he said, swallowing hard, "I peed the bed."

Someone, almost certainly the nuns, had given him the idea that he had violated the sixth commandment. I tried to untangle that one, thinking of it as some kind of exception. But the parade of youthful penitents showed me it was close to being the rule. Youngsters confessed to biting their nails, cursing. The words they used turned out to be something like, "You dirty rat!" hollered on the playground.

"I screamed at my sister. I broke my brother's toy." These at least were shadows of sins and I could cope with them.

Then came the ladies.

A priest is cautioned never to go into detail with women about sins against the sixth commandment. If a priest wavers from this rule, a woman penitent may report him to his superiors and he is in real trouble.

But when a woman decides to regale her confessor, no matter how he tries to stop her, there is never any way of shutting her off.

There were women who enjoyed talking sex and insisted on giving every detail. Most difficult were those who insisted on confessing the same sin with elaborations and additions to each new version. This practice was rationalized in their minds with the excuse that they had no new mortal sins to confess.

The younger men of the parish rarely had any reason for coming near the church, so I got into the habit of dropping in to the social and athletic clubs in the neighborhood. Ordinarily I heard the confessions off in a corner with two chairs arranged for the purpose. There would always be a few who would refuse. I would follow them around the pool table and in whispered tones ask them about certain sins and whether or not they were sorry for having offended God. When they admitted there was nothing else in their lives that was sinful, I would tell them they had just gone to confession.

Each week also, there would be men and women who rarely came to confession. Deeply troubled, they were searching vainly for some realistic answer to the problem that haunted all married Catholics. Usually it would start like this:

"Father, I have not been to confession in two years because we have practiced birth control. I want, we want so much, so very badly to receive Communion. I go to church most Sundays. In every other way I believe I am a good Catholic. But we just cannot afford to have another baby. I am working and my husband is working. And we have a rough time now taking care of our three children. I feel deep down God knows I love Him and I'm trying. Father, can you help me? Can you give me some kind of permission? We

151

tried practicing rhythm after the first baby but it just doesn't work for us. Is there some way I can make up for this? I will do anything."

Or: "Father, my doctor has told me I'm not to have any more babies. I have two now. Must I put them in danger of losing their mother?"

Men would say: "Father, my wife doesn't want any more children. Does this keep me from being able to receive the sacraments?"

These people were looking for help. They drove me deeper and deeper into volumes of theology and philosophy looking for an answer. I discussed it with Father Joseph, with other priests. They had lived with it far longer than I. But the answer was always the same. *Roma locuta est. Causa finita est.* Rome has spoken, the matter is finished.

All I could tell these people is what I had been told in the seminary. Pray and have faith.

Two painters are working high on a scaffold. Their rope breaks. Both men dangle perilously. Soon it becomes clear the rope can only save one man. One man lets go and falls to his death below. In sacrificing his life to save his fellow man, he is committing suicide without sin.

This was one of the seminary classroom examples illustrating the principle of "two-fold effect."

Our instructors used to analyze this neat little episode as an example that was supposed to guide us in the confessional. It seemed to have little relevance now, since the man who dropped to his death would never have a chance to confess what his "intention" was. For all we knew he might have been waiting for weeks for a chance to commit suicide to get away from the loan sharks. And the only problem a pastor might have would be with his family: whether he was entitled to be buried in the Church. And even there the principle of two-fold effect would make it possible for the pastor in question to accept the fee for the funeral in good conscience.

Another example was the classic one of removal of a tumorous ovary from a pregnant mother. The resultant abortion was not sinful since it could be justified on medical grounds. The "intention" of the surgeon's knife was removal of the tumor. The bad effect (abortion) followed the good effect. Therefore there was no sin for him or for the mother or for the husband who approved the operation.

I reached the point of desperation in stretching the principle of two-fold effect to cover the problem of birth control as it was continually presented to me in the confessional. When my penitents were searching for "some way" to limit the size of their families and still be eligible to receive the sacraments, I discreetly asked them whether or not they needed a lubricant to facilitate the marriage act. If they answered yes, I would ask them what kind they used. If they replied that they used a kind which also had contraceptive side-effects, I would give them absolution without any comment. The principle of two-fold effect was present; the church's teaching was stretched to the absolute limit. Later on I became more brave and when some of my penitents stated that they used no lubricant at all, I used to suggest they try the brand which had contraceptive side-effects.

Many husbands neither attended church, nor cared a whit about what their wife's confessor had to say of their marital problems. The husband was firm and definite: he would not perform the marriage act without some contraceptive. This left the church-going wife in a dilemma: for her to refuse intercourse would be a mortal sin in the eyes of the Church; for her to engage in intercourse under her husband's conditions would also be a mortal sin. If she refused, and her husband were to seek sexual solace elsewhere, she was not only endangering the permanence of the marriage, but she was indirectly responsible for driving him to adultery. Countless cases like this and even more complicated cases confronted me every week. Many times the principle of two-fold effect applied, many times it didn't. But rare indeed were the women who did not go away feeling they had some kind of way out. And if there was any sin involved, it was mine. The problem of Church doctrine was mine, not theirs.

The effect of my willingness to take on this burden was immediate. The lines in front of my confessional box grew longer by the week. Soon even my group of older ladies got the message and began steering their granddaughters and their friends to me. I became the most popular confessor in the parish. Parishioners began to recall one of my predecessors who merely listened and routinely gave absolution because his English was inadequate for anything else.

I was helping the people I had come to love. But I could not fool myself very long. I was preaching a doctrine of casuistry which I believed to be foolish. I knew where that could lead.

Hearing the interminable confessions of the children was a matter of routine scheduling. But the confidence of the old ladies was something that had to be earned. They had plenty of time for shopping. If your confessional manner did not appeal to them, they would quickly let you know and try someone else.

For the women in their old-country black, the church provided a very real haven and a source of comfort—especially for the older ones who were no longer needed by their children and grandchildren. They found it natural to spend their entire mornings in church. In spite of the rule that Communion can be received only once a day, there was always someone who tried to receive it at every Mass.

To them, the confessional was not a place only for absolution; it was a place where they could let fly all their complaints. They would gladly have spent an hour. The signal for a long session was always a certain amount of huffing and puffing as the penitent installed herself comfortably. While I was hearing a penitent on the other side of the confessional box, I could hear the long-suffering lady adjusting herself for a visit. I would slide open the door that blocked her off and would barely have a chance to finish the opening prayer.

"Padre, tengo na nuoro. . . ." she would begin softly. "Father, I have a daughter-in-law. . . ." This was always declared as a kind of prologue, to prepare you for the worst.

"Quello marito mio, ubriagone, avvocato del diavolo, mi fa santa," would come the announcement. "That husband of mine, drunkard, advocate of the Devil, he's forcing me to be a saint."

A select group of girls over eighty, long graduated from the league of saintly complainers, as practical old souls made it their business to teach me to speak Italian properly.

They would relive all their old transgressions confessing pungent and dramatic sins of their youth—all in the guise of giving me Italian lessons. When I first arrived at St. Rocco's my Italian was slim and in certain areas at least, non-existent. Some of the old girls would come to confession three times a week in order to turn the confessional sessions into a regular Berlitz school.

When I asked a question, or interjected a thought, they would say indulgently, "No, Father, you say it like this." I would try and they would say, "Now, try again. Repeat after me."

I'm sure each imagined herself my chief instructor. Some of them lived outside the territorial limits of the parish. They came miles because they were made to feel unwelcome in the Irish parishes where they lived with their children or grandchildren. They came back to St. Rocco's weary of trying to do things in what they called the "Ayerraize" or Irish way.

Sometimes when we had missions and a visiting English-speaking priest would be installed for an evening, the first penitent would withdraw from the confessional with a long sour face. The others would look to the first for the verdict and when she turned down her thumbs, they got the message. They would leave in disgust rather than submit to a formal, by-the-book confession.

"He didn'ta wanna talk," I used to hear them saying. "He only tella me whatta sins? I no make sins, I wanna talka to him. He no wanna talka to me? Only he ask whatta sins? I tell him I got a real pain in the ass for a daughter-in-law anda he's aska me whatta sins. Whatta he wanna me to do? Go home, smacka her in the face and then tella him all about it. He wanna me to do that, he no wanna talka to me now, that's easy. . . ."

After a few weeks of lessons in the confessional, my over-eighty club encouraged me to try speaking Italian from the pulpit. They all showed up at six o'clock Mass, bristling with pride when I made my debut.

One of the announcements on my schedule was a reminder that the parishioners were to bring their monthly collection envelopes. In Italian the word for envelopes is "buste." I knew I had done something wrong when tiny Vincenza jumped excitedly from her seat and made wildly exaggerated gestures of a woman tugging at her girdle. When I looked blank she shouted out, "Padre, mio figlio. . . ." "Father, my boy, you're asking us to bring our corsets to church for the collection!"

There were roars of laughter from the other ladies

as she explained that I had said "busti," girdles, instead of "buste," envelopes.

Somewhat red-faced, I started over. But I was trying, learning, letting them teach me.

Most of the older people of the parish had come to America in their teens and twenties right after the First World War. The women often came as a result of pre-arranged marriages. Sometimes they had met their intended husbands in Italy, and this way two people passed immigration regulations instead of one—it was one way of beating the system. Others arrived like Grandma Rose, and married men they had never seen, on the docks at Hoboken. Many of the people at St. Rocco's came from the same general area of Italy; they shared a strong attachment and feeling for the same home town. Whole Italian towns lived on in their imaginations amid the northern New Jersey landscape.

Nothing rated higher on the ecclesiastical calendar than the celebration of the feast of the patron saint of their town of origin. This was the custom they clung to with tenacity. Christmas and Easter and the other big church days barely mattered beside it. One day a year, the paisani from the same village took over completely. They organized the day—the Mass, the street parades, the dinners and the dancing—into a complete holiday atmosphere. The feasts were always arranged to take place during the warm weather, for, in the old country, virtually everything of consequence took place out-of-doors.

Mass was the high point of the feast. For many nominal parishioners, especially men, it was the only time they set foot in church all year. Before feast days, I often got the opportunity to hear the confessions of fathers and husbands—something more often reserved for the deathbed.

They revealed the other side of the story, the notion

that church-going is something to be attended to by women.

The old-country fathers were more concerned with the failings of their sons than their daughters-in-law. A father would extract from me promises to "knock my stupid son's head off" when he was no longer available to do it himself.

"I worka so hard," he would say without really complaining. "I worka so hard to senda him to school to get a little education. An whatta happens? Eh Padre, whaddaya think? He'sa went ana married some citrool Merigan, anna she maka the stupido into himself a citrool, too."

It was considered a sign of weakness for a young man to be dependent on anyone for anything, except in pursuit of higher education. This was the only status symbol.

Sometimes an older man would insist that I take two dollars. One dollar was to be pinned on the statue of his patron saint during the next feast, in case he were not there to share in the ceremony. The other dollar was for me. It was understood that on the occasion of his funeral I was to take time out from the "fesserie" and have a good glass of wine—on him.

In my early parish days, with post-seminary fervor, I had fostered a special devotion to the Immaculate Heart of Mary. It centered about receiving Communion on the first Saturday of each month, just as devotion to the Sacred Heart of Jesus makes first Friday a special day. This was another way I made extra work for myself. I spent most Saturday mornings taking Communion to the parish shut-ins. The invalids, those in wheelchairs, the hopelessly ill, were always the first recruits.

Patty was only eighteen years old, in a wheelchair with multiple sclerosis. I would arrive, hear confession, give Communion and then I was trapped into a discussion of her personal concerns. Desperately lonely and longing passionately for the problems of a normal girl, Patty always raised havoc with my schedule. But we both knew she didn't have long to live. All she wanted was a chance to have an affair with a boy, any boy. A delivery boy, the iceman, the TV repairman, her cousins—or me.

Then there was Josephine. The moment I arrived she fell to her knees. I didn't dare move. If I changed position, or walked three steps, Josephine would leap up to her feet, run ahead of me and plunge to her knees again to make sure every single "holy word" was pronounced directly over her. What mattered most to Josephine were the broad ecclesiastical gestures. If I didn't make a wall-to-wall sign of the cross, Josephine felt cheated and could punish me, when I was in a rush, by making amendments to her confession. She felt the potency of absolution was related in some way to the choreography. Like most invalids, she usually got her way.

Eleven years seniority as a polio victim with partial paralysis entitled Millie to have a "regular confessor" who came to her house. This was another of the duties that befell me. It was difficult to tell which Millie enjoyed more, polio or privilege. Millie also had her little tyrannies. Since modern medicine had failed her, she had taken up with a neighborhood sorceress who was also a member of the parish. As the anthropologists are forever rediscovering, remnants of pre-Christian religions survive under the veneer of Roman Catholicism.

Millie was always in fear of the "evil eye" and the sorceress was credited with the power to drive it off. Millie shrewdly played the sorceress against me, and me against the sorceress. I prevailed on her to save her money and accept the approved blessings.

Each time, after I had read her the blessing, she

insisted her headache had gone. Finally I showed her the place in the Ritual I had read from: a blessing for airplanes, for fire engines, newborn babies or pregnant women. Millie was angry with me for weeks.

I suspected that her paralysis might submit to the same therapy as her headaches. So when it came time for the Holy Water, instead of the usual few sprinkles, I began to let the water fly liberally when Millie wasn't expecting it.

One time she shielded her face with her supposedly paralyzed arm. Once I saw her move her legs to avoid getting drenched. The next time I arrived with Communion I stood by the table, and shouted sternly:

"If you want to receive Communion, come over here and kneel where you're supposed to."

I turned my back so she could save face. When I turned around she was on her knees, four feet from her wheel chair.

One of my special duties was that of spiritual director to the Maestre Pie Fillippini convent. I never looked forward to my regular visit there. One brush with the dictatorial Mother Superior was always enough to ruin my day. Whatever I attempted in the way of teaching in the confessional or at spiritual conferences in the parish was always undone by the nuns. I sometimes spent ninety percent of my time in the confessional re-educating tiny penitents who had been led to believe that bed wetting, fingernail biting, gum chewing, or nail polishing were sins that had to be absolved.

The only way I could counter the heavy hand of the Mother Superior was in periodic spiritual talks I gave to the nuns. Conscious as I was of my own confused feelings in this area, I tried to get near their feelings of guilt and fear that surrounded even mention of the word sex. I tried to explain that they had been born women and they had to stay women—not neuters —or they could do all sorts of harm to children in their tender care. I tried to be firm, explicit, but I felt we were talking across a massive gulf.

My visits to the nuns always brought me a laugh as I recalled the stories about priests fooling around with nuns. It had been a subject of gentle jesting even in the seminary. I never forgot one instructor, citing examples of sins committed by two people in tandem, who said, "Now, take the ordinary case of a priest and a nun."

Ordinary? What an absurdity! Heloise and Abelard, Martin Luther and his fat and ferocious Mother Superior paramour belonged to another time. With the real temptations which beset every priest in this day of automobiles and motels, it is amazing that the old legends persist.

I knew priests who were tempted by socialites, call-girls, waitresses, ladies in their parishes, teen-age girls, teen-age boys—even priests who were tempted by other priests—but I never heard of a priest who had been, or could be, tempted by a nun.

"Father, I have to go see someone in City Hall. Will you come with me and talk English?" "Talking English" was a kind of convention. I knew many of them could talk English as well as I could talk Italian. But they knew, as I learned, that the presence of the priest at their side in some government bureau brought a kind of magic reprieve from petty tyranny and the run-around. So I was happy to show my face in their behalf.

Il Formo del Gubernamento to them spelled trouble. "If you no pay, they maka you in jail," they would say. I was the expert, I could read the form. If I took the matter lightly or tried to tease them about it, they would become very annoyed. If it was something simple, I straightened it out myself. If it was complicated,

I would show the form to one of our ushers, who worked at the I.R.S., and he would fill it out for them.

Many of the older parishioners lived on tiny social security payments; a few had pensions. Some lived off their children. Those who had no income at all would come to the rectory with their Il Formo del Gubernamento because they saw the others do it. Sometimes they pretended to have government troubles merely to keep up appearances.

"Excuse me, Father Longo, but I have to talk to you."

This skinny pimply high school boy must have been waiting in church for me on his knees for a full hour. His had been one of the first confessions I heard when I began at seven. Now it was almost nine o'clock.

"Of course," I said. "I have someone waiting at the rectory already. If you don't mind waiting. . . ."

"Oh no, Father," he said. "As long as I know I can get to talk to you privately."

The boy was getting to be a problem for me. He wanted to talk about becoming a priest. I had been trying to discourage him, without being obvious or unkind.

"Why don't we walk back to the rectory and talk along the way?" The rectory was about two hundred feet from the church. Maybe he would take the hint.

"You know, Father, since I joined the Knights of the Eucharist I've been going to Communion almost every day."

"Yes, I noticed." And going to confession at least every other night, I might have added.

"Oh, did you?" he said, beaming. The Knights of the Eucharist was an idea to foster more frequent recourse to the Sacraments. I used to speak at the meetings of the parish group. This boy never missed one. Every time I walked to the altar rail, he seemed to be there.

Every time I installed myself in the confessional he seemed to arrive. He used to get so carried away confessing the explicit details of his homosexual sins, I often had to cut him off sharply. He had a piercing feminine whisper that reminded me of some of the seminary flits. I had been pitching the Sacraments to him because I couldn't think of anything else to suggest. Now he had become a pillar of the Knights of the Eucharist and I noticed more and more flits coming to the meetings.

Even more unsettling was the way he insisted on introducing all his recruits to me, making it embarrassingly clear that I was his idol, and that his great goal in life was to be another Christ like me. He made it all sound very sick, very sick indeed.

"If you stick with the Sacraments," I said, "I'm sure Our Lord will help straighten out your problem."

"Oh yes," he said enthusiastically, "I think He has."

"I'm glad."

"Oh yes, Father Longo," he said. "But the thing I wanted to ask you about is in connection with that."

"Oh?" I said.

"Yes, Father, sometimes I think I love Christ too much. I got too excited about it at Mass. I love Him as the Son of God who died for us. But after all, He was a living man too, wasn't he Father?"

"He became man to die for our sins."

"I could just die myself sometimes thinking about it. My love for Christ is the biggest thing in my life, Father. I hope you understand. I worry if it might not be a sin to think about *Him* in *that* way."

The whole thing was suddenly as clear as one of my own nightmares. This boy was daydreaming about sex and Christ. Right at the altar rail, probably. Right under my own stupid nose. And the next thing he would tell me was where I fit in. I wished the sidewalk would open up and swallow me.

"Well, Fred," I said, "I think the thing for you to do is stay with the written meditations in your Missal. That might keep your mind from wandering."

"Yes, Father, I've tried that. That's all right before Communion and after. But when I see you coming toward me with Communion—knowing you are bringing me the Body and Blood of Our Lord Jesus Christ who died for my sins—oh Father, I can't help it. Something happens. I'm embarrassed sometimes to walk down the aisle. That's why I always kneel at the rail so long if you noticed."

There I stood, almost thirty years old, and if it hadn't been for those filthy comic books I wouldn't have had the slightest idea what was going through this poor boy's mind. I knew I was blushing and all I could do was blow my nose.

How could I have been so blind and stupid as to assume that all the priest-teasers would be women? Or was it even more stupid to assume this boy was teasing me? He might be perfectly sincere. The flits in the seminary might have felt this way, for all I knew. Maybe that's why they were such Holy Joes, such model benders to the Rule. Maybe I should just close my eyes, swallow hard and quit discouraging this boy from trying for the priesthood. The flit painters and artists of the Renaissance started turning Christ into a faggot; Irish hierarchy and homeletics had succeeded in finishing the job. Fred was the natural result.

"Fred," I said, "have you ever made a retreat?"

"No, Father, you think it might help me?"

"It's something you should try. You can go for a weekend or if you can manage it, for a full ten days. It's a change of scene. You get away from companions and temptations. And besides, at St. Dominic's Retreat house they have some confessors with wide experience in all sorts of problems. As you know I'm barely out of the seminary, without too much experience. I think you need someone older and wiser."

"Oh, Father, nobody has helped me more than you have."

"Well, I'm not so sure about that. If you think I have helped you, then that's one more reason for taking my advice."

"If you think so, Father."

"Yes I do, Fred. I really do."

I was just ducking and I knew it. Probably he di' too.

I was fifteen when I started at Seton Hall—when my studies began and my education ended.

In our last year at the seminary we had taken a special six-week course in clerical economics. Our beginning salary as parish assistants was to be one hundred dollars a month. Out of that, our first responsibility was to repay the Archdiocese of Newark for our education. In my time that debt was calculated at five thousand dollars. Repayment was guaranteed by something called the Docier system: each priest was obliged to take out a twenty-year life insurance policy with the Archdiocese as beneficiary. At the end of twenty years, the Archdiocese received back its five thousand dollars. If a priest died before that time, the Archdiocese got more. Either way, it couldn't lose.

Later phases of the course dealt with how to save money, how to plan insurance policies, how to manage investments. We were drilled to beware of traps, ruses, and con games especially designed for priests. We were told to beware of people coming in off the street with sob stories. Anyone asking for charity was to be referred directly to Catholic Charities.

The first Saturday night at St. Rocco's when Father Joseph reached into his pocket, peeled off over a hundred dollars in bills and handed them to me, he turned the Archdiocesan fiscal policy on its head.

"My dear Gabriel," said Father Joseph, "whatever you do, get rid of the money quickly. Get rid of it foolishly. Make sure by morning you are a poor boy."

"But Father Joseph, in the seminary we were told to open a bank account, and pay our insurance. . . ."

"I know what they tell you, my dear Gabriel. It is for that reason I make sure to tell you differently at the first opportunity. The check book is the worst occasion of sin among priests. Ah yes, the worst."

"Then maybe I should arrange to make some investments. We were taught how to manage our investments."

"Investments!" He almost spat out the word.

"Let the Bishop handle the investments. The Archdiocese already owns the Hudson and Manhattan tunnel and railroad and how much of General Motors and the Empire State Building God only knows. How much of American industry does the Church of Christ own? I'll tell you, Gabriel. Too much, *per Baccho*."

Per Baccho, was Father Joseph's favorite expletive. Whether he was calm or excited, he aways took the name of the ancient Roman gods in vain.

"If you want investments, I'll show you how to make investments. Just answer the rectory bell when it rings and learn how to invest in people.

"You will learn, my dear Gabriel, the only thing to do with money is to give it away. The faster the better. The most foolish thing you could possibly do with this money is wiser by far than holding on to it. Aha, the check book. I'll tell you what happens when you have a check book. Not many years ago I was called to pray with Monsignor d'Aquila as he lay dying. One day when I die, you will come pray with me and you will know what it is I am talking about. The good Monsignor had been dying for many days and I had been praying at his bedside. The doctors had given him up to God already so they no longer even came around. I noticed while I was saying my prayers that Monsignor was stirring in his bed, reaching under the pillow, searching for something.

'What is it you seek, my dear Monsignor?' I said to him. I found his rosary and handed that to him. He shook his head. So I handed him his Breviary. Again he nodded no. I put my head close to his chest, as he seemed to be speaking. *Per Baccho*, even today, years later, I can hear his voice. With almost his last breath, so weak, so feeble, he growled to me: 'Give . . . me . . . my . . . check . . . book. . . .'

"It was like the voice of the Devil himself. I stood back from his bed and looked at him in horror. Then he shouted: 'Give . . . me my . . . check book!'

"God is good, I thought. We were alone in the room. What a scandal it would be to die in the street, with a throng of unbelievers around, screaming for the president of his bank. I didn't know what to do. Where would I find the good Monsignor's bank books? I was ashamed to ask his housekeeper. I was ashamed to ask his nurse. But I wanted to stop him from screaming. Oh, Gabriel, what a scandal! So I looked around and with the Devil himself guiding my eyes, I found on his dresser a small black book in alligator leather with solid gold ornaments at the corners and the cross of our Lord Jesus Christ on it. The check book. Monsignor took it in his hands and he clutched it to his chest. It relieved his pain and quieted his soul.

"The good Monsignor died with the book in his hands. Hundreds of thousands of dollars he left—close to a million. . . .

"Oh, my dear Gabriel, I can tell you stories they won't tell you in the seminary. Get rid of the money as fast as you can."

167

It wasn't easy. As fast as I could get rid of it, the money rolled in. I had received almost five thousand dollars cash in gifts at my ordination. Even after buying my new car, I still had almost four thousand. I had spent a few dollars on clothes, but how much can you spend on black suits? In my short time as a priest I had already learned that the Roman collar is better than any credit card. You get instant service everywhere and at the end of the month, instead of getting bills, you get more gifts. Unless you yanked off your collar, got into your golf clothes and went somewhere where nobody guessed you were a priest, it was virtually impossible to pay for anything.

You didn't pay for parking tickets, because you never got any. You had privileges even a politician doesn't have. If you smashed into a baby carriage while driving drunk, the woman with the baby carriage would get the ticket. If you drove into the middle of Journal Square in Jersey City at the height of traffic, some cop always stuck his face in the window to tell you that he would take care of your parking problems. Restaurants were a problem. Even if you went into a place for the first time, the manager was apt to make a big scene if you tried to pay for a meal. If you went into some place where you were known, the argument began at the door, and you were reminded of the last time you attempted to pay a check. You were expected to be a free loader. Waiters were humiliated, waitresses were insulted if you left a tip.

If you took your car into a service station for repairs, they charged you only for the replacement parts, and were apologetic about that. If you went to the movies, before taking your money, the cashier would buzz the manager. In an instant he was out in the lobby glad-handing you, telling you he hoped you liked the picture, promising you he had booked a cleaner "family-type" picture next week, and complaining that the movie moguls were buying too many Tennessee Williams' properties.

Jewish merchants were the softest touch of all. If you walked into a Jewish store, chances were the manager or owner would be out there quoting special discount prices on everything in the place. If you bought anything at a discount, he was apt to load you down with more things gratis.

Hotels, bars, and public places were hopeless spots to spend any money. If you had to go to a doctor, you never got a bill. It was the same way with the hospitals.

What wasn't on the collar was on the cuff.

For centuries good Catholics had had bred into their bones that the quickest way of acquiring grace was to endow the clergy with financial gifts. Princes did it with gold and precious stones, masonry and architecture. Peasants did it with bread and wine. I was always embarrassed when gifts came from people who had far less than I. Even my Mother's friends, emancipated as they were, still forced money and cigarettes on me. People knew they were acquiring grace—whether by refusing a tip or handing me a crumpled five-dollar bill. To refuse to take it was to deny them heavenly favors.

A priest lived in opulence on credit in the outside world. And he lived opulently at the rectory besides. There were a few unlucky seminarians who landed with parsimonious frost-bitten old tyrants, but they were exceptions. Boys from working-class families who had never seen a servant in their own homes, who had lived austerely for a decade in the seminary, ended up living like young potentates. There was always a housekeeper who managed everything: cleaning, laundry, darning, shoe shining; meals were extravagant with wine, whiskey, champagne and beer; there were snacks and special lunches at all hours. Cooks, maids, receptionists, phone-answering services, even private secretaries—all on the house.

In the beginning it embarrassed me. I was used to a family atmosphere where everybody pitched in to take the heat off Mother. My impulse was to pick up after myself, to rinse a glass, to dump an ash tray, to make a dirty towel do a second day. But I learned quickly enough to do everything the lazy way. The first thing that happens after a priest settles down to his first pastorate is that he starts putting on weight. As athletic as I was, it even began happening to me.

Out of my hundred dollars a month salary, I paid virtually no income taxes, and a nominal amount on my insurance policy every quarter. That was the limit of my outlay.

On income there seemed to be no limit at all. At St. Rocco's the going rate on an offering to God for a low Mass (without singing) for the repose of the soul of a dearly departed, or for any other intention—announced from the pulpit in advance—was five dollars. The stipend for a High Mass, sung by the priest, was ten dollars; for a solemn High Mass, with three priests in attendance, twenty-five dollars. Announced low Masses at St. Rocco's were so rare as to be unusual. High Masses were the custom and solemn High Masses were very common. There were always more Masses than we could possibly squeeze on our calendar. We drafted priests from nearby St. Benedict's preparatory school to handle the excess business, and gave them the five dollar stipends—which they were happy to get.

Every time I said Mass in the morning, I cleared ten dollars. Technically this was an offering to God with the priest as an intermediary and custodian, so there were no taxes to pay. If after a ten dollar Mass, there was a solemn High twenty-five dollar Mass on the calendar, the additional stipend was split three ways. Eighteen dollars a day was not uncommon.

Offerings to the priest for weddings and baptisms

went for the support of the rectory—food, salaries for servants, and the booze bill. But offerings for celebrations of solemn High funeral Masses—the most lucrative of all, running from twenty-five dollars up to over a hundred—went directly to the priest's pocket.

Father Joseph knew what he was talking about. Money was a problem. In addition to my salary, I was soon clearing well over a hundred dollars a week in stipends. Later when I got special Archdiocesan jobs, I received additional stipends. The next year it doubled and soon it doubled again. I didn't need it. Father Joseph didn't want me to have it. I couldn't spend it. It was goof money all the way.

Father Joseph enjoyed raking it in and he enjoyed giving it away. His favorite saint was St. Martha, the patroness of rectories, who always took care of the household while Mary Magdalene and the others were traipsing about after Jesus and his disciples.

"A la bella Santa Marta," he would chant over a particular collection, light on coin and heavy with green. "She takes care of priests who put themselves in her hands."

Since St. Rocco's was an old parish, it was free and clear of debt with no running expenses except plant maintenance repairs and the salaries for the sexton, the organist and the choir. They were all paid by the job, by the same kind of parish offerings we received, plus a small additional official parish salary.

On Sundays when on duty, standing by for hospital calls, baptisms and marriages, it was customary to help the pastor count the collections. He had coin-counting machines and bill wrappers and all the technical conveniences, but Father Joseph had an eye like a pawnbroker. He could take one quick glance at a collection pile and tell you within a few dollars how much the total was. If his estimate was more than five dollars under what the take turned out to be, it meant he was playing games underestimating the amount to prepare for himself a tailor-made surprise.

As Director of Pre-Cana Conferences for the parish, it was my duty to instruct couples about to enter the marriage state. In this situation I always felt like the lifeguard who couldn't swim. I could remember Monsignor Fulton Sheen giving his long television lectures on Catholic marriage, studded with fairy tale stories of princes and grandees and other wax figures of the European nobility. This was great fodder for television, and proved that the Monsignor had a great acquaintance among the married nobility. But sitting down with young couples in the rectory was quite another story.

The younger ones seemed to have no idea of what they were getting into. The course included a briefing on the Catholic position in marriage, the physical aspects of marriage, the economic considerations, and the sanctity attainable through the married state.

The "rhythm method" or periodic continence was tolerated rather than recommended by the Church and it was a mortal sin to employ it in marriage unless a specific set of conditions were present. The use of the rhythm method must always be a temporary expedient; the couple must have a serious reason for employing it, and be willing to plan their sex life around the calendar. If it was their intention to use it to avoid having children, they were frustrating the primary intent of their marriage vows and were in as much trouble as those who employed other less complicated and more efficacious methods of contraception. For even the *thought* of enjoying sex combined with any scheme for avoiding pregnancies was a mortal sin. In my experience, the rhythm method was so complicated and so beset with difficulties that most couples didn't even want to try it.

Much more to the point was a pamphlet called "Happiness in Marriage," an English translation of a very sensible manual written by a French Catholic doctor. It was plain, down-to-earth and very French; it treated the whole subject of the marriage act respectfully but very sensibly. One could give this to any young couple with the confidence that it was not beyond their understanding, that it would afford them real practical help no matter what their level of ignorance or sophistication. "Happiness in Marriage" was our ace in the hole. And then we began to hear gossip to the effect that it was going to be banned in the Archdiocese. Sure enough, one day we received a letter: it had been banned by Rome on the grounds that it put too much stress on the sexual aspects of marriage. We had given out as many as we could when the rumors started; our supply was practically exhausted; now there would be no more. They were only available to French Catholics who probably had little need of them in the first place.

After our French pamphlets were banned, we had to deal with the physical aspects of marriage face to face. I discovered myself getting very glib on the subject, especially if the young bride to be was attractive and not pregnant already.

The old man was in an oxygen tent after a massive coronary attack and would not last very long. I checked the name plate at the bottom of his bed. It was a Northern Italian name, so I greeted him in Italian and he smiled. I suggested he save his strength by not spelling out his sins in any detail. The important thing was that he feel sorry for having offended God and ask his pardon. He nodded and reached for my hand.

It was always the same: with their last breath these

men would insist they had harmed no one. He began explaining to me in Italian that he had always supported his family; of course to do that he worked hard and often his only chance to relax was on Sunday morning when he sent his wife and children to church. But, he explained to me, God understood all that, so he had nothing to confess.

I asked him again to save his strength. "You are sorry for having offended God. You don't have to say anything. Just squeeze my hand and God will understand."

"Eh, all right, Father," he said vehemently in Italian, "I'm sorry."

Then the oxygen tent shook with something between a laugh and a cough; I looked anxiously for a nurse. Then I heard him speaking in broken, but clear, English:

"Eh, Father, what do you think of my Italian?"

"Take it easy," I said. "You had me fooled. You're *not* Italian?"

"No, Father," he said. "I'm a Slovak. But I understand it and I speak pretty good, don't you think?"

"Excellent."

"You know, Father, you remind me of Father Basil."

"Father Basil?"

"My priest. Father Basil. My priest from my parish. St. Ignatius in Down Neck Newark."

I had never heard of a St. Ignatius parish in Newark and I didn't know any priest by the name of Basil. I wondered if it was his first name or his last. But I didn't want to use any of the poor man's strength to answer my questions. Perhaps he was delirious already. Often when people are dying, youth, middle age and the present all merge into one. Basil might be a priest in Europe and St. Ignatius might be a parish in Czechoslovakia.

"St. Ignatius in Down Neck Newark," I repeated. "Father Basil."

"That's right, Father. You remind me of him."

"I'd like to meet him."

"When you do, you'll see what I mean, Father. Tell him Miklov said he was sorry."

"I'll do that, Miklov. But now you take it easy and try to get some sleep."

"No, Father, I don't want to sleep. I want to die wide awake."

"Receiving Last Rites doesn't mean you're going to die."

He reached out from under the plastic tent, stretching a strong right arm to the white enamel table, pulled open a drawer and extracted a couple of dollar bills.

"Wanna bet, Father?"

Before I could get the money out of my pocket to back my wager, he was gone.

On my way out of the hospital that night, I passed a telephone booth. The Newark Directory lay there with a light beamed on it. Something possessed me to take a look. If Miklov were not delirious, St. Ignatius parish would have to be in the Directory. And there it was. As big as life. I wrote the number down in my book. One day I would telephone Father Basil.

More than ever I began to take stock of my own position. I was still preoccupied with my desperate search for the meaning of faith. The love that I sought in the priesthood and in the Church was a word reserved for sermons: it wasn't really there.

People around me noticed I was disturbed. I found myself more nervous and edgy every day, and tried to find some outlet golfing, skiing, fishing, even racing sports cars. When I couldn't get away from the parish I would go down to the rectory basement and play out my feelings on a saxophone until I was exhausted.

175

Temptations grew stronger and more frequent. The rectory seemed always to be filled with young women, assisting with arrangements, committee work, secretarial chores. I became more aware of the fact that some were prettier, more pleasant, and some were sexier than others. Reading or music had been able to dispel sex fantasies before, now I could only rid myself of such thoughts by plunging into an ice cold shower. And my trips to the shower gradually increased.

mcmliv

FATHER JOSEPH and I had lived together for over a year. He saw me as the young man he used to be. I saw him as the wise old saint I could never aspire to be. He heard my confession at least once a week— sometimes once a day. I forced him to share all my torment, all my despair. I unloaded on him every thought, every impulse, every movement, every misstep. And in return he told me how he had suffered all this himself, and managed somehow to survive.

I felt very close to him because I felt my days as a good priest were numbered. As long as I had Father Joseph to lean on, I would keep going some way. But it never occurred to me that his days were numbered too.

Of course, he was no longer young. Even that great vitality sometimes flagged and he lapsed into being the man in his late sixties. He had been a diabetic for years; every evening Angie Amato came in to give him his shot of insulin. He had always smoked huge misshapen wiggly cigars of a special old country brand. One day I noticed the cigars seemed to have vanished from the rectory. When I asked him about it, he said he believed they were giving him trouble and the doctor had recommended cutting them out for a while.

Then one day Angie told me the doctors had taken a test and the grim results had swiftly shown up. Cancer of the jaw and throat.

Still, with blind faith in the doctors and their knives, I managed to believe that somehow, some way, Father Joseph would be spared. I talked to the doctors. They recommended that he visit the hospital in New York where Evita Peron had been treated. I wanted to take him there but Father Joseph wouldn't hear of it. Angie went with him. They recommended surgery. They talked of removing a piece of his hip bone and making a replacement for his infected jaw bone.

When Angie told me about it, I appointed myself a medical committee to sell him the idea of surgery. *He* could live without hope of recovery but I couldn't face it. Not yet.

I talked to him about it after breakfast. I talked to him about it when I took him to the country for a drive. I lobbied unceasingly, trying to sell him the idea of giving the surgeons a chance.

When I was going to him for confession one evening, I broke down in the midst of my recital and begged him to set a date to go to the hospital.

"Gabriel, my dear Gabriel," he said to me, "now I will confess something to you. You are a brave boy. A boy who has had many operations. I am an old man and I confess to you that I am a coward. I am more fearful of these New York surgeons with their knives than I am of my own disease."

"But Father Joseph, you're already in pain. You're already suffering. Even if the surgery only relieves you for a while. . . . And many times these operations are successful. Many, many times."

"No, Gabriel, everyone must listen to his own body. I know these old bones of mine. Perhaps they might have success with someone else, taking a piece of the ass and making him a new face. But not this old sinner."

That night when Angie came with the insulin I noticed she had two needles. They had started the morphine already.

"Gabriel has been trying to talk me into going to New York for the operation," he told Angie. Angie looked at him and looked at me and said nothing. I knew she was against it.

He had some kind of primitive instinct about the roots of disease which came to him from way back in the hills of Tuscany. One night at dinner he looked at me. He held a knife in front of his face. The light shone on it as he twisted and turned it in his hands.

"My dear Gabriel," he said solemnly, "cancer is a disease of the cells of the body. Cells so tiny they can only be seen through the strongest microscope. And you expect the doctors to fight it with *this?*" And then he put the knife down at the side of his plate. My argument for surgery was demolished.

Father Joseph believed, like many old country people, that most diseases had their origins in what we eat. He had little faith in modern science. He would often compare the life spans of country people who lived a simple frugal hardworking life in their farms and farms and villages in Italy, with their relatives and descendants who immigrated to this country, lived in relative luxury, and then were plagued by degenerative diseases in their forties and fifties. He undertook to simplify his own diet; he refused thick steaks and rich pastas. He cut out all tomatoes. He started eating plain macaroni with white sauce. He even ate tripe and other organ meats without tomato sauce.

But the cancer grew on him. One side of his face began swelling. This disturbed him. He was in very severe pain but he never complained. For many hours a day we tried to keep his swollen jaw under external

179

applications. It became virtually impossible for him to shave. I tried not to notice, but I couldn't help it. I tried to think of something I might do, but what was there?

I thought it would make him feel useful to worry about something besides himself, so I began asking him to hear my confession every night. Since Father Joseph seemed already to have one foot in eternity, it was close to confessing to God himself. He no longer had the strength to remonstrate with me, to protest that my own personal future was not as dark as it seemed to me. He would just nod and shake his head in bewilderment and say:

"My dear boy, you must not depend on me so. It is time we found someone else, some other priest to give you strength and comfort."

Soon it became an ordeal for him to talk, torture for him to move his jaws, open his mouth. Even a swallow of water was a trauma. We could delay no longer: he had to go to the hospital. He fought the idea for a few more days, then he suddenly didn't argue anymore. Angie packed a few things and we took him to St. Michael's Hospital in Newark.

His illness had virtually doubled my duties at the parish and in the rectory but I would hustle over to the hospital whenever I had twenty minutes or a half hour free to sit by his bed or to stand with him or just to hold his hand.

His nephew, his relatives from the Bronx, came, if at all, during formal visiting hours. I always tried to come at odd hours when no one else was there. For days I felt Father Joseph was on the verge of telling me something, but that he was stalling, waiting until the very end. The wait became a kind of game I played. Maybe he will tell me today, I would say to myself as I raced up the hospital stairs. Then when I found him, he would be too drugged, too stuporous from the pain.

And I would just stand there, and tell him what the old ladies of the parish asked me to say.

Now he was on the critical list. Arrangements had been made for a cadre of other priests to be with him constantly to perform the rituals for the dying priest. They started coming in shifts of twos and threes in the morning. He was in a coma from time to time and no one knew whether he would open his eyes again.

That night I had gone on sick call to City Hospital. I gave Last Rites to two old women and a young boy and death was very much with me. It was almost midnight when I left the hospital. I decided on impulse I would stop by St. Michael's and look in on Father Joseph. He would probably be in a coma. But it was my last chance to be with him alone before the ritual began in the morning.

When I walked quietly into his room, he held out his hand to me before he opened his eyes. His effort to speak triggered a spasm of coughing.

"Please don't waste yourself, Father Joseph," I whispered. "Save your strength. I will be back tomorrow."

He shook his head impatiently.

"My dear boy," he began slowly and painfully. It had been days since he had spoken three words. But he kept trying.

"To die," he said, "can for me . . . be . . . fortunate. I do not want to live. . . ." I started to protest but he hushed me. ". . . to see the day . . . when you will leave . . . the priesthood."

So that was it. All the hours and days he had spent trying to save me, he knew he was wasting his time, and yet he never permitted me to doubt his faith in me. Until now.

He took my hand. Tears spilled out of my eyes. I turned my head and started to protest but he would not permit it. He squeezed my hand until I shut up.

"Make no vows to me, Gabriel," he whispered. "Not

here. Not now. My sadness is to know what will be. My happiness is being able to die before that happens. You have been my young self over again. All over. I hope I can help you when this happens. I will . . . *if* there is a heaven."

His calmness, his clarity, the bare economy of his words made the shaft sink deeper. I felt it might have been better had I not haunted the hospital during his suffering. I only added to the pain. The tears hung on to my stubble of beard like basketball sweat. Father Joseph smiled at me with his eyes. He raised his hand to bless me and then he sank into what seemed like a coma again.

When I got back to my room at the rectory I was too shaken to do anything. I poured myself a stiff slug of Scotch and then took an endless shower.

"I will help you any way I can IF there is a heaven."

His words became so important I had to write them down. I studied them as if they were a passage in the scriptures. Then I tore them up. Father Joseph was telling me I would need heavenly help *after* I left the priesthood. He took my departure for granted.

"You have been my young self over again." Had he ever left? In Italy, during the First World War, anything was possible. Had there been a woman? Had he left and *then* come back? Would I leave and come back too?

Why hadn't Father Joseph told me this before? Why had he waited?

I couldn't sleep so I tried to read. I had finished my Breviary at City Hospital but I read it again. The Lives of the Saints might put me to sleep. I put on my robe and went downstairs to get Father Joseph's copy. I wanted to read it in Italian.

The Lives of the Saints had become like Mother

Goose to me. Born of noble parents, took a vow of virginity at the age of two. . . . I didn't believe any of it anymore. The martyrology, that saga of blood and gore, had been drained of all meaning by repetition. The blood and gore of the mystics and heretics and visionaries spilled by the Church during the Inquisition and since would make just as gruesome a horror story. No rational soul could be exposed to one without thinking of the other. But the constant descriptions of weird manifestations like levitation, ecstasy and visions remained with me as some kind of intellectual challenge. They were like drugs: something unknown and untried. The common denominator was always some measure of consecutive physical torment. Father Joseph was in torments of suffering. Maybe I could stay closer to him in his last days if I were suffering too.

I had laughed at the kooks in the seminary who practiced self-torture. Maybe I shouldn't have. Maybe this was a short cut to some kind of understanding, vision. At least I could do penance for the small sins of Father Joseph and the larger ones of my own.

I started with scalding hot showers followed by cold ones. I didn't eat and drank nothing but a little water. Then I gave up standing, sitting and lying down. I knelt straight up for hours until I keeled over. Then I took the water torture again. I pulled all the blinds so there could be no distractions. I lost track of night and day.

I had to be very cautious about making noises in the night. I knelt for hours looking at a blank wall waiting for something to happen.

On the way out of the shower I noticed the crucifix on the wall, so I moved it to the wall in front of me and began to concentrate on the face of the suffering Jesus. God Almighty, did anyone ever look at these grotesque sacred figures, mass produced by the thousands? Did anyone ever *look* at them? They had turned Our Lord into a cock-eyed bearded lady with a pathetic clown face.

Judas always appeared very manly in all the stories and pictures, but from Sunday school through the passion plays and the seminary, Jesus and his buddy John the Evangelist always came off a couple of flits. This pious blindness bred satisfaction with plaster junk! I tossed the bearded lady with her crown of thorns under my bed and put it out of my mind.

I pushed at the limits of consciousness. My head was swimming, my stomach was yawning, my body creaked with stiffness and then suddenly the wall opened up. The paint peeled off like flakes of dust and I was kneeling before a shimmering gauzy white curtain. Behind it was a woman, her naked pink plaster body suspended in an odalisque position. Barely moving. There seemed to be acres of First Communion veiling between us.

"Please, Father Longo," a voice whispered, "this is an emergency. This poor soul needs extreme unction. Last Rites." It was the Devil dressed in a white coat pretending to be a Catholic doctor pleading with me to have sex with this woman. He said he had a dispensation from the Bishop. It might bring her back to life.

He held up something but through all the veiling I couldn't make out the signature.

"If this isn't an emergency, nothing is," the Devil Doctor Satani said. "We've tried everything. This woman doesn't care if she lives or dies. *In extremis*, Father. There is no time to be wasted."

Her body stirred. I clawed through the acres of veiling trying to get near her. Her lashes fluttered, she smiled. I could see her eyes. They were the eyes of the virgin at St. John's in Jersey City, right across from

Dickinson High School annex. Our Lady's virgin eyes. Her hair was black and shiny as a funeral limousine. I recognized it: the hair belonged to a woman in St. Rocco's parish, the one who used to bug me with made-up stories in the confessional. The arms were pink and soft and rounded—Chickie! Chickie Formato, dream girl from P. S. 35. And Eileen. The legs belonged to Eileen. You could tell from the tiny scar on the knee. But no, the hips were Angela. Angela moving the way Angela moved. They didn't go with the eyes. Not at all. But the hair down there, the black curly hair down there belonged to the society debutante on the curved stairway under the chandelier. Rubinoff and his magic violin!

I turned to denounce the Devil and all his works but there was too much veiling. I ripped at it and tore and it was as hard as plaster. I scratched and clawed at the plaster until my hands were bloody.

There was a knock on some distant door.

"Father Longo. Father Longo. Are you resting?"

"Doctor Satani?"

"No, Doctor Stapleton, Father. Mrs. Perrazini has taken a turn for the worse and they want you at the hospital right away. May I say that you're on your way?"

"I'm coming," I said. "I'll be right there."

I tried to stand but I could barely make it. I snapped up the window shades and the daylight almost blinded me. I looked at the clock. Then I checked the reading with my wrist watch lying on the dresser. It was almost noon. Hours and hours of hot and cold running showers. Hours on my knees. And my ecstatic transcendental spiritual vision turns out to be a slow motion Playboy pin-up!

St. Vincent Ferrer, *ora pro nobis.*

Somebody needed a priest and this lousy priest

needed a shave. He also needed to soak that plaster First Communion veiling out from under his bloody broken nails.

St. Francis of Assisi, *ora pro nobis*.

Father Giuseppe de Sanctis, Holy Father of the Saints, dear old man who changed his name from Putzalente, little stinker, to de Sanctis, of the saints, pray for me.

The sight of your death, the ordeal of your death— even that sacred moment becomes for me the occasion for fantasies of coupling, mating, fornication. And then I remembered a woman in the confessional who spilled out the story of burying her husband, and that very afternoon, going to bed with the undertaker's assistant. I thought she was just another priest-teaser, but maybe what she had told me was true. Maybe death does this to you. It could be a natural reaction. A matter of life and death. One more thing I should have learned easily at seventeen. Instead I was learning it the hard way at twenty-eight.

I needed desperately to confess all this to Father Joseph. I telephoned St. Michael's and asked about him.

"He went into a coma last night shortly after you left, Father Longo. We don't expect him to recover consciousness. There are four priests with him now saying the prayers for the dying. He is *in extremis*. Why don't you get some rest?"

Rest. Rest! No rest for the wicked. I had something to confess that only Father Joseph could understand and he couldn't hear me. He would never hear me again.

When the pastor of a parish dies, the senior assistant automatically succeeds him, until such time as the Bishop names his successor. Father Frank Masiello was appointed the new temporary administrator at St. Rocco's. He had already made a few small changes in rectory routine—portents of things to come, like giving Angie Amato the boot—when he got a call from Paolercio asking him to come to the embalming room to assist in the vesting of the body of Father Joseph. When a priest dresses for Mass in the sacristy, he dons each symbolic garment to the accompaniment of an appropriate prayer. When he is dressed for the last time, another priest has to be on hand to make sure the vestments are properly worn, and to say the ancient prayers. Father Frank was very unsettled, he didn't want any part of this eerie ritual, so he asked me to go in his place.

The blue-white body of Father Joseph lay there naked on a draining slab. The place was lit as brightly as the back corner of a supermarket and it smelled like a morgue. It was an air-conditioned nightmare. When I edged closer to look at his poor tired face, the skilled embalmer ran around the draining slab and slapped the left side of Father Joseph's face. The surgery that he had refused to permit in his lifetime had been routinely performed by the embalmers. The swollen side of his face had been replaced by a free-form sculpture of flesh-colored wax. They had difficulty keeping the wax in place and each time it slipped someone would reach over and wham it into place.

When I saw the embalmer tugging with the pants and the underwear, I checked over the vestments. At last they were ready. I kissed the Cross on the Amice and touched it to Joseph's head, then placed it on him. The embalmer tucked it into his collar as I said the prayer "Impone. . . ."

Then I placed the Alb and said the prayer "De Alba me. . . ." I tied the Cincture while praying "Praecinge me . . ."; while pinning on the Maniple, "Merear . . ."; and adjusting the Stole, "Redde mihi. . . ." And last the Chasuble, "Domine qui dixisti. . . ."

187

That afternoon they brought his coffin to the rectory.

The place was still and empty. Father Frank had given orders to the housekeeper that no meals were to be cooked or served until further notice. All parish meetings and affairs were cancelled; all rectory routine was suspended. Even the phone stopped ringing. The stillness was very unnerving.

Angie was in tears all the time, and Father Frank couldn't stand that. The old ladies of the parish came, dry-eyed and realistic. They talked of Father Joseph's death as a happy deliverance from the doctors and the hospital. The cousins and the nieces came all the way from the Bronx. His nephew, Father John, as a priest and next of kin, began immediately to dispose of his personal effects.

Before he died, Father Joseph told me I could have anything of his that I wanted. I had always refused to discuss it. But that very afternoon Father John brought me his black cape and told me Father Joseph wanted me to have it.

It was a long full black cape, as heavy as a blanket, ancient in cut and vintage. We used to call it his Batman outfit. It had been given to him by an older priest who died shortly after World War I. It had been a gift to the older priest from His Eminence Cardinal Gaspari. I knew the history of the cape from memory. I knew the cape meant something to him, whereas money didn't. So I felt honored, but embarrassed to have it. I felt Father John might be embarrassed to have to give it to me.

Father Joseph's bank book showed a balance of fourteen dollars. Father John had his hands full consoling the cousins and the nieces and their husbands who were in a state of shock, having finally realized the full extent of their loss.

I began to feel that Father Joseph must be enjoying

all of this hugely. The hoboes, the derelicts, the winos, the gypsies and the drunks, all his friends, as the people of the parish called them—none of them turned up. There was no way of notifying them. During his period in the hospital, Angie and Father Frank had discouraged them from coming around. Few of them would be brave enough—or feel steady and well dressed enough—for the solemnity in the rectory. They would hear about it eventually somewhere, sometime, and—if Father Joseph had any powers of heavenly intercession—they would be provided the wherewithal to drink a toast to him with a decent glass of wine.

Even after his nephew had disposed of all Father Joseph's effects, Father Frank still avoided his room as if it were haunted. He kept the door closed and never went near it.

There was hardly anything there except a plain glass-topped desk, an old bed and a couple of dilapidated chairs. Already the austere poverty of the surroundings seemed to belong to a long gone time. The whole character of the place was changing and changing fast. The speculation over who was to be the new pastor had already begun. But the money was riding on two priests who had come from that parish originally, had been born and raised there. The leading candidate was Father Mike Fuino, an assistant at a parish in Down Neck Newark.

Within twenty-four hours my sense of loss became complete. Our new pastor, whoever he was, couldn't replace Father Joseph as my Father Confessor.

"I will help you any way I can *if* there is a heaven." For the moment I had to believe there was.

That night I decided I should try to talk to Monsignor Artioli. After all, he had known me since I was a boy. I *was* still the boy he knew from Mt. Carmel. That was the trouble, fifteen years later I was still a

189

boy of fifteen. Could he understand that that was the trouble? But how could I be anything else! All my emotions—if I ever had any—had been put in the deep freeze. I didn't know what emotion *was* any more. I couldn't tell honestly how I felt about anything. I was playing games. Was Monsignor Artioli too close to me to see that? Could he help me?

It was late, much too late to call him. But I couldn't wait until morning. He might want to see me this very instant. He had always encouraged me to call on him at any time. This was no night to stand on ceremony.

I went to the telephone and called the Mt. Carmel Rectory.

The telephone seemed to ring forever before there was any answer.

I imagined poor Mrs. Artioli, probably I was rousing her from a sound sleep. I looked at my watch. It was still only twenty minutes to midnight. Finally someone picked up the phone. It was a strange voice.

"This is Father Longo," I began. "I'm sorry to call at this hour but it is important that I reach Monsignor Artioli tonight if possible."

"I'm sorry," said the voice. "But I am afraid that is impossible."

"Is he out of the city?" I asked.

"Yes."

"Can you tell me how he might be reached?"

"No, I'm afraid that is impossible."

I explained that I was one of Monsignor Artioli's boys from the parish, that I had a problem he had asked me to take up with him and it was important to know how I could reach him.

"I'm afaid I can't help you. There is no information I can give you on that. Nothing at all . . ."

This was all mighty mysterious.

"Is he ill?"

"He has not been well."

"Can I talk to his mother, Mrs. Zita Artioli?"

"I'm sorry, Mrs. Artioli is not here at present. There is really no information I can give you. If it is urgent I suggest you write directly to the archdiocese and they will refer the matter to the proper person to handle it."

It was like talking to an answering service. I put the telephone down. I had forgotten all about my own problem, absorbed in this new mystery.

I would call Father Joe. The later it was the more apt I was to catch him. I dialed his number and he was on the phone in a flash.

"Look, Joe," I began, "something strange is going on. I called Mt. Carmel and asked for Monsignor Artioli and some guy answered. We talked for a couple of minutes and—"

"Gabe," he said, "I thought you *knew*. The Monsignor has had a nervous breakdown."

"A what?"

"Well, they call it a breakdown. He is in a hospital somewhere, getting the best treatment. That's all anybody knows."

"Joe, I'm sorry I bothered you. I guess I'm just out of touch."

"When did you see him last?"

"I don't know. It couldn't be more than a couple of weeks."

"Well, it was kind of sudden, I guess. If I hear anything more I'll let you know."

"Thanks, Joe," I said.

I put down the phone and fell back on the bed. I was holding my breath as if breathing would bring on some unimaginable pain.

If only, I always thought, if only I could be like him. Maybe now I really meant it—all the way.

191

mcmlv

"ARE YOU going to be in, Father?" "May I stop by?" When one priest telephones another, that's all that needs to be said. It is just assumed, whatever the hour of the day, that the caller needs a confessor and will show up promptly after having driven as carefully as possible through the perilous highways and the treacherous intersections.

I thought I might find a good confessor at St. Lucy's, an Italian parish in the next ward, where Father Artioli had served his first assignment. I gave two priests there a try and went back to the telephone. I tried the priests at St. Benedict's Abbey. Then I used to get up early when Father Mike Fronzak came to say early Masses.

It began to dawn on me that all a priest really knows anything about is playing the role of a priest. Unless he's leading a double life. At least that gives him some experience—the kind of experience that would have been helpful to me in the confessional. But the priests that *were* leading double lives (at least the ones that I knew about, the ones that were talked about) seemed to bend over backwards for fear that some of their worldly experience might show up in the counselling they gave me. After a year with Father Joseph it was hard to take seriously anything these new confessors had to offer. I rarely confessed to the same priest twice. I continued shopping.

Late one night, while making a sick call at Newark City Hospital, I remembered Father Basil at St. Ignatius. I had written down his telephone number somewhere and promptly forgotten about it. So I looked it up again, and dialed his number.

A lilting, softly accented woman's voice answered. She didn't sound *super adulta*. Not *super adulta* at all.

When Father Basil picked up the phone I introduced myself and said, "Are you going to be in, Father? May I stop by?"

"Come right over, Father," he said, "by all means."

There was something about the way he walked, something in his handshake, his voice, a certain something in the way the weight of his body was centered below the belt, an indefinable kind of strength in him that spelled not just guts, but balls. When I followed him into his study I saw the Byzantine crosses and I knew what I should have remembered. He was a priest of the Eastern Rite, with just a hint of indefinable accent which I guessed to be Middle European.

He sat in the chair at his desk. When I began to kneel down he motioned me to another chair. There was something in his eyes, in the way he spoke the words: "Now, let's talk." I knew somehow Father Joseph had a hand in our meeting. I said, "Bless me, Father, for I have sinned" with one breath. Then I took another deep breath and really let go.

When he raised his hand to give me absolution, I noticed the fingers of his right hand were missing.

As soon as the confession was over, we really got down to cases. I was completely at ease for the first time in weeks.

"Gabe," he began, with a casual look over his shoul-

193

der toward the open door of his study, "when I go to Rome, I can't take my eyes off the ladies in the Via Veneto. Va-va-va-voom!" he exploded, as he threw his chest out, "the tits on those Roman prostitutes. When you go over there, I'll tell you where to head for, but you got to be careful. Oh yes."

"Maybe I'll wait until I'm excommunicated," I said. He laughed. "I've never been to Europe. Dad has family there. One day I'll get there."

"There's nothing to stop you."

He noticed me looking at the missing fingers. He gave a sketchy explanation; someday when he had the time I would get the whole story. I was sure it would curl the hair. Paratrooping for the CIA, cut off behind Russian lines. Caught, tortured, escaped, back at least four times. Now he was a colonel in the U. S. Army Intelligence. His knowledge of Central Europe and his fluency with all middle European languages made him a kingpin in our set-up over there. Whatever it was one could only guess. He underplayed it so completely I began to imagine all sorts of things. He had to be at least a triple agent. Vatican Intelligence. CIA. U.S. Army. God knows what else.

I could guess, too, that he ran some kind of recruiting and underground employment service that was worldwide. He was already the regular confessor of innumerable priests. His suggestions and advice all began where the average Roman priest feared to think.

He talked about the Vatican as if it were a rundown, rotten Jersey political machine. The politics of the Curia, the Council of Bishops, his own Church, the Pope—all these he discussed as candidly and knowingly as a politician discussing Mayor Kenny of Jersey City.

According to him, all I had to do was make up my own mind about what I wanted.

"If you want to just play around with women, that's one thing. You can play around, either in or out of the

Church, as you know. You don't need me to tell you that. You just need someone to brief you on how to be careful, how to beat the system. If you have some girl in mind—but you apparently don't—and want to marry and have a family and still stay a priest, you can do that too. It isn't always easy. It takes a little money here and there. But it can be done. You just need someone to tell you how and how much."

Then he began to outline the ways. I could join the Eastern Rite, preferably in Europe. Then, when I dissolved my affiliation with Rome, get married, preferably over there, being careful to pick the right country, and being careful to have the right documents—preferably two of everything, one fake and one real.

"After you are married, you can petition Rome, if you want, to come back under the Roman Rite. Or you can wait it out until the inevitable reconciliation. Pacelli is not long for this world and with him out of the way—may his soul rest in peace—it's just a matter of, well, decades. You're young enough. You'll live to see it."

He began to sound like the bossman of all the clerical James Bonds on this planet. He had me dazzled. Other people looked at a closed door and saw the door closed. Father Basil looked at a closed door as a challenge.

"But," he said finally, "if you don't mind my saying so, I think you should spend a few years seeing a little more of this wicked world before you think about getting married. Shall we put it this way?" he mused. "In spite of all your very real torment over some very real imaginary situations, you are still a very young man. And you have led, what is that phrase, a very sheltered life."

No one ever called a thirty-year-old man an adolescent with more finesse.

"You see, Gabe," he said with infinite sadness, "it's

wonderful to be an honest man. But in your—our—
Holy Roman Catholic Church, being an honest priest
is absolute *hell*. Nobody ever told you that, did they?
Come on," he said, "I want you to meet my wife,"
calling her name.

On his desk he had pictures of his teen-age daughter
and a son in the paratroops. His wife walked in, a warm
lovely woman. She suddenly seemed too good to be
true.

The notion of having a wife at your side in the
rectory was absolutely fascinating to me. She couldn't
miss being a great asset to him in his work. The parishioners would have to be crazy about her.

So what was all the torture about? Here was the
alternative, fifteen minutes away from that room in
the rectory at St. Rocco's where my hormones were
driving me crazy.

I felt like a man from Mars taking a look at this
planet for the first time. When Father Basil's wife invited me for dinner, I felt as awkward and as curious
and as full of awe as I had at Mt. Carmel when Mrs.
Artioli served me Coca-Cola in a wine glass.

I accepted the invitation. I thanked her as politely
as I could. But I was absolutely stumped about the
proper form of address for the wife of a priest. The
Pope was Your Holiness, a Cardinal was Your Eminence, a Bishop was Your Excellency. But a priest's
wife? My seminary education didn't cover that social
eventuality.

HEADQUARTERS CONTINENTAL AIR COMMAND
AIR RESERVE RECORDS CENTER
3800 York Street
Denver 5, Colorado

PERS-A 1-10 LONGO, Gabriel A. AO 3059646
SUBJECT: Appointment as a Reserve Officer of the Air
Force

TO: Chaplain (1st Lt) Gabriel A. Longo, AFRes
    AO 3059646
    Jersey City, New Jersey

1. The Secretary of the Air Force has directed me to inform you that, by direction of the President, you are tendered an appointment as a Reserve Officer of the Air Force, in the grade and with service number shown in address above, for an indefinite term. The Secretary of the Air Force has designated you to perform the duties of a chaplain (PAFSC 792C).

2. There is inclosed a form for Oath of Office which you are requested to execute and return promptly to this Office. The execution and return of the required Oath of Office constitute an acceptance of your appointment. No other evidence of acceptance is required.

3. You will not perform the duties of an officer under this appointment until specifically ordered by competent authority.

4. Authority for this appointment is the Armed Forces Reserve Act of 1952.

BY ORDER OF THE COMMANDER:

James T. Quirk
Colonel, USAF
Asst. DCS/P

The forms had been filled by the thousands in sextuplicate, the interminable interviews endured, the tests surmounted, the doctors had looked into all my grey crevices and pronounced me a specimen suitable in every respect. The machinery had ground relentlessly on; only one detail remained: I had to tell my parents. I had to tell them something.

I had buried all my doubts and difficulties whenever I came home, or tried to. They had nothing but glowing reports from the parish. Dad's heart attack had been my excuse for telling them nothing.

I started explaining it to Mother first; I thought she would be the best one to break the news to Dad. His greatest joy these days was to walk down the street with me in my Roman collar. Friends greeted him, not with an inquiry about his own shaky health, but the more pleasant: "How's your son, the Father?"

"I think a change will be good for me, Mother." I was telling her in the kitchen. "You know I never got a chance to travel very much. I always felt sort of left out of things during the War. It's something I'd like to experience while I'm still young enough, you know. . . ."

"Gabriel," she interrupted, "are you in trouble with a girl?"

"A girl? Mother, where did you get that idea?"

"What's crazy about a mother asking her son a personal question? Because if you are, I want to know. Carrie was telling me about some priest from Paterson, a very good looking fellow, who got into trouble with a woman in the parish. So he got into uniform and she went somewhere in Arizona and they were living together in a trailer and the whole parish was talking about it."

"Mother, there is no girl."

"If you did anything like that, you know it would be the death of your father."

"Mother, there is no girl."

"I'm only asking. I just wanted to be sure."

"Well, you can be sure."

I had brought my uniform in its box. My car was full of clothes, books, skis, a trumpet, my saxophone, and the chalice my parents had given me at ordination. I unloaded everything into the basement and came upstairs with the single box under my arm.

"That's a pretty big box. Why don't you leave it in the basement with your other things?"

"Mother, this is my new uniform."

"Oh, you got the clothes already before we knew anything?" she said. "Well, go ahead, try it on. Let's see how you look in it."

I went into my old bedroom and put it on. When

I got the angle of the hat adjusted just right I made my entrance. Mother was standing in the kitchen. Immediately she turned away.

"You look awful in that thing. Absolutely awful. Black is the only thing looks right on you as far as I'm concerned. I just don't understand whatever put this silly idea in your head." In an instant she was fussing with the silver first lieutenant bars.

"You've got them on all crooked." She stood back and took another look. "Hold your chin up, Gabriel. You got the tie crooked too." She started adjusting the knot at my neck.

"Don't forget, Mom, it's been quite a while since I knotted a tie."

She looked at me and then turned away. How many years exactly? When I put off my priestly clothes and went skiing, boating, or golfing, I always wore a sport shirt open at the neck. It had been exactly nine years since I had tied a tie.

Dad walked in the front door and Mother rushed out to meet him, waving me out of sight until she had broken the news. She shrewdly turned the announcement on its head and made it sound as though the assignment had come out of the blue; it was none of my doing. The Air Force needed young chaplains and I had been elected.

"Where are they going to send you?" my father said when he came into the kitchen.

"Well," I said, "I have to report first at Lackland Air Force Base in Texas for basic training. After that I suppose they'll assign me to a base here in the States for a while. After that, your guess is as good as mine."

As soon as I said it out loud, I knew in my bones I was never going to Texas. I wasn't going to go, that's all. I wasn't going to run away. Why was I changing uniforms? I wanted to wear a tie, why not be honest about it?

"Will you have to do a lot of flying in those jets?" Mother wanted to know.

"Don't be silly, Julia. He's not going to be a pilot."

"Oh, I don't know." I laughed. Never say never. I might end up with American Airlines yet. To fill the awkward silence I began lecturing them how being a chaplain is very much like serving in a parish. A chaplain functions as a parish priest for all Catholics and their families stationed at these bases. Chaplain's quarters were very much like military rectories. Then I realized I was talking about some other guys, not me.

"Will we be able to come visit you from time to time?"

"Oh, Julia, nowadays the boys in service seem to be on furlough half the time. That's what they call it, don't they, Gabe? Furlough, or leave, A.W.O.L. Leave."

"Leave, furlough, it amounts to the same thing, Dad," I said.

An indefinite leave of absence, that's what I'd ask for.

Dad was standing very close to me. I could see the bulge in his shirt pocket where he carried those nitroglycerine pills for his heart. I wanted to blurt out everything, pour it on the kitchen floor. But I looked at the bulge and didn't.

I went into my bedroom and got the letter Father Basil had drafted for me, just in case. I read it over.

Archbishop Thomas A. Boland
Archdiocese of Newark
31 Mulberry Street
Newark, New Jersey

Your Excellency:

I wish, your Excellency, to withdraw my appointment to the Air Forces; instead I wish to have an indefinite leave of absence. My reason for asking withdrawal of the appointment is that I do not feel I am fit at the present time for such service.

I wish to state here categorically to your Excellency that I am most grateful to Almighty God, Our Blessed Lady, and Your Excellency for paternal handling of my situation.

In return, I promise to your Excellency that I shall never fall away from my faith, and that I shall never bring shame on Holy Mother the Church, and I shall be loyal as I know in my heart and my soul that the Catholic Church is the only Church that offers mankind salvation, and only through the Catholic Church can I be saved.

Begging your Excellency's further paternal attitude, guidance, prayers and blessings, I am an unworthy son of your Excellency in Christ's vineyard.

Sincerely,
Rev. Gabriel A. Longo

I couldn't sign my name to a letter like that. Not anymore. Loyal in heart and soul? I shall never fall away? "Never say, 'never again' again" was a song Helen O'Connell or somebody used to sing. I had taken too many vows in my lifetime. Never again. I hadn't taken the Air Force oath of allegiance to the U.S. Government yet and wasn't about to.

I rewrote the letter:

Archbishop Thomas A. Boland
Archdiocese of Newark
31 Mulberry Street
Newark, New Jersey

Your Excellency:

I wish, your Excellency, to withdraw my appointment to the U.S. Air Force, of which I am not yet an official member, not having been sworn in.

Instead, I wish to have an indefinite leave of absence.

My reason for asking for the withdrawal of the appointment is that I do not feel that I can be fit for such service at the present time.

Yours in Christ,
Rev. Gabriel A. Longo

I changed clothes, walked to the mailbox and dropped the letter in. That was that.

The bishop had given me the names of a couple of psychiatrists, one in Newark and one in New York. Both were Catholics and specialized in the problems of priests. One day, to get it over with, I called the Newark doctor. I expected he would be booked for days or weeks in advance, but when I gave him my name he suggested I come in the following afternoon.

That seemed almost too easy—too automatic. The bishop had probably given the psychiatrist my name. Maybe they even put a red check mark after Longo which meant: get to work on this one immediately.

The doctor was about fifty. I had no idea where to begin. I felt the first move was his. He seemed to feel the first move should be mine. My don't-give-a-damn attitude certainly showed because one of his first questions was:

"Do you resent being here in some way, Father Longo?"

"Yes," I said. "I'm afraid I do."

"I don't think there's any reason you should," he said.

"I probably shouldn't. But there are a lot of things I feel that I shouldn't, that's why. . . ."

"That's why you're here."

"That's why I'm here."

"So you resent the circumstances which bring you here as well."

"I don't resent them so much as I don't understand them."

"You resent needing help."

"Perhaps."

"But if I'm to help you in any way, it depends totally on your cooperation. You understand that."

"Of course I understand that."

"Then will you cooperate with me?"

"Yes," I said. He looked at me and smiled. My reply certainly sounded like a "no," possibly a maybe. He kept looking at me until I repeated the "yes" with a little more conviction.

"It's just that I feel I could be totally cooperative if I had decided to see you on my own."

"And you didn't?"

"This was the bishop's idea. Certainly there is no use in fencing about that."

"No. Of course not."

At that point he pulled a form out of his desk and began jotting things down on it. That didn't relax me any.

"Did your resentment of authority begin in the seminary or did you have problems before that at home? With parental authority, for instance."

"Who says my problem is resentment of authority? I have no problems with authority. I was assigned to a parish where assistants came and went, where the pastor was supposed to be a regular ogre, and I found him to be one of the finest men I had ever known. I didn't even begin to have problems really until he died."

"You had no problems in the seminary? You were able to adjust completely there? I find that difficult to believe. If that is true, you are certainly the first priest in my experience who did."

"The seminary seems pretty far behind me. It doesn't seem to have very much bearing on the present. At least not to me."

"Then you're critical of your seminary training?"

"I think there's no substitute for experience and in

the seminary that's exactly the one thing you don't get. Can't get."

"You mean sexual experience?"

"I wasn't thinking about sexual experience."

"Do you resent talking about your sexual experiences?"

"I can't talk about them because I haven't had any."

"And you resent *that*."

"I'm adjusting to that. Or I have adjusted to that. At least I haven't had any. At least that's a fact."

"You're sure."

"It just happens to be a fact."

"But before the seminary you were attracted to women?"

"I was always attracted by women."

"You were never attracted to men? To boys? Now don't be in a rush to answer. Think back a ways."

"That's one thing I don't have to think about."

"You're sure."

"Of course I'm sure."

"You don't have to shout, Father. I'm ready to believe you."

There was such condescension about his answer he made me angry. He seemed to feel that was some kind of coup.

"You see, doctor, it has been years since I talked about anything like this outside of the confessional."

"And you resent the fact that I'm asking you questions without being a priest?"

"I don't resent anything. That's what I'm here for. To answer questions."

"Oh, you've decided that, have you?"

"What else?"

"There are no questions you want to ask me?"

There was one question I was dying to ask him and I decided to risk it.

"Doctor, to be perfectly honest, I keep looking at that form you're filling out. And wondering what's going to happen to it after we're through."

"The relations between you and me are confidential. There doesn't seem to be much point in continuing if you don't have the confidence in me to believe that."

"Doctor, I've never been to a psychiatrist before. But I have heard a few thousand confessions. I don't think it would help if I carried a pad and pencil and started writing things down. It seems to me, if I were you, I would wait until after I'd left before I started making notes. Or at least you might wait until the second visit. Maybe even the third."

He smiled and slipped his pen back into his breast pocket.

"Well, perhaps we should adjourn until another day. Do you want to make another appointment now or would you prefer to call me?"

"I think it would be better if I telephoned."

"As you wish."

At least the Archdiocese could put in their records I had reported. I couldn't imagine this doctor being able to help anybody.

But talking to him helped me to decide one thing: I wanted to see a head shrinker on my own; somebody I picked out of a telephone book, a hat, anything, so long as I was sure he wasn't the official psychiatric arm or ear of the Archdiocese of Newark.

I tried to remember someone I knew or heard of who had ever gone to a psychiatrist. And I couldn't think of a soul.

I parked my car in the garage at Rockefeller Center, walked east on 48th Street to Madison Avenue toward the offices of the Military Ordinariate in the New York Archdiocesan Chancery Complex behind St. Patrick's

Cathedral, between 50th and 51st. I walked up the steps but I didn't open the door. I just stood there. Then I turned around and walked down.

The Madison Avenue crowds seemed to be moving with more drive than usual. Or maybe I was slower because I didn't know where I was going. An old lady smiled as she turned to avoid walking into me. I used to feel genuine warmth and security from such deference but now it irritated me.

If she knew what the Devil and I were thinking she would be gasping for air, I thought. The parade of pretty girls made me conscious of my collar. I crossed Madison Avenue, wandered into the lobby of the New Weston Hotel, found the public phone booth and dialed the Chancery office. When I got the secretary in the office of the Military Chancellor, I didn't recognize my own voice.

"I'm terribly sorry," I said. "Please apologize to Reverend Moriarty for me, but I won't be able to keep my appointment. Something has come up."

"Oh, I'm so sorry, Father Longo. But thank you for calling."

It had been so easy. Something had come up. I was going to spend a night on the town. I wasn't due back at the rectory in Newark until early Mass the next morning. I wasn't due back at the Chancery office ever again. I felt as though my private world had just changed back from daylight saving time to eastern standard and I had a bonus of fourteen hours for which I was accountable to no one. With the possible exception of my exhausted overworked conscience.

I buttoned my black raincoat at the neck to cover the Roman collar and walked over to the desk. When they handed me the registry, I was stumped for a name. Then I wrote G. A. Long and added my parent's address. Play it safe! Dropping one little "o" made me somebody else.

Since I had no luggage, I handed the clerk a twenty dollar bill before he could ask me to pay in advance. When the cashier gave me my change, the bellboy was standing there with the key. I knew perfectly well he was going to ride upstairs on the elevator, look around the room knowingly and then stand there waiting for his tip. I was always a generous tipper but I didn't like his style. He was reading me, casing me, wondering what he could do for me. It was a little too obvious, a little too insistent. Or perhaps I was a little too sensitive. Maybe he had seen me come in with my topcoat collar unbuttoned. Some of the midtown bellmen never miss a trick, I had heard.

It was an uncomfortable elevator ride. When I got rid of him with a half dollar I thought I would feel more comfortable, but I didn't. I wondered why I had paid fourteen dollars for a hotel room in the first place. There were better places to hide. I decided to take a walk.

It felt good just to wander aimlessly looking in the shop windows. The windows at Rogers Peet & Co. were a friendly reminder of the good old days. A week before I got my official acceptance for ordination, I had received a letter of congratulations from Rogers Peet. They must have a regular pipeline to the Chancery offices. It never occurred to me before. But I was so impressed at the time I let them sell me a new cassock. Their clerical clothing department is a very *in* place for the clergy. I was surprised to find no cassocks in the windows. Tweeds, white-on-white shirts, tab collars and a little beachwear.

That brought up the subject of clothes. I had a uniform I would certainly never wear. I had three black silk suits, cassocks and clerical clothing to burn. Now I caught myself looking at a couple of sports jackets. Maybe I could unload my whole wardrobe on some tall con man, size 42 long, and start anew.

I didn't feel up to shopping in Rogers Peet, but I kept looking at clothes. It was almost closing time when I spotted a beautiful grey jacket in a small shop near the hotel. It just happened to be my size. Sixty-five dollars was too much, but whatever my other problems were, getting rid of money was the only thing I had mastered. After I bought the jacket, I let the clerk sell me a shirt and a tie. It was a contour shirt, cut wide at the top and narrow around the hips. I had never owned one before. When he suggested I might want to try it on, I knew what he was getting at. He thought perhaps I didn't have a hotel room, and wanted to make a quick change. It was amazing how accommodating the shops seemed to be in the Cathedral area. Why not? He showed me to the dressing room and I came out without my Roman collar. The clerk seemed so pleased with my confidence in him, he unloaded three or four sport shirts on me.

Well, I thought, at least I gave him something to discuss with his roommate later.

When I walked back to the hotel, I thought I noticed a couple of old ladies staring at me. Had they seen me go into the shop in a Roman collar? It wasn't possible. I had had my topcoat buttoned right up to the chin, I was positive. Anyway, to make sure, I buttoned it up again, hiding the new maroon striped tie I had paid six-fifty for. Even one little button was giving me trouble.

When I walked into the lobby carrying my package, the same bellhop was on duty. The package gave him an opportunity to move in on me. I wasn't ready and before I could fend him off he had grabbed my bundle, and stood by the elevator pushing the button.

He trailed me down the hallway to my room. I thought I heard "Oops, sorry," but I ignored him. When he said, "I'm sorry, sir," I looked around.

My Roman collar, my rabbat, and the sport shirts

were spread out on the carpet. He didn't say a word as he carefully picked them up and stuffed them back into the box. He didn't have to. I wanted to let him know I suspected him of cutting the string but I decided not to get into it.

Priests are trained not to allow themselves to be treated like "regular guys." But coping with bellhops should have been a special course.

When we got to the room, he treated me like I was a fellow-member of a counterfeiting gang. He sat down on the bed and I knew I was in for a hard time.

"This hotel's got nothing except location," he said. "I don't know why anybody would want to stay here unless they wanted to commit suicide. But the Waldorf still gets most of that business."

I ignored him and reached into my coat pocket: nothing but bills. When I gave him one, he brightened up immediately. "Is there anything else I can get for you, Sir? You know what I mean?"

"Not a thing," I said. "Thanks anyway."

"No, *sir*, this is a dull place, but if there's anything you want, you know what I mean? There's nothing that can't be had. All modern conveniences."

"Thanks very much," I said. "But I have a date for dinner."

"You got a reservation?'" he inquired.

"No, I'm just going to wander into one of the places around here."

"If you want to see an interesting place, walk over to Lexington Avenue. You ever been in Jimmy's Keyboard Lounge?"

"I don't think so. What kind of music do they have there?"

"Music?"

"The name sounded like it might be a place where you could relax and listen to a little music. Like the Embers."

"Oh, sure, sure," he said. "It's very relaxed around there." He felt he had made a sale, I guess. At least he got up off the bed and moved toward the door. Then he paused, looked back with a sly smile and said:

"When you drop in there, say hello to the hatcheck for me. Her name is Lois. Tell Lois Wayne says hello."

"Thanks very much," I said. Then I bolted the door.

I didn't feel like having dinner alone in my room. I wasn't up to coping with a waiter who was apt to be as wise and helpful as the bellhop. I felt like that Nazi spy who landed on the tip of Long Island during World War II, came to New York, took one look at the strange enemy town, panicked and turned himself in. But I didn't know where to surrender. In Stockholm you can dial SUICIDE and somebody will talk to you. In New York you can always call A.A. I started reading the classified directory page by page. Why hadn't I bought an evening paper, a copy of *Playboy* or the *Reader's Digest*?

I tried to take a nap but I felt worse with my eyes closed. So I headed for the shower. It seemed as though I spent half my time under the cold shower and the other half in the confessional. But instead I ran a hot tub and just lay there. I could have used a shave. What would it matter? Jimmy's Keyboard Lounge was bound to be as dimly lit as the law allowed.

You know you're going to end up there sooner or later. The bellboy is Satan and he's already scored, so why not give him credit?

When I walked into the Keyboard Lounge some guy was playing musical comedy tunes on the piano. Half the kilowatts that lit the place seemed to be focused on the spot where his hair was thinnest. The rest of the place was as dark as a tomb.

"Check your hat, sir?"

I never wore a hat but I surrendered my topcoat to the woman in the checkroom. She wasn't the type to be in league with a bellhop, not the type at all. She looked more like a high school science teacher than a hatcheck girl in a glamorous Lexington Avenue bistro, dimly lit to accommodate cheaters, shoppers, merchandise and refugees from the Archdiocesan Chancery. Maybe Lois was off tonight or maybe the checkroom was a two-girl operation. The place was beginning to get crowded. When she handed me my numbered chit I was terribly casual. "Wayne told me to say hello to Lois. Is she off tonight?"

"She'll take care of you in a minute," the woman said. She slammed the door of her little cage and led me to a small table in the back, right on top of the small bandstand. Two obviously unescorted ladies were hunched over a nearby table. One looked like a natural blonde, the other was a dyed brunette. The hatcheck girl turned, caught me looking at the girls, and said:

"I'm Lois. I want you to meet Peggy and Celeste."

When the brunette turned around to look me over, I was amazed to discover she was wearing stage make-up, thick pancake with false eyelashes. My reaction must have showed because after a round of glances, Celeste rose grandly from the table and walked off. I sat down with Peggy. Satan had scored again. The waitress materialized out of nowhere.

"Good evening," she said brightly. "May I help you?"

"*J and B* on the rocks," Peggy said. "Better bring me half a dozen." Wow, I thought, I was misreading the signals again. Maybe Celeste hadn't gotten lost on purpose. Maybe she was expected back from the ladies' room in a minute with the rest of the softball team.

"What are you having, darling?" Peggy inquired. "Your usual?"

"I'll have *J and B* on the rocks also."

"Seven is not a lucky number for me, darling. Eleven would be more like it."

If this was going to be her speed for the evening, I would be under the table and Satan would feel terribly cheated. I had to watch myself carefully. I had to eat before midnight, and stop eating and drinking at midnight. Otherwise I couldn't say Mass in the morning.

Mass in the morning. I had to have excuses ready. How could I possibly explain that I had to stop drinking at midnight without giving myself away?

Probably the whole set-up had my name on file already, my parent's address, a police teletype of my wardrobe. They had probably already had a good laugh over the story of my clothes spilling out in the hotel corridor.

"I have to take it easy. I have an appointment for a basal metabolism test early in the morning." My unconscious was obviously never very far away from the smell of ether and the sound of hospital bells whenever I got within a female aura.

"Oh," said Peggy, "those can be very exciting. My girl friend had one of those. How soon will you know what type you are? I can't stand waiting. How long do you have to wait?"

Her honesty and brass entertained me. "I have no idea. I've never had one before," I said.

When the drinks arrived, Peggy quickly downed two. If that's the way she earned her commission, she was a hard worker. With four shots left in front of her, she casually recalled the waitress and ordered a full bottle.

"Sometime you must tell me all about it. I'm an absolute *freak* for case histories. I could listen to doctors all night. But you're not a doctor."

"Not really," I said. "But you're close." Before she turned on any of her antennae I thought I would throw her a few false clues. "But I have to do a lot of listening in my work too."

"Oh, I got you, Harry. You're a lay analyst on the town. My dear," she said, "are you having separate conventions or something?"

"I don't know what you mean."

"Last night, darling, I had four psychoanalysts on my hands at one time or another. All M.D.s. But I'm not prejudiced against lay analysts. As a matter of fact, my analyst is not an M.D. and I wouldn't trade him for any of that bunch from the convention."

"How long have you been going?"

"This one is my new love. About seven months, I guess. Before that, well, you might say I've had a couple of analysts shot out from under me. This one is a psychologist really, I believe. He's on lower Fifth Avenue, near Washington Square. Maybe you know him."

One thing was certain: if I got a referral to a head-shrinker from a B-girl whom I met through a hatcheck whom I met through a bellman he wouldn't turn in reports to the archbishop. "If I don't, I'd like to," I said.

"Give me a piece of paper and I'll write it down," she said.

The orchestra moved in and began to play so loud I couldn't hear anything. This was a relief. By the time I had finished my one drink, Peggy was well on her way to getting thoroughly smashed. Soon I was busy trying to think of ways to keep her quiet. The idea of inviting her to go back to the hotel with me—that important apex of temptation—was so fleeting and so tepid as to be absurd.

I caught myself praying—not to get rid of the temptation, but to get rid of this loud, drunken woman. As soon as the solo piano went back to work, I was in trouble. Every word she uttered could be heard all over the club. I tried to pay the check and sneak out, but as soon as she saw me reach for my wallet, she was

213

on her feet, slobbering over me. I was so concerned about the scene she was making, I didn't even complain about the size of the check.

"Let's go to your hotel, darling," she kept saying at the top of her lungs. I decided not to protest until we got into the street. Then I might be able to get her into a cab. When I agreed, she threw her arms around me and started to plant a wet kiss on my right ear. What began with sloppy tenderness turned into the loudest belch I had ever heard a female deliver. When we got into the street, she made it plain she would never desert me. It seemed quieter on Lexington Avenue than it had been in the club. The pet names she showered over me—sweetie, honey, darling, baby, sugar-lover—rang out as we walked along. I kept looking around to make sure no one had noticed my predicament. I turned off Lexington into a side street. Park Avenue is more deserted, I thought, maybe I can get a cab there. When we passed St. Bartholomew's Church, she complained of being dizzy and sat down on the steps.

"I'll get us a cab," I said, as I started pacing up and down at the curb.

"You're not trying to get rid of me are you, sugarlover? She got up and staggered toward me. I caught her just as she was about to fall.

I had to get back to Newark in a hurry. Maybe I should just skip trying to get rid of her and take her to the hotel. If I intended to get rid of her and couldn't, that certainly lessened my transgression.

Now, when I would have been delighted to meet the nosey bellhop who steered me into this predicament, of course he was nowhere to be seen. The night clerk stared at us as we navigated the lobby and got to the elevators. I kept talking to her quietly, trying to keep her from loud-talking until the elevator arrived.

The elevator man didn't bat an eye. When I finally maneuvered her into the room, I was perspiring visibly. I sat her down on the edge of the bed where she swayed precariously. One tiny push and she was flat on her back. One shoe fell to the floor with a clunk. Now all I had to do was make a quick change and get out of there. I stripped off the jacket and the new shirt and tie and slipped into my rabbat and Roman collar. Just as I whipped on my topcoat and buttoned it under my chin, I could hear her retching. She opened her mouth as if she were going to cry out, then she collapsed like a spent balloon.

I grabbed my package and opened the door quietly.

The elevator man remained impassive. The night clerk was on the telephone. I was holding my breath. It was like swimming a last lap under water until I felt the fresh air of Madison Avenue. As I walked west on 49th Street to the garage, I began to unwind. The NBC marquee reminded me of Monsignor Artioli, his sister Elda used to work there. I had to get to confession immediately before going back to the parish. The thought of getting involved with Peggy had been fleeting, but time didn't matter. For one second I could roast in hell for an eternity. Had the thought been pleasurable? I had to be free and clear of everything before I walked onto the altar.

I climbed in my car and put the top down. Ordinarily when I was wearing my Roman collar I drove with the top up. This morning I needed as much fresh air as I could get. I made it in seconds to the Lincoln Tunnel and roared through; there was virtually no traffic at that hour. It was almost dawn and I was alone on the highway. Soon I had the tachometer way 'round; I was hurtling along at almost a hundred miles an hour. Wait! I was in a state of mortal sin. An accident at this speed, and I was asking for fire and brimstone. I took my foot off the accelerator and started to recite the Act of Contrition aloud. I decided to stop off at the Benedictine Abbey in Newark.

Driving slowly, I began another examination of conscience, preparing for confession. With all my doubts about doctrine, with all my wrestling over the contradictions of dogma, the hold of the confessional was still unshaken. I was doubting wherever it was comfortable to doubt, but where it got to my personal survival, I was playing it safe. A hypocrite, if there ever was one I was defiantly doing 95 again when I approached the Newark exit. I had to make two racing drift turns on the S-ramp in order to make it. As I sped toward the toll gate, I had to rev the powerful engine to down shift and break my speed. The valves floated with a shrill "ping." Over the screeching brakes I heard the toll gate attendant whistle.

"Jesus H. Christ. . . . Oh, excuse me, Father. You must be on sick call. Go right ahead." Then he waved me through without even bothering to collect the toll.

Driving along Raymond Boulevard, I noticed the steeple of Father Basil's parish. Then I was within sight of the Benedictine Abbey. Just as I parked my car in front, a black sedan arrived and came to a slow stop. I was heading for the entrance to the Abbey when I saw a priest get out of the car. I was relieved at the timing. I recognized him. I had been hearing about him for years. Someone had once ranked him with Monsignor Artioli as one of the most sincere and holy priests in the diocese. That settled it. I would ask him to hear my confession. When I waited and spoke to him, he nodded his assent. We walked silently to the room reserved for that purpose at the Abbey. It was simple and bare—with no furniture or adornments except a confessional screen and a plain wood crucifix on the wall.

I knelt silently at the confessional screen. The other priest took his place behind it. I began.

"Bless me, Father, for I have sinned. It has been five days since my last confession. Last night I touched a woman and took great pleasure in the sensation, for the moment. I made no conscious effort to avoid or overcome any of the temptations that were set before me. I invited impure thoughts. Our meeting was not accidental. I wilfully managed to bring it about. I enjoyed impure thoughts in advance especially at the idea of having intercourse with her. . . . I am sorry if I offended God, but I am confused, Father. I don't know where my confusion began and I don't know where it can end. I have allowed myself to question Church doctrine, and question it liberally. I have been liberal even to the point of advising young couples in application of the principle of two-fold effect where they confessed to a problem with birth control. I honestly do not believe and cannot accept the Church's arguments against birth control. I have repeatedly told my past confessors about my doubts in several matters of faith and morals. I have doubted the infallibility of the Church and in all honesty and truth I must admit that the more I stifle these doubts and try to erase them, the more they persist. These doubts have led from one matter to another until there is barely one facet of Church doctrine which has not come under scrutiny. I am afraid to think about my doubts or to deal with them rationally. For I am afraid of what I may doubt next. I pray as I have prayed through high school, through the seminary and my days as a priest. I have prayed as I was told to pray that my faith might increase. But Father, I am terribly afraid. I feel so dishonest, so ashamed, confused and dirty. Today I found myself actually mocking a woman on the street who treated me with the reverence which a priest of God is usually accorded. Not a word was spoken between us, but the mockery was there, unexpressed. How can I teach our religion any longer? How can I continue this way? Whenever I speak of these doubts to my confessors, I have been assured that they aren't doubts, but difficulties. I have been told to pray in order to receive the grace necessary to overcome them. I love the people of our parish, and I would never do anything to hurt them, but I know I am hurting them. Today I felt I was a hypocrite for even trying to continue as a priest. Even now when I put this into words to you—the decision that I must leave the priesthood—I can feel the sweat pouring down my back. May God give me strength to avoid scandal. May God forgive me. May God give me strength to know what I must do. And will you please, Father, give me your absolution. I will willingly submit and gladly perform any penance that you can suggest to me."

When I stopped I could only hear the pounding in my chest and the sound of breathing on the other side of the screen.

"God is all goodness. We must learn to understand and believe in the fullness of His Mercy, the amplitude of His grace. . . ."

He could have been talking to anybody. It was as if he hadn't even heard me. It was a prepared exhortation which never touched the realities of my confession.

I knew his predicament and I knew it well. Before he could grant me absolution he had to satisfy himself about my intentions.

"Are you willing, Father, to make arrangements to make a private retreat within ten days?"

"Anything, Father. I will do anything, willingly, gladly."

I meant it. But I had come to doubt my intentions. They were as feeble as my powers of resolution.

I began my Act of Contrition calmly. Then I tried

to do what I was always recommending to others in the confessional. I tried to summon some freshness, some vigor of feeling. I spoke the words slowly, trying to find solace in the ancient phrasing. It was no use.

When I rose from the kneeler, I was so preoccupied that the voice of my fellow priest startled me.

"Father," he said, "now hear *my* confession."

Unceremoniously we exchanged places, without a glance in each other's direction. I raised my hand in blessing and began:

"Dominus sit in corde tuo, et in labiis tuis ut rite confitearis omnia pecatta tua. . . . May the Lord be in your heart and on your lips that you might properly confess all of your sins. . . ."

"Bless me, Father, for I have sinned . . ." he began. "It has been twenty-four hours since my last confession." His recital blotted out for the moment all the confusion over my own problems. He confessed his problem as though he had confessed it a hundred times. He had lived with it for more years than I had been a priest. He knew what the solution had to be. He had known it from the beginning. It was as clear as it was terrible. He was not wrestling with fantasies, or bungling around like an adolescent with a Lexington Avenue lady who had an infinite capacity to booze her way out of tight spots. He was in love with a girl. I didn't know whether to feel compassion or envy.

It was only a few minutes drive to the rectory where I slipped into my room without encountering anybody. It was a First Friday of the month, one of those days when the church is on a rigorous assembly line schedule. Quickly I showered, and as usual I said morning prayers while shaving. Then I proceeded to my daily meditation. This spiritual exercise is an important part of priestly routine. One sets a scene in his imagination, preferably from the life of Christ. One selects a detail

219

from the scene for deeper meditation, attempting to apply it to his own life, hopefully to overcome some weakness, to work on some imperfection. There had been moments when I thought of vivid imaginary scenes from the Scriptures, inspiring vignettes fraught with parallels in my own life. But when I was rushed or preoccupied, I would always depend on one scene which Da Vinci had made possible to conjure quickly and without strain: the Last Supper. For years the Last Supper had evoked images I found most engaging. The total giving, the outpouring of unrestrained Divine love.

But this morning my subconscious was caught up on the mysterious figure near the end of the table, the most despicable traitor who ever lived—the first spoiled priest.

For years I had unquestioningly accepted the notion that Judas had been temporarily insane after betraying Christ. Whenever someone known to me personally had left the priesthood, I often took the easy way out. Unhesitatingly I had compared him with Judas. Now what could I say for myself?

Now that I was on the edge of leaving, as sure a candidate for the Catholic classification of a traitor as ever wore the collar, I was drawn to the figure of Judas. Why hadn't I made a serious attempt to read some of the Catholic literature on Judas, especially from those quarters in which he was later regarded as a saint—having made a last-second repentance as he dangled in the noose?

I had been taught that Judas' suicide and his most serious sin had been despair—despair and lack of faith in the infinite divine capacity for forgiveness.

Perhaps despair was another temptation. If I decided I could not remain a priest any longer, perhaps I could summon the dignity to make a clear decision and leave out of love. Love for God, for my neighbor and myself. Silently I repeated my habitual prayer: "Help my unbelief." Then I walked to the church to say Mass.

Every priest has moments when the great miracle, the axis around which the priestly life should revolve, becomes a matter of routine. Assembly-line Masses are said hurriedly so the communicants can catch their rides, meet their buses, get to work on time.

Behind me in the church there would be a hundred people who believed that when I consecrated the bread and wine, I was performing a miracle, causing it to change in everything except appearance, to the reality of Christ in the flesh.

One day soon they would hear about what happened to me and they would think back and wonder. They would, wouldn't they? Perhaps they were wondering now. There was no time to think about it. The bell rang and I walked to the altar.

I made all the arrangements necessary and left on Sunday morning for a retreat at Spencer, the Trappist Monastery in Massachusetts. The prospect didn't appeal to me in the least, but I fully intended to keep my word—until I saw the snow.

I turned off the highway and headed for a small ski lodge in Bellayre, where I'd been going during the season for the past two years. No one who ever went there, except the owner, knew I was a priest. I could rest and relax and not be treated in any special way.

The skiing exhilarated and refreshed me; the girl named Marilyn did not. She was small, blonde and sexy; the moment I saw her I mentally undressed her. I skied an extra day to find out her address and phone number in New York and thought about her all during the three-hour drive to Spencer.

By the time I arrived at the Monastery I was scarcely in the proper frame of mind for a retreat. After confession, Father Raymond, who was my spiritual

221

guide, launched into a "fire and brimstone" exhortation. It had practically no effect. The spiritual exercises of the retreat were continually interrupted by reminiscences of the two days I had spent skiing. When I tried to meditate, I fell asleep. Father Raymond tried diligently, not only to dissuade me from leaving the priesthood, but also to adopt a life of penance to atone for my sins of "intellectual pride." I packed up early on the last day of the retreat and his last words to me came as no surprise: "Go fall on your knees before the Crucifix, you Judas!"

I drove back to Bellayre, grabbed my skis and rode the chair lift to the mountain peak. For the first time, I savored the beauty of the scene for itself, not as a part of the perfect beauty found only in God. I thought about Christ, about Monsignor Artioli's sermon at my First Mass: "Behold him, another Christ!" I knew that I had never really identified myself with Christ, that I had never really known or loved Him as a Divine person. Suddenly, all my other doubts seemed infinitesimal as I admitted to myself that I did not believe Christ was God!

A cold shiver crept up my back and my teeth started chattering. I should never have become a priest, not without that vital ingredient—the ability to believe, to accept, without question.

I raced to the bottom of the slope, kicked the skis off and rushed to my car. I was sure of one thing: I had lost my entire way of life.

I drove back to Newark in a daze all the way. At the rectory, I took my skis upstairs. Trapped. What to do? Outside. Still didn't know what to do. But I couldn't stick around. Didn't want to think. *I did not want to think anymore!* I did not want to admit that I had ever said to myself, I don't believe Christ is God!

I was ashamed, distraught. I felt like the dirtiest man on earth. The most despicable I had ever known!

When I realized I was outside again, I climbed into my car. I didn't want to be around the rectory. I drove down to the seashore. Bleak and barren. Drove all the way down there, but no peace, no anything! Finally I had been honest, admitted this thing. But I was ashamed to think it. Ashamed that I continued to think it.

So I drove and drove. New Hope, Pennsylvania. New Hope! The outskirts of Philadelphia, back to New Jersey, the seashore again. Cold. Wind whistling past me as I sped through the night. I tore through Asbury Park. Then it started to get light and I automatically headed back to Newark, in time for Mass.

I went into the rectory and brushed past Mike, the pastor; he gave me a strange look. Who cares? Out all night, I should have felt guilty. But who cares? Went up to my room and put on my cassock automatically, then came down again and went to the sacristy to get ready to say my Mass. I didn't even see Caesar, the old sacristan. Didn't say anything to anyone. I just went in. Who could understand my mood? They all thought I had had an argument with the pastor. I went out to say Mass then. *Introibo ad altare dei.*

I wanted to run off the altar and grab Mike or any priest I could find, and confess. Right there. And say, bless me Father for I have sinned. *Kyrie Eleison. Christe Eleison.*

You don't believe Christ is God. What are you doing on the altar? *Munda cor meum.* Run off and tell someone, anyone. Go to confession. Get cleansed. I couldn't. This is the most sacred thing in your life. *Suscipe, sancte Pater.* I'm married to it! *Deus qui humanae substantiae.* Part of it. It's me. A dozen years of my life aimed at becoming *alter Christus,* another Christ! How

223

could anyone be so stupid, spend so much time living a mistake! *Veni, Sanctificator.*

The Mass had been the prime thing in my life. *Lavabo inter innocentes.* It *was* my life! This was all I had! But now I did not believe. Run off the altar and fall on your knees in the confessional. *Suscipe sancta trinitas.*

Almost all your sermons were on the Mass. The Eucharist. Making love with Christ. You had told all these people. Everytime you talked to them it was something about the Eucharist. The supreme act of love. Total union. All the love you wanted and needed. All the love anybody wanted. Right here in the Eucharist. Enough to supply infinite worlds. More than enough.

But you don't believe that now. What does it matter?

The Devil's playing tricks on me. *Orate fratres.*

You'll never get me! *Sanctus.* I'll never leave the faith. *Sanctus.* I'll never lose the faith. *Sanctus. What faith?*

I was holding the wafer in my hand. I looked at the missal. *Hoc est enim corpus meum.* This is my body. The words that change the bread into Christ. I held it in my hand. And I bent over the altar staring at the round wafer of unleavened bread. I was just about to say *Hoc est*, when I realized I was at the Consecration.

The intention. This was a necessity, the intention of changing the bread and wine into Christ. Not necessarily to make it right there; it was perfectly proper to have made an habitual intention. At ordination I had made this habitual intention. When I come to this part, it's automatic. I want this bread to change into Christ. Fortify the habitual intention when you're a priest.

I can't see the Missal. Tears again. Soaking wet. Chills. Drops of perspiration were pouring off my head.

I couldn't see the book. I tried to focus on the wafer. Foggy. *Hoc est enim corpus meum.* I said it, and said it again, over and over, the Devil is not going to win out on *this* one.

I knelt and held the wafer up in the air. I was going through the roof. Bells. Bells. Bells. Up there on the altar, looking up at it, I said to myself, infinite love? I don't believe it. I can't believe it.

I pitched forward and dropped the wafer on the altar cloth. Hold on! Another genuflection. Pull the chalice over so that you can genuflect over the wine. Because then I had to change the wine into the blood of Christ. The complete Christ!

I looked in the chalice. The wafer. Unleavened bread. It's a piece of bread, it's not Christ! This is love. Is this the Devil, is it really? Do I believe?

I looked into the chalice again. That's wine. There had been no words spoken. Nothing!

I'm going to say words and all of a sudden it's going to become Christ? Because some bishop held hands over me?

Hic est enim calix sanguinis mei. This is the chalice of my blood. And every Catholic *must* believe this. That this is really Christ now. All love. I looked at it. I cannot believe. This is no devil tempting me. Pray! To the Blessed Mother, to Christ, to God the Father, the Holy Ghost, *to anybody*—to get me through this somehow!

Maybe I'm too tired. I shouldn't have driven all night. It all came back to me, the whole day. I leaned over the chalice. I leaned over it and, oh God—I'm grabbing a ski pole!

This is wine. I can't change wine into Christ. My beloved. I don't believe Christ is God. I don't believe *He* could change anything into Himself. God! God! God.

Hic est enim calix sanguinis mei novi et aeterni testi-

menti. Things began to swim. I saw red, orange, every color of the rainbow. The chalice my mother and father had given me when I became a priest. The large diamond from her engagement ring sparkled in the base. And the diamonds from my brother's and sister's rings. Raise the chalice. My fingers touched the wedding band fastened under the base.

How proud it made them feel when I was ordained. *Pater noster*. Tears. *Suscipe*. Suddenly I was sobbing. *Agnus Dei*. Right up there on the altar. I was crying, me. *Quod ore sumpsimus*. It wasn't loud and it wasn't phony. It was as though I had opened a pair of faucets in my head. *Ite, Missa est*.

When I finished that Mass, when I got up to my room, I could only remember Caesar, the sacristan, wringing out the vestments. *Ite, Missa est*. I couldn't even remember walking into the room. *Ite, Missa est*. I was drenched from head to foot. I remember wringing out my socks, underwear, cassock. *Ite, Missa est*. My cassock had big cuffs on the sleeves, like a topcoat, and they were completely soaked. I left it on the floor. *Ite, Missa est*.

The room was bare. There was nothing but the furniture and the pile of soggy clothing. I changed back into ski clothes, without even bothering to shower. Stuffed the wet things into an old canvas bag. The teeshirt was an old one so I dropped it. Wait. It's dirty under the armpits. The black cassock must have stained it. But the stain—reddish, like blood. Burn it! Before some *super adulta* starts having hot flashes and technicolor visions at the laundromat.

mcmlvi

On a navy blue convertible sofa in the cabin of somebody else's cruiser, drydocked like a fish out of water on the Jersey shore—that's where it was going to happen.

"Oh, we're going to have fun on Saturday night, Gabe honey. I can't wait for Saturday." Ever since she said that I had been reading "Happiness in Marriage." Sometimes I had to put the book away. I began to understand why the Archbishop had banned it. It got to be very stimulating.

I had headed for one of my favorite spots on the Jersey shore to lick my wounds and get rid of some of the cobwebs. While beachcombing, I got the chance to do some odd jobs cleaning and refurbishing, caulking and painting, installing new equipment, engines, radios, canvas tops and sides, and general cleaning up for the coming boat season.

I was less nervous at ordination. There my lines were all written in Latin. We had rehearsed for weeks. I was lost in the crowd scene. All I had to do was follow the leader and not pass out. Here I was on my own with nothing but a how-to-do-it manual.

Sherry wouldn't be through work at the diner for another twenty minutes at least. I went up onto the rear deck of the drydocked cruiser.

The spring evening was warm and there was practically no breeze. I took off my shirt to catch the last of the sun. I tried to relax but stretching out reminded me of what was going to happen, so I went back down into the main cabin. The convertible sofa was all made up. I had a clean sheet under the slipcover. I slammed the pillows into place, moved the ashtrays. I put out the bottle of Scotch and the glasses. I took ice out of the trays in the galley and put it in a bowl so it would be handy. There were two permanent fixtures on the walls with shades. I unscrewed one bulb so the lighting would be a little softer. The cabin seemed a little stuffy so I opened one of the hatch-covers a crack.

If I let go for a minute the same vision always blacked out everything else: the picture of me taking off Sherry's panties. Sherry was very clear, but the pants were fuzzy. It had been so many years since I had seen any panties, and then they were in a store window or hanging behind the shower curtain in somebody's bathroom.

"Hiya, Gabe honey." There she was. Right on the dot, waving from the jetty. She wore her sandy-colored hair in a pony tail. At thirty-five, she probably shouldn't have. But maybe she wore it that way in the diner to keep it out of the soup. She hadn't even bothered to change. She still wore the dark suit and the plain white blouse and the flat shoes she wore at work.

I waved to her and she ran down the causeway to the dock.

"You're not one of those girls who keeps a guy waiting," I said. "You're right on the dot."

She pouted a little. "Yeah. Dolores is always telling

228

me how to play hard to get," she said. "But that wouldn't be *me*, Gabe honey."

When I reached out to help her aboard my hand was trembling. She jumped onto the deck and grabbed my other hand. It was shaking, too.

"Gee, Gabe honey," she said, rumpling the hair on my chest, "be careful, don't try to get tanned in one day. I get the shivers all the time when I've had too much sun, do you?"

"Maybe I better put on my shirt," I said. Now my teeth were chattering.

"You're sure you're okay?" she asked. When she stuffed my shirttail in the back of my pants, I really began quaking.

I grabbed her around the waist and held her close. I never realized she was so tiny. In the diner she always seemed a fairly good size, but then I was sitting on a low stool. The second time I went in there she had leaned across the counter and pulled my head toward her and kissed me. We seemed to be on a level then. Now her head seemed down under my armpit somewhere. Her lips were soft and spongy, I remember. I didn't dare kiss her; my jaw was quivering so, I might chew her to pieces.

"It's too cold out here," I said. "Let's go down to the cabin."

"Maybe we better," she said. "If you feel cold then you've had too much sun. It can do that you know, honey."

"Mmmmmmm," she said when she saw the cabin. "Isn't this cozy though?"

"Yeah," I said, "I've got to get warm." I reached into the locker and grabbed a sweatshirt. It smelled like the whole CYO had played a tournament in it, but I had to get warm.

"How about a drink?"

"Gee, honey, that would be nice. Feel better now?"

I was shaking more than ever and beginning to get embarrassed. When I opened the refrigerator to get the ice my hand was trembling so much that the ice rattled and a chunk spilled on the floor.

"Gee, honey, maybe I should make you a hot toddy or something. What kind of hot plate do you have?"

"I'm fine," I said, as she came toward the galley. I got an ice cube into a glass and it rattled so loud I put it down. "You want to pour?" I asked her. No sense spilling good Scotch.

She poured the drinks. I was leery about picking up the glass.

"Gee, honey," she said, "you're still trembling."

"All I need is a good slug." Quickly I grabbed the glass and downed a burning swallow straight.

She picked up her drink daintily and held it up as a toast. "Chin Chin."

"I'm sorry," I said, picking up the glass. "Chin Chin." Then I put it down again and grabbed her. If I held her tight it might stop the trembling.

"Easy, Gabe honey," she said, almost spilling her drink. "I'll tell you when."

I pulled her over onto the sofa, drew her head toward mine and tried to kiss her. I was shaking. She was startled but replied gently, "Go slow, Gabe honey. Don't rush, honey. There's no rush, sweetie. We got all night."

All night? If I trembled like this for five minutes I'd come apart at the seams.

"Don't you have any family or anybody to worry about getting home to?"

"I'm free as a bird. Until eleven tomorrow morning. I hate quickies, don't you? I think one of the nicest things about sleeping with a man is, well, sleeping with him. We got the whole place to ourselves. You said so yourself."

"Oh, sure," I said. "I told my assistant Bunky not to come in tomorrow."

"Oh, that's great, honey. Then you hate quickies, too," she said, giving me a big squeeze.

I tried to unbutton her blouse in the back but my fingers were so shaky I couldn't tell whether I was fumbling with buttons, zipper or snaps. I remembered that girl from Staten Island who had grabbed my hand and stuffed it down the front of her dress.

I started kissing her again so I could try the front of her blouse. But there were no buttons there. So I tried the back again and found the zipper. Suddenly Sherry was sitting there in her brassiere and her white blouse was waving like a racing flag in my hand. I dropped the blouse and made a grab for the clasp of her brassiere.

"Gee, honey," she said, "we got all night. We can have loads of fun if you'll just calm down." Her face twisted into a thoughtful expression as she undid the back clasp of the brassiere.

This was the first time I had seen so much of a woman naked. I didn't realize there could be that much to them, uncaged. I reached out to touch her and she fell on her back. Then she grabbed my stinking sweat-shirt and pulled me down against her.

"I'm sorry, Sherry," I said. "I've been working in this for days." She helped pull it over my head. I was freezing to death in my flannel shirt and she was hot as a pistol stark naked. I lunged across the room, got my heavy black pullover sweater and grabbed my elbows to keep from trembling.

"Go slow, Gabe honey, and everything will be dandy."

"What do you mean go slow?" I said shivering. "I want you. I want *all of you*."

"Yeah, honey, I know. I know," she said. "But good

231

things are better if we're a little patient, you know what I mean?"

This sounded like preaching to me and I wasn't in the mood for any preaching. If she knew how long I'd waited, if I could only tell her how important this was to me, if she had any way of knowing, if anybody had any way of knowing. I was a drowning man, freezing to death, I had walked across the Sahara for twenty years, torturing myself, denying myself, mortifying myself. Who was she to tell me to go slow?

"I'll be right back," she said as she got up from the sofa.

For an instant I thought maybe she was offended. But she wouldn't walk out on me, not now, not without her brassiere. But where was she going? What was she looking for?

"Where's your john?" she asked.

Jumping Jehosophat! The one thing I hadn't taken care of. With the cruiser in drydock, the toilets are out of commission. You'd think a woman who worked in a diner next to a yacht basin would know that.

"What are you going to do?" I asked her.

"Never mind," she said grinning, swinging her handbag behind her. "You just leave everything to me."

"Well, you know, the john, with a john on a boat in drydock, you know how it is. I've been using the one at the gas station."

"Don't worry, silly," she said. "You just show me where it is."

So I showed her. I wondered how long she would be. I grabbed a blanket from the back of the convertible sofa and wrapped myself in it, right up to the chin. I knew I'd be all right in a minute if I could just get warm. When I found I couldn't pour another drink without trembling, I grabbed the bottle and tried to down a slug. I almost pushed a tooth down my throat. I got scared when I felt it and got a little blood on my finger. I was afraid to touch it for fear it would wiggle. Soul-kissing might get very bloody if I wasn't careful.

Then Sherry walked out of the head in her bare feet, with nothing on but the bottom half of her slip. The pony tail was gone and her hair hung almost to her shoulders. She seemed tinier than ever, a completely different person. I was so struck by the change in her appearance, I forgot I had been waiting to hear her unlatch the door. That was going to be my signal to ditch the blanket. But it was too late now.

She was almost naked and I sat there like a fullback warming up to go into the game. She was steaming and I was shivering. She walked over to the sofa beside me, not saying a word. Then she laid down on her side, peeled her slip down to her knees and kicked it off. She opened her arms wide and reached toward me. *Adolorata.* I let go of my blanket and she lifted up my sweater and pulled it off me. She opened my shirt, grabbed a handful of hair and pulled me toward her.

It was like trying to breathe in a typhoon. Could nitro-glycerin pills save me now? With a coronary you only have an instant to make an Act of perfect Contrition. I needed oxygen. Adrenalin. Help. It was too late. I could hear my own death rattle. I grabbed Sherry's naked shoulder as all the blood rushed from my brain to my crotch and I jackknifed. My knees hit my chest.

Per omnia saecula saeculorum.

I was astonished to be able to hear Sherry moaning, "Oh no!"

I was lying in this puddle, but I could feel her holding me so I couldn't be dead. My grey cotton pants were wet and moist against my stomach and it wasn't perspiration. I wasn't trembling anymore.

Sherry seemed to know what was happening. I

didn't. I only knew I was exhausted from working too hard and tomorrow was Sunday, a day of rest. Should I go to Mass or shouldn't I, that was the question.

I heard her get up and pull on her slip. "Gabe honey," she was saying, "you better let me take care of those pants."

I didn't know what she was talking about. "Roll over, honey, and we'll slip them off," she said. I rolled over and she started tugging at the bottoms. "Ooops, honey," she said. As she tugged at them, her breasts bounced in thirteen directions. I undid my belt buckle, slid out of the pants and grabbed the blanket.

She smiled bravely and said, "Don't worry, honey, the night is young. Where can I find a towel?"

What had happened finally dawned on me when I saw the shiny Rorschach all over the front of my grey dungarees. This was my first conscious score sheet and the score was a big zero. Sherry was busy, bustling around the cabin like my mother preparing for company. She bounced back and handed me a dirty towel. "This is all I could find, Gabe honey. You really need some looking after, I can see that. Who's been taking care of you, for crying out loud?"

I wished I was trembling so I'd have some excuse for lying in bed with the blanket over my head. I could hear her in the head. She had found a pail of water I had stashed in there and she was sloshing the pants in it. Why did she have to be so damned *understanding?*

"If you soak them in cold water first," she explained, "it don't leave rings." Helpful household hints, yet. I pulled the blanket over my ears.

When she came back she had her hair in a pony tail again and her brassiere was in place. I couldn't even face her. "Happiness in Marriage" was such a great little manual, I thought it covered everything. All my years in the confessional, listening to other people's troubles, nothing had prepared me for this. All you had to do, I thought, was have the time, the place and the girl. I hate quickies, she had said. What would she call this?

Now she was pulling on her skirt and slipping into her shoes.

"Where are you going?" I asked her.

"I better go back to the diner and get a few things, Gabe honey." Then she ran over and gave me a spongy peck on the cheek. "Somebody's got to take care of you."

"I'm okay now," I said. "I'm sorry." I wanted to explain but I didn't know where to begin. "Sherry, there's something I want you to know. That was the first time for me."

"Oh, Gabe honey, it can happen to anybody if they don't take care of themselves."

"No, I mean it was the first time in my *life*."

"Don't worry about it, Gabe honey. Don't get a complex about it." She was zipping up her blouse and putting on a little lipstick.

"Would you believe me if I told you I was a Catholic priest and you're the first woman I ever saw naked in my whole life. . . ."

"Where you been living, Gabe honey, with the Eskimos?" she asked. "Wait a minute!" she gasped, putting down her lipstick. "A real honest-to-God Catholic priest?"

I nodded.

"Oh, my poor baby," she said as she sat down beside me on the bed. "You never even been *married?*"

"Roman Catholic priests are not allowed to get married."

"Of course, honey, I know *that*. But this girlfriend of mine, her mother had a very steady, very lovely affair with a priest. It went on for years. He left her an awful lot of money. She ended up very well fixed.

But he was quite along in years, I guess, and one of those priests who's his own boss. He had a church of his own and a car and nobody to tell him what to do. I don't say every priest has a steady thing going, but I mean in this day and age, a priest who's young and good-looking, well it's none of my business, honey, but I always figured a priest had more chances than an average John. Well, live and learn. Of course, I knew you were a very sincere person. I didn't have you figured for an ordinary cheater, but still. Dolores thought you were a very sincere person too. Well, I can see there's a lot of things I have to teach you, Gabe honey."

She gave me another spongy peck on the mouth and then she was gone. Taking it in her stride is, I guess, the way you'd describe her reaction to my momentous announcement. The most embarrassing thing that could possibly happen had already happened and Sherry had taken it in stride. I got up and stretched myself. No more chills. The cabin seemed stuffy so I opened another hatch. I found a pair of dry pants and poured myself a drink. My first big love scene was a fiasco, and I was back in fantasy land, flat on my back being ordered around by the night nurse.

Within ten minutes I could hear Sherry's footsteps on the dock. I ran to help her aboard. She had a shopping bag in one hand and a bundle in the other.

"I brought a little supper." She smiled. "And something for breakfast."

"Wait a minute," I said. "I have a supply of things on board."

"But you've been eating the wrong things, Gabe honey. That's part of the trouble. No more sandwiches for you. No hamburgers. No meat at all. I brought fresh clams and eggnog with nutmeg. Lots of nutmeg."

Then she launched her crash program to make me a man of the world. Within a few hours I began to

236

have a sneaky feeling that she knew what she was doing.

Occasionally her tutoring would remind me of the hours I had spent in the confessional passing out advice to married couples who were having troubles. When I remembered some of my glib counsel, I didn't know whether to laugh or cry. Sherry was a patient, devoted little Miss Fix-it-all. Before long she had me feeling as ballsy as Adam in the Garden. Sunday morning I woke up feeling like Aly Khan.

On Monday I felt New York couldn't scare me. I began packing my things, ready to make a do-or-die try at building a normal life for myself. A few days later I breezed through the Lincoln Tunnel, drove up near the Hotel Paris on upper West End Avenue, parked my car, and checked in as Mr. G. A. Longo. That night was like old times. I slept alone.

When I came downstairs the next morning, my car was gone. All my worldly goods were in the trunk except my little black bag. When I called the police, I had to become a priest again. The car registration was in the name of Reverend Gabriel Longo. I hoped it could all be settled over the phone. If they asked me to come to the police station to make out any papers, I would have to wear my black raincoat buttoned up to my chin. I didn't have a Roman collar with me.

The police were very relaxed about the entire matter; they took the information and told me they would check on it and call me in a few days.

That meant I needed a New York address until the stolen car had been recovered. Staying at the hotel where they would take phone messages would be expensive. It would lower my cash supply in a hurry. I had to start looking for a job immediately.

For days I had been re-writing my life history, trying to stress the social service side of the priesthood so it might qualify me for something in that field. Now I didn't have enough money to get the resumes typed. I thought I'd better start with a sure thing—the place where most priests started when they left—teaching school. I called the teaching employment agency that had placed some fellows I knew. They cooled me off in a hurry. It was June. School was almost out. They couldn't hope to place me anywhere until the fall. I didn't even know what month it was. Or maybe I thought all schools ran the year around like the seminary. I needed a job tomorrow morning. The first agency I tried directed me to a financial district placement bureau where they hired trainees for the Wall Street brokerage houses. Each one was the same. When they spotted Immaculate Conception Seminary as the source of my college degree, eyebrows were raised. Things got very vague. I tried to pass as a seminarian who had left to teach school.

"But were you ever actually ordained?" When the question came up I couldn't lie and the interview was over. One firm actually hired me and fired me the same day. The man in charge of the training program was apologetic but frank.

"Mr. Longo," he said, "let's not kid ourselves. No firm like ours is going to take a chance on offending any customer by employing an ex-priest. There are places I imagine where it wouldn't matter. But this just happens not to be one of them."

When I got back to the hotel after three weary days of turn-downs, there was a call from the police. The car had been located. Hallelujah, at last I didn't need to stay in an expensive hotel. When I called the station to find out where I could pick up the car, I got my first experience in being treated like an ordinary citizen. My car had been towed away to the city pound by the Sanitation Department for having been illegally parked on that particular day at that particular time. It had been years since I had paid any attention to the fine print on NO PARKING signs. I had never paid a traffic ticket in my life. The first one would be a whopper. Fifteen dollars fine and ten dollars for towing charges.

I checked my wallet. There was the little note I had written: "In case of accident or injury, please notify Mr. and Mrs. Bernard Longo, Jersey City. Please, if it is anything serious, break the news gently. My father has a serious heart condition." My social security card was a relic of the days I worked at bingo. And twenty-seven dollars. There was no way of getting the car out of hock and paying the hotel bill too. I had no choice. I had to check out of the hotel immediately. I packed my little black bag and went downstairs. When I finished paying the bill, I had less than ten dollars left. I was tempted to make another try with the police department. But to do that, I'd have to become a priest again. It amounted to too many quick changes for one day. I wasn't up to it. I had to get something to eat, find a place to stay and find some kind of job. It didn't matter any more what kind.

I had never been in New York without a car. I don't think I had ever ridden the subway more than once in my life. So I got on a bus heading downtown. It crossed Forty-Second Street to the East Side. I didn't want to go too far east; there was nothing there, so I got off at Third Avenue and walked. I kept walking, looking for a cheap hotel or rooming house. Each one seemed more forbidding than the last. I recognized the edge of the Bowery. It gave me the shudders. By then I was really famished so I ducked into a cheap diner and ordered a hamburger and coffee.

There is some kind of telepathy at work in that part of town. The guy next to me immediately became friendly. He eyed me up and down, from my black moccasins to my red rooster tie. I wondered if the knot looked amateurish. Maybe he had his eye on the suit. It was an expensive slubbed silk dupioni suit I had carefully chosen as the most unpriestly thing, the most neutral thing in my wardrobe. Here it seemed as conspicuous as all get-out. Then he eyed my black bag with all my worldly goods. I kept trying to keep it close enough so I could keep one foot on it.

"From out of town?" the guy asked me.

"Yes," I said, "as a matter of fact I am." Since he had struck up the conversation, I might as well ask his advice as anybody's. I told him I was looking for a room that was reasonable.

"Well," he said to me, "you can try the place I stay at. I pay eight bucks a month."

Eight bucks a month. I had been paying almost that for one day. I had only ten bucks left but having a place to stay for a month would take a load off my mind. Eating could wait until I got a job. The place was only a block away so he came and introduced me to the landlord. I gave him the money in advance and the man tossed me the key to number 14.

I walked down the darkest dirtiest hall I'd ever seen, littered with garbage. The door opened into a closet about five feet by eight. The only air in the place came over the transom from the stinking hall. The furnishings consisted of the bottom half of a daybed covered with an old tablecloth, and one wooden chair. A water faucet protruded from one wall, but there was no sink, no drain. A light bulb dangled from a cord in the ceiling. When I turned it on, nothing happened. The bulb was burned out.

What a stupe I was to give the guy the money before seeing the place! The guy in the diner must have been a shill, looking for greenhorns from out of town with one piece of luggage. Probably they rented this room for a month once every day. Who would stay here?

I walked back down the hall in search of the landlord.
I rang his bell but nobody answered. I was scared to
ring it again. I was sure the man had not been the
landlord at all. It was probably a con game played by
two fast Bowery operators.

There was nothing to do but try and get some rest
on that crummy bed and get up as early as possible
the next morning and get going. If I was the first one
on tap at one of the employment agencies on Forty-
Second Street, I might have a chance.

I hated to rumple up my only suit but I was afraid
to undress. I was afraid my two friends might return
and relieve me of my suit and bag. So I put the bag at
the head of the bed between me and the wall, and
collapsed.

Just before nodding off to sleep I remembered Marilyn, the pretty blonde I had met at Bellayre. She
lived in a hotel on West Seventy-Second Street. Tomorrow I would give her a call.

I woke up in the middle of the night, sure someone
was in my room. I felt for my black bag. It was still
there. I felt a thud on my knee and I ducked. A huge
rat, the size of a Pekingese, scampered into the corner.
I kicked the chair against the wall and tried to move
the bed. I lit a match and peered around the closet. It
didn't matter, I knew what I had seen. I threw on my
jacket, grabbed my bag and ran through the dirty hallway into the fresh air of the street.

I started walking west, keeping close to the curb,
on the lookout for rats. When I was a kid we used
to go to the city dump and shoot them with B-B guns.
Once I got bitten through my sneaker and I never
hunted rats again. At Seton Hall I had gone to the
basement kitchen one time to get some milk for the live
animals in the Christmas creche and when I turned on
the lights, a posse of rats went scurrying across the
overhead pipes to their holes. Sometimes on hot nights

as a priest, I had gone to the Jersey shore at Sea Bright to sleep on the beach. One night I had seen a horde of rats running through the rocks of the sea wall. The rats at Newark City Hospital used to hang around the autopsy room. Doctors would throw knives at them but they always came back for more. Big-city rats I didn't know much about and I didn't want to learn.

I kept walking and walking until I came to a small park. There were two empty benches. It looked like a real oasis. I was so tired I used my bag as a pillow and stretched out. I had never slept on a park bench and didn't intend to. I was just resting and thinking.

When the traffic wakened me, it was daylight. I snapped up to a sitting position and noticed I had a bench mate. He was still sleeping with his head on the edge of my soft black leather bag. I wanted to get up and get out of there but I felt it would be rude to waken him. He had a good face, crew-cut iron-grey hair. He wore heavy work pants and an expensive grey golf jacket. Could he be another priest? He had a copy of *Turf* magazine on the bench beside him. I picked it up and flipped through it.

This was ridiculous. The guy had moved my bag to make a pillow for himself and he might sleep there all day. If the traffic and the sunlight didn't wake him, he had to be pretty far gone. It was only seven o'clock. No employment agencies would be open before nine. I walked to a street sign to make sure where I was. Abingdon Square Park. I'd never heard of it. Forty-Second Street couldn't be more than a half hour's walk. Carrying a bag, forty-five minutes maybe. The bag! I had left the bag on the bench under my roommate. Maybe he was playing possum waiting to make off with it. I rushed back to the bench and he was awake. Now I'd have to prove the bag belonged to me. Well, that was easy. My papers were in it. But my papers were all made out "Reverend."

"I really hoped you wouldn't mind," he said when I faced him. He had an Oxford English accent. We had a priest with an accent like that at Seton Hall. He was from Hoboken and his accent was phony. This one sounded real.

"Not at all," I said. "I was amazed to find out how comfortable the bench was."

"Come on, friend," he said, "I'll buy you a cup of coffee. I've been around a bit more than you have. Where are you off to?"

I told him my plans and he interrupted at key points with practical advice. To get a shave, go to Penn Station or one of the good hotels. The way I was dressed no one would stop me. Check your bag at Penn Station and don't carry it around while looking for a job. It makes you look desperate. "If you don't connect with anything today, meet me at the same bench in the same park around ten tonight."

We walked toward the river, to a little carry-out coffee shop. I was never much on coffee and I was accustomed always to picking up the check. He ordered me a couple of doughnuts and insisted on paying for everything. He didn't make any move to introduce himself so I kept calling him "Friend," which seemed terribly cold and distant. He played it very close to the chest. He was kind, helpful, but he kept his mystery to himself. I couldn't help noticing that the man in the coffee shop, who saw him from the waist up, kept calling him "sir."

He talked of nothing but essentials. Unless a miracle happened, I knew I would be back in the park to meet him later. "Good luck," he said and walked off.

I started up Eighth Avenue toward Penn Station. I knew I had time to waste now, and had better hang on to the fifteen cents for the subway. The bag got heavier and heavier. I wished I could carry it on my shoulder. I was weary and sweaty when I got to

Thirty-Third Street. The last time I had been in Penn Station was in 1939, on my way to the World's Fair. I headed for the men's room to shave. The station was deserted but the men's room was jammed. When I found an empty bowl I didn't know where to hang my jacket. There was a gang of sailors laughing and talking and one of them was being sick in a corner. I didn't like the crowd and the next time, I decided, I would brave it and walk into a hotel.

I got my shaving things out of my bag, but there was no place to put anything. I didn't want to ruin my coat, or risk having it disappear. I resorted to the old priest's trick of folding the collar under and shaving with my shirt on. I felt very bashful and embarrassed, sure that everyone was watching me. Then a guy moved in next to me, ran his sink full of water, peeled off all his clothes down to the waist and proceeded to slosh water all over himself, me and everyone else. He dried himself with miles of toilet paper. I didn't have a towel in my bag. That was stupid. I had marriage certificates, baptismal certificates, resumes and all sorts of useless things. But no towel. I took my extra T-shirt, daubed myself dry, and got out of there in a hurry.

The next problem was checking my bag. I walked up to the row of wall lockers, read all the instructions, found an empty ten-cent locker. Foiled again, the bag was too big. I turned it sideways, upside down, tried squashing it on top, but there was no way of wedging it in. It would cost me a quarter, one-eighth of my cash balance, just for storage. Before I sprang for the quarter, I sat down and tried to take an inventory of everything I might need which could be stuffed into my raincoat pockets. The papers, Marilyn's telephone number. I felt very conspicuous in the waiting room early in the morning. I stuffed the papers in my jacket pocket and put the bag in the twenty-five-cent locker. Using that quarter meant going without lunch, but at least I didn't look like a traveling salesman any longer. I walked across the street to scout the Hotel Pennsylvania men's room while I had time, to see if the accommodations there were any better. It was immaculate and quiet. That's where I would wash and shave tomorrow. I bought a *New York Times* at the newsstand and sat down in a luxurious comfortable chair in the lobby to study the HELP WANTED MALE columns. I checked off every possibility and routed them geographically. I figured I should be able to cover at least twenty agencies in a day. I decided I wouldn't emphasize the priesthood, merely claim a college education, four years of social work and settle for anything.

Some of the ads really made me feel as though I had nothing to worry about. These wonderful experienced people called Career Guides, and so on, were waiting to welcome me with open arms, ready to plan my future.

I was waiting in the hall when the receptionist opened for business in the first agency on my Forty-Second Street list.

"Are you registered with me?" she asked me. I had to answer no, so she handed me a bunch of forms. I began to study the system. While I was filling out the forms, other registered people were showing up waiting to be interviewed. By the time I had my papers filled out, I was last in every line. I had no time for waiting, so I left the papers, made an appointment for the next day and started the same routine all over again in the next agency.

Fortunately, one interviewer was late. He came in just as I finished filling out my forms, and there happened to be no queue in front of his niche at the counter. While I stood there, he turned his back on me and started haranguing the receptionist because she had forgotten his coffee. I finished filling in a few more

245

blank spaces on the form, meanwhile keeping first place in the line. He seemed to be making a point of not acknowledging my presence, looking right past me like a snow-blind waitress at the Chock-Full-O-Nuts. Finally and wordlessly, he picked up my set of forms and began scanning them. While he was reading I tried to look past him and just listen for his comments.

"Oh, you were a Catholic *priest?*" I heard him shrieking. I could sense other necks straining and I could feel my own neck getting red. I didn't look right, I didn't look left. I didn't even nod. I felt like crawling. "Why did you *leave?*" he asked me. Suddenly everyone else stopped talking. You could hear a pin drop.

"I just left, period," I said.

"Please Mist-er Long-go," he said. "You'll have to talk up a little. I can't hear you."

"I left, period," I repeated.

"Well," he said, "the only reason I mentioned it is because I know a fellow who's a priest and I thought maybe he could help you."

"I know quite a few priests myself, as a matter of fact. But the reason I'm here is I want to start a new career that has nothing to do with religion. And I have to find a job immediately."

"Well, that's what I mean," he said. "I have a cousin who's a rabbi and believe me, when it comes to being influential and powerful, one word from a priest in the right place at the right time, and you're in, Jack. I mean IN!"

"Perhaps," I said, "but some of the downtown agencies advised me not even to mention the priesthood. On Wall Street I was told very explicitly they couldn't hire me because it might be considered an affront to their Catholic customers."

"You mean Catholics would discriminate against

you? I think that's ridiculous. I know some Catholics who are wonderful liberal people. It seems to me if any one should help you, they should. After all, you spent some years working on their behalf, so to speak, don't you know?"

"Well, sometimes it doesn't work that way. All I can tell you is I've been advised to forget about the priesthood, not even mention it, and to consider my background from the point of view of social work."

"Sure, social work is fine. But all your experience has been with Catholic agencies. That's the advantage you have. You understand those channels. Why throw that away?"

We went round and round. It got to be a debate. I had gone to all the trouble of sweating out a night in the park, traipsing uptown to save subway fare, shaving in the railroad station, filling out acres of forms, only to have some jerk tell me to go to the telephone and call the Bishop. It was ridiculous. I walked out.

The big problem was the absence of an address. I never knew what to put down. Until I could establish some sort of residence, or a telephone connection, I would have to stay with one agency and wait all day for them to send me out for an interview. I had never looked for a job in my life before. The simplest mechanical problems were mysteries I had to uncover by myself, one at a time.

I counted my change and fingered another dime. I had Marilyn's telephone number. She had said to give her a ring anytime and come up, and that she cooked a great spaghetti dinner. She might be able to help me. She might even take phone messages for me, she might even let me use her address on the forms. But I had to think carefully before I made the call. If a girl lives in an apartment and she's not home when you telephone, you get your dime back. If she lives in a hotel, it costs you the price of a cup of coffee to find out she's not in. And I had no message to leave them except my name.

I had more to gain than lose so I called her. It was my first break of the day when she answered. I decided to be very casual and just say I happened to be in Manhattan for the day, so I wanted to call her.

"That's very sweet," she said. "I'm cooking Italian spaghetti tonight in honor of you so you have to come." My second break of the day. I was so hungry I could already taste the sauce. When I asked her what time I should come, she said:

"I'm home all day, darling. The earlier the better." It was practically *carte blanche*. I began to feel she would understand about the address business if I asked her. The telephone calls would be the most important thing. If I could just use her telephone number and she would take the messages, I was halfway toward an executive trainee connection.

I felt better already. When they handed me the set of inevitable forms in the next agency, I wrote out Marilyn's address and phone number. The rest was easy. When I faced the next interviewer, I was relaxed and confident. While he studied the forms, I studied him. I was an unemployed social worker from New Jersey who wanted to work in Manhattan. I had all the phony answers ready. But his first question came from way out in left field.

"There's something here I don't understand, Mr. Longo," he began.

"Yes?"

"If you own 226 West 72nd Street, what are you doing here?"

My neck was getting red again. I'd never make it as a liar. "I'm sorry," I said.

He pointed to the box on the form where it said

DOMICILE: OWN OR RENT. I had stupidly checked in as a homeowner.

"Ah, you made a slip there," he said, sympathetically. "You *do* own your own home but now you're staying at a hotel. That means marital trouble," he said smiling. "You're in the same boat as me. What court has she had you in?"

He was ready to recruit me for an anti-alimony club right on the spot. "Let's not talk about that," I said bravely.

"When I first picked up these forms, I knew there was something in here that just didn't hang together. I couldn't quite put my finger on it. First, I thought you were a doctor in trouble. Then I realized you were acting the same way I acted when my wife got me fired and I had to go out and start over. God Almighty, if only I'd had sense enough not to get married," he said, holding his head in his hands.

He really went to bat for me. While I sat there he made four telephone calls. From listening to the way he sold me, I learned something about how to sell myself. Each time his tack was slightly different. He gained something from each response. When he felt a door opening, he slammed his palm over the receiver and said: "Cross your fingers. This is International Paper. They give trainees eight thousand a year. It's the highest paying position we have listed."

I was on the edge of the chair. He kept nodding. I crossed my fingers. When he put down the telephone he was beaming. "You've got a date with the head of their training program. I really pushed."

"I know. Gee," I said, "that's great. When is it?"

He wrote it all down on a pad and handed it to me. The name, the address, the time, the date. My heart sank. I expected it would be today. I couldn't wait three hours, let alone three days. I needed a job this

249

afternoon. I had told him I was desperate, had no money left. Now I couldn't even hint I was disappointed or *that* desperate.

"What's the matter?" the interviewer asked.

"I'll be there," I said.

"Come in the afternoon before," he suggested. "I want to talk to you about how to handle the marital thing, if it comes up—and it always does. I've got a few hints on how to look stable while you're on the run."

"Thanks very much," I said.

He had done his best. I had to keep going. It was almost lunchtime. But most Forty-Second Street and Madison Avenue agencies have their heaviest traffic during lunchtime. People already employed have the luxury of holding one job while scouting for another. Lines got longer, interviews got shorter; but questions on the agency forms stayed the same. I could have filled out the forms in my sleep. I kept going until three o'clock. I filled out complete sets of forms in at least twenty-five agencies. I was interviewed a half dozen times. But my only accomplishment was an appointment three days off. With a dollar-sixty in my pocket. I knew I'd be sleeping in the park again so I began thinking about Marilyn's spaghetti. She had asked me to come early but five o'clock would be ridiculous. I had to hold out at least until six-thirty if dinner was scheduled at eight. I started walking toward Central Park, pleasantly killing time, trying not to think about food. I saw a man carrying an umbrella. What should I do if it rained? That's one detail my roommate at Abingdon Park had neglected in his briefing.

By six o'clock I was exhausted and I decided to go directly to Marilyn's hotel. I called her from the lobby and went right up.

Her peppermint striped pants were tight enough to stop her own blood circulation and rev up circulation around her. Her idol and namesake was in the middle of rebellion against Hollywood then and Marilyn II acted like a precinct worker running a boycott against Twentieth-Century Fox. Every other word was a bulletin on the struggle between MM and Mr. Zanuck. Every detail of make-up and hair coloring was borrowed from Monroe. She had just heard that MM and Sammy Davis, Jr. were an item and she regarded this as the greatest symbol of democratic progress since the Supreme Court decision of desegregation in 1954. She wanted me to be among the first to know.

The living room walls were painted blood red with black ceilings, red and black awning striped drapes, black furniture and very low indirect lighting. The whole place could have passed for the ladies room in a cheap night club. In the darkness I tripped over a couple of dogs. Marilyn collected dogs, cats, soldiers and musicians in imitation of Brigitte Bardot, whom she also admired tremendously. Her make-up, false eyelashes, and wig left her almost unrecognizable.

She had two musicians staying with her, in addition to her sister and a small baby. The telephone rang continuously and the traffic in and out of the bedrooms and bathroom was constant. Dogs, cats, a crying baby and strange people competed with the telephone for Marilyn's attention.

"Now tell me about you, Gabe," Marilyn would say as she ran from the telephone to the kitchen. "What do *you* think about Marilyn and Sammy Davis going steady, isn't that just too marvelous?" Then she would disappear. Each time she talked on the telephone she would take an oath that she was the most discreet and closed-mouth girl in town. But when she hung up, she proceeded to drop names, details and gossip items like ashes from her cigarette. She had just posed for a billboard effigy of Gina Lollabrigida because Gina wasn't available and they had the same size bust. A friend had promised to get her into the Actor's Studio.

She had a chance to do a single at a posh East Side nightclub but she didn't know whether the Mafia would allow it, because they owned the hotel around the corner where she had been offered a larger suite, but she didn't want to get too deeply involved. After all, when she was designing wreaths for a Madison Avenue florist, she received a commission to design special funeral wreaths for Johnny Dio two days before he was killed. She knew too much, that's why she had to be so careful and close-mouthed. She had been invited to a private party at the Warwick where some Tammany judges were hosting Senator Kennedy from Massachusetts and she thought he was a real doll. She had terrible problems because her singing teacher and her psychoanalyst didn't get along and the simplest conflict in appointments was apt to bring two dear friends to the edge of blows. She couldn't live without either man, and what was she to do?

I sat there sipping cheap wine in an expensive glass feeling like a visitor from Mars. I wanted to ask her if she would take telephone messages for me but I decided it was hopeless. I managed to mention I was job-hunting and she asked for a copy of my resume. When I said I didn't have any extras, she immediately went to the phone and called a friend of hers, a model who had just had a nose job and was going insane staying home every day waiting for the swelling to go down. Her friend would be happy to type the extras as a favor.

Marilyn was hungry to do things for me and everybody else. She was warm and generous on the surface, but there was something very cold and calculating about each apparently impulsive move she made. I decided I'd better keep my troubles to myself unless I wanted them spread all over town.

Eventually the five of us assembled in the kitchen for the famous spaghetti. As hungry as I was, I could barely eat. It was limp and mushy; the sauce reminded me of the seminary. But since it had been concocted in my honor I had to eat every scrap and smile when it was over. When I told Marilyn I had an appointment downtown at ten, she made a show of being furious. I would have invented one just to get out of there. The quiet and privacy of a bench in a park began to look very inviting.

Marilyn insisted on walking me to the subway. She put her best looking dog on a leash, curled herself onto my arm and off we went. In the hotel hallway under the bright lights, I got a good look at her. Actually she was a painfully ugly girl with a fantastic figure. But the blond wig, the eyelashes, the heavy make-up were startling enough to turn her into a looker. It was the first time I had ever walked in the street with a girl who looked like that. She could turn every head. The sloppy sweater she wore featured her bosom without overemphasis; it was just long enough to bounce across her behind as she moved her body along in imitation of the famous MM motions. It was a mystery to me that Marilyn, who seemed to be the sexiest thing on two feet, merely reminded me of how exciting Sherry had been, who made no effort to be a sexpot at all. I decided I had plenty of research to do in the comparative study of girls.

The subway trip downtown cost me thirty cents. I had to stop off at Penn Station and pick up my black bag. When I got to the park my new roommate was just ready to leave. He hadn't expected me to show.

"Come on," he said, "I'll buy you a sandwich." I wondered how he spent his days. At some race track probably, but I never asked. When I protested I had just had a free spaghetti dinner, I couldn't have been very convincing. "You can always use a sandwich," he said. Again he insisted on paying. Then we started walking downtown. I noticed he was wearing those expensive space shoes and instead of his golf jacket, a beautiful sweater. When we got closer to the whole-sale market section of town, his British accent seemed to dissolve and he began to talk in rugged American vernacular.

As we walked along, I kept an eye out for rats. The tall shuttered loft buildings made the night seem dark, but electric bulbs glared beneath the canopies that over-hung the sidewalk out to the curb. Trucks were be-ginning to arrive at the stands. They dominated the sounds in the night. Doors and tailgates slammed. Men shouted directions to drivers as they attempted to maneuver their vehicles in the narrow streets. Cases and cases of fruits and vegetables piled up on the side-walks.

My British friend seemed to know his way around. He chatted pleasantly with the men who were hanging around waiting for their trucks and vans to arrive for unloading. But whenever he spotted someone who seemed to be in authority his manner changed com-pletely.

"Hey, motherfucker," he would greet a supervisor as he threw an arm around his shoulder and drew him into confidential conversation. He was putting on an act, but it was a good one. It made me feel very much like an outsider and I stood there wondering what to do.

"Hey, where's the chief fuckoff? He's late tonight," my British friend was saying. The men accorded this title, I discovered, were the platform supervisors in the various market stalls. My friend kept moving from one quarter of the market to another. He was acting as my agent, trying to persuade someone to take me on as a laborer, apparently without success. I was very conscious of my clothes. I tried to leave my bag some-where out of sight.

Men were unloading heavy crates of vegetables and

fruit from trucks and vans, hauling them in and out of the market stalls; I wondered if I was up to that kind of physical work. All day I had been saying glibly, "I'll do anything." Now "anything" turned out to be hard labor. I opened my bag, fished out a couple of dexedrine tablets and swallowed them dry.

"Hey, Chubby!" my British friend hollered as he walked into another stall. I followed along after him. Chubby was a fat and angry-looking Italian about five-foot-six and all of two-hundred-fifty pounds. He turned around and took us both in. "Listen, motherfucker," my friend greeted him, "I brought a friend down for you. A paisano. If you don't put him to work tonight I'll have to cut off your goddamn balls."

Chubby smiled and I smiled and then the two of them walked off into a huddle.

I stood there waiting for the dexedrine to take effect.

A feeling of deep embarrassment swept over me at the thought of meeting anyone who might have known me as Father Longo, and even deeper concern over the shame and humiliation that it would bring to my parents were they to hear of me in this situation. I surely could not contact them again until I was into something on a higher level. It was difficult to become accustomed to anonymity. Nobody along our path had saluted me with, "Hello, Father." I was sensitive to the missing respect with which I had been treated.

"I don't know, pal," Chubby greeted me after my friend waved me to come inside. "It looks like a slow goddamn night around here. But you can hang around if you want and you might make a night's pay."

"It's in the lap of the gods," my friend chimed in. "I'll see you later, friend. Good luck." With that he walked off. I had figured on our working together, counted on having him around to show me the ropes. But I was on my own.

"Jesus Christ, pal, ain't you got no work clothes in that goddamn bag of yours?" Chubby asked.

"This is all I happen to have with me. I'll just get rid of the jacket," I said. When I started to stuff it into the bag, Chubby said: "Naw. Naw. Hang it on the rack in the back. Nobody steals nothing from me. Goddammit, they know better."

While I was hanging up the jacket he threw me a flannel shirt and an old sweater. "This here is one of mine. It's big enough to fit any goddamn body, pal," he said.

"Thanks, Chubby," I said. "Where do I start?"

He wanted me to try to create some order in the back room where crates of fruit, opened and unopened, were thrown around in wild disarray: grapefruit, melons, lemons, oranges, avocados. He handed me a broom and I went to work. No interviews. No forms to fill out. No training program. No career guidance. No questions.

"You got enough there to hold you until the new loads start coming in." Chubby himself was examining written orders from French restaurants and hotels.

I attacked the storeroom mess as if my life depended on it. In a half hour it looked like a Gristede's window. When the big trucks arrived and Chubby was checking papers with the driver, I began to unload the crates of new fruit. Most of it, like me, was from New Jersey. At the end of the first hour I began to wonder how much I had earned. Every hour had to mean at least a dollar. Twenty-five hours of this—three days or four days—and I would have enough to get my car out of hock. I could find a place to park it somewhere downtown. My British friend was bound to have some ideas on that. Then at least I would have a place to sleep. As far as eating was concerned, I could at least get fruit wholesale. Then there was that appointment coming up at International Paper. Three days began to seem less and less like forever.

Around midnight Chubby announced he was taking a break to have coffee at a nearby diner with one of his customers. I was astonished that he seemed to be leaving the entire enterprise in my care, without any questions.

"Can I bring you back something, fer Chrissakes, pal?" he said.

"No, thanks, Chubby." Hungry as I was, I didn't want any deductions from my first night's pay.

"I should learn to control myself too, pal. Look at this belly," he said, thumping his paunch. "I always get two meals a day just outa what's lying around here. So help yourself, pal. The best food in the world comes from here. Even if you was used to eating at Voisins and Chambord, just remember it all comes from here. Whyn't you knock off while I'm gone and sample the merchandise? That guy across the street," Chubby said in farewell, "he supplies the Morocco. Down here you can eat good as anybody."

He just assumed I was hungry. I looked at the mountains of delicious fruit. This was like a wholesale version of the Garden of Eden. I didn't know where to begin.

I worked until almost four the next morning. Chubby paid me eleven dollars. It was the first money I had ever really sweated for in my life.

He had a hyphenated name. I remembered that much about him. The night that girl in the bar had written down the address of her psychiatrist for me. It was a hyphenated name, British-sounding. And his office was on lower Fifth Avenue, a number between one and ten. If I had to look at every name on every bell in the block, I knew I could find him, and I did. When

I called I spoke to him directly and he gave me an appointment the next day.

There was something about his voice—the phrasing, the inflections, that rang a bell—but that was unimportant. The main thing was he was very receptive and cordial and, well, sympathetic. And one thing was certain from the accidental referral: there was no possible connection between him and the Church.

When I saw the layout of his office—a huge penthouse, terrace apartment, black leather furniture against clean white floors and walls, floor to ceiling indirectly lighted aquariums full of exotic fish—I decided I'd better waste no time in telling him I didn't have any money.

He was fat and sloppy, and looked out of place in the beautiful environment he had created.

When I blurted out that I was a priest on the run and without any resources, he seemed more sympathetic, more cordial and more receptive than ever.

"I wouldn't worry about that at all," he said. I felt he was sizing me up physically when he took a second look. "If you need a place to stay for a few days, or if you should need a New York address, please feel free to. . . .

"Well, anyway," he continued after interrupting himself to lead me out onto the terrace, "as you can see, I do have certain natural advantages and plenty of room, heaven knows."

The view from the terrace was something. I could see across the Hudson River to Jersey City.

"If it's a question of ready cash, I'm sure we can work something out. We should be able to have a decent position lined up in no time."

Either he was a mind-reader or very perceptive. Were all non-Catholic psychiatrists this sharp? "A few days ago I thought so too," I said, "but I got over that in a hurry."

"I suppose I've had rather more experience at this sort of thing than you have. It's difficult, I know, to beat the system all by oneself."

It was a strange phrase. Father Basil used to use it. The two men weren't alike at all in manner, yet they had something in common. I couldn't figure out what it was.

"Since this *is* an emergency, perhaps we'd better get cracking," he said as he led me into a library. He gave me some forms to fill out—extremely long ones and very complicated.

"I'll leave this to you while I make a couple of telephone calls," he said. Again I caught him standing off and looking at me rather like a tailor figuring what kind of alteration a suit might need. I began on the forms. If I had had any kind of active sex life, the job of filling them might have taken hours. I had to leave so many spaces blank that I began to feel underprivileged. I was through in about twenty minutes.

When he came back, bringing the forms for a Rorschach test, he seemed slightly surprised that I was finished with the first set. But he restrained himself from any comment.

"You just whip through these; don't give any of them a second thought. Try and let me have the first thought that pops into your head. That's what I'm after." He smiled. "You'll be appropriately rewarded when you join me on the terrace. Gin and tonic, or would you rather have something else?"

"That will be fine," I said. He took the completed forms and disappeared again while I went to work on the Rorschach. When I stared at the blots, I felt, what the hell, give it to him straight. Every weird smear on the paper reminded me of some part of some girl, so I identified the blots as a kind of road map of my sexual fantasies. Then I joined him on the terrace.

He seemed strange. I didn't altogether like him, but

I was sure he was someone who could be trusted, so I started blurting out all the details of my recent experiences in New York—the things I couldn't tell anybody else. I had just begun when he interrupted and stopped me cold.

"My dear boy," he said. "I'm sure you're acquainted with that apocryphal story which tells of Mrs. Henry Luce, after her reconversion, having an audience at the Vatican and nailing His Holiness the Pope to the wall with the intensity of her newly discovered faith. And the Pope replies, 'Please Mrs. Luce, I'm a Catholic already.' "

I had heard the story but I still didn't get the point. My blank stare must have revealed as much. He leaned over, put his hand on my knee and said wearily, "My dear boy, I was a Benedictine myself. I had been a priest a good deal longer than you, if I may say so."

I don't know why I was surprised, but I was. Now it all added up. He had treated me like a Dutch uncle from the minute I walked in. But he was actually the first ex-priest I had run into by accident. I would have to learn to trust my own instincts. After all, if one out of five American priests leaves, there are quite a few thousand wandering around. I would have to learn to spot *them*, instead of worrying so much about being spotted myself.

"You see, my dear boy," he continued, "most of my optimism is based on hard fact. I didn't leave until a good ten years after I should have. Still, I managed to survive. Good heavens, difficult as it is, things are a good bit less sticky than they were right after the war. On top of that, Gabriel, you're barely thirty. Timing is everything, my boy. You still have your youth. You're not rotted with alcohol. You've not consoled yourself with calories and run to fat. You're young, you're apparently healthy, you're extremely good-looking and my God, an old goat like me can only envy you. To be able to experience one's youth at a time one is old enough to appreciate it—good heavens, how I envy you. Truly I do."

It was quite a switch. He just assumed I had done the wise thing, the healthy thing. I was braced for an argument. I half expected to be told I needed six months on the couch before making so momentous a decision.

"I will do everything I can to help *if* there is a heaven," Father Joseph had said. Suddenly I wanted to tell him all about Father Joseph. When I began, he interrupted me again as he poured himself another drink.

"Now, if you should feel you can trust me slightly more than when we first met," he began, "I would like to give you an opportunity to amend this little questionnaire."

"Of course," I said, "in what way?"

"Let's try to fill in some of these blank spaces," he said. "Let's try not to take it so seriously as to conceal things which may seem inconsequential but go to the root of the problem of belief."

I wasn't sure what he meant. "Can you be more specific?"

"For instance," he said wearily, "you certainly cannot expect anyone in my position with my experience to accept this comment as altogether responsive, now can you?"

I looked at the form. He had his finger on a little square which asked at what age you had your first homosexual experience. I had left it blank and in the next box I had written NONE. If it hadn't been for Sherry the whole page would be blank. I didn't know what to say. I was sure I was blushing.

"That's one thing I never expected you to be embarrassed about. We all hide things, even from ourselves."

"But I'm *not* hiding anything. I'd be happy to tell you some stories but I'd have to make them up. And I'm not very good at that."

"Come now, my dear boy. Try and remember. It is just not possible. It's not possible at all with your particular background and experience and, if I may say so, your temperament. If not with an older compatriot then as a boy with other boys. Something must have come about in the way of homosexual adventure."

I saw him studying the Rorschach.

"What do you base that statement on?" I inquired. "On the Rorschach test?"

"These tests are rubbish in most respects. I don't credit them as being much of any aid at all, really, just between us. What I do credit is my own experience, in many ways similar to yours. Good heavens, man, the nature of the beast doesn't change that much. Some things we all have in common. And this is one of them. Whether we'll admit it or not."

I didn't know what to say. "If there's any other kind of test, I'd be happy to take it," I volunteered.

He laughed. "Well, I'm not at all sure there is one. But if you insist on maintaining this unusual posture, I may have to devise some kind of maze to run you through."

He was downing two drinks to my one. When he gave me a second one, I wasn't sure I could handle it. I would have much preferred a ham sandwich or even some peanuts. In trying to bring up the subject of food, I mentioned the Washington Market. When he found out I was working there, he was horrified and insisted I should quit. He wanted to start sending me out for interviews immediately. This brought up the problem of clothes. When I explained most of my wardrobe was at my parents' home, he was ready to send someone to get them.

He had worked out an entire plan of attack. He was going to arrange some sort of academic affiliation immediately. I told him I had already scouted that market and found that no agency was placing any teachers until next fall.

"Well, I don't expect to work on that level, my boy," he said. "Not at all. With three or four of the right kind of letters, and a recasting of your seminary training and pastoral experience, we can turn you into an experienced clinical psychologist in no time. Then we take the high ground and sit here quietly having our gin and tonic while several colleges fight over you. You have to be careful to start with a decent post at a decent salary. You're going to be shocked to discover how much money you need just to live. I know I was and, good heavens, that was fifteen years ago. Things are a good bit more expensive now."

Suddenly I knew what I didn't like about him. This was where I came in! Sitting there like a fifteen-year-old kid and letting some older priest tell me, "Look, Gabe, you're young and good-looking and I like you. All I want to do is to arrange your life for you." He was showing me his five-hundred-dollar-a-month apartment like Father Artioli had showed me the seminary. He had me up on top of the mountain and he was showing me the world. If I needed money, he would arrange it. If I needed clothes, he would arrange it. If I needed letters of reference or a fake background, he would arrange it. I would become one of his boys, just the way I had been one of Father Artioli's boys.

"Of course," he was saying, "you'll have to go into analysis immediately. We can begin whenever you like."

The trouble was, at the moment, I had no alternative. I needed help from somewhere and there was no doubt that he had connections, influence. He could help me. But why should he want to?

Because he was still a priest. The apartment, the hyphenated name, the guise as a psychoanalyst—none of this changed anything.

He was acting like a very wise bishop, very worldly, very righteous, very sure of himself. What we used to call the "de Fide" type. Meaning "you must believe in me."

His phone rang and he went inside. In a moment he came out again. "Gabriel, this is going to be a long call. I'm talking about you to the dean of a college, an old colleague of mine. So make yourself comfortable. Why don't you go into my bedroom, take a shower. Let's get rid of that black suit and see what you look like in something else, shall we? What about dinner?" He left without waiting for an answer. Maybe he wanted me out of the way so he could talk freely.

Heaven knows I needed a shower. But for some reason I didn't feel too comfortable about taking one. I had my bag with me, with another shirt in it and a sweater.

But I didn't move. I finished my drink and I just sat there thinking. I didn't trust him. I liked him but I didn't trust him. Still I was going to play along with him until I found out what there was about him that made me uneasy. Then I would charge it up to experience.

He had already given me one answer I was seeking. I had gotten assurance from left field—from someone with professional competence—that I wasn't in the middle of some kind of breakdown, and that my decision to leave the priesthood had been arrived at rationally. He had given me his answer in spades.

I begged off dinner, I ducked the offer of a shower, I promised to begin analysis the next week and I took him up on his offer to meet with the dean of a nearby college that afternoon.

He gave me a build-up as one of the most eminent

men in the field of clinical psychology. The object of my visit with the dean was not to get a job, but to persuade him to sign a personal letter of recommendation which would be drafted carefully to make it sound as though I had been a practicing psychologist for four and a half years, instead of a practicing priest.

My fat former Benedictine friend, father confessor and future psychoanalyst suggested I wear a sport jacket and grey slacks and loafers if I had them.

I tried to thank him for his time and all his help but he pushed me off. There was only one thing he asked in return.

"When I told you about my former life as a priest, I had a very specific purpose in mind," he said. "Needless to say, I don't like it bruited about. I've spent a good many years escaping the pernicious designation of 'former,' or 'ex,' or whatever they call it. And I wouldn't like to think about the consequences of its becoming current public knowledge. I know you, above all, understand that. I mention it only so we both understand each other."

"I understand completely," I said.

"Call me the instant you can. I'm terribly anxious to hear that everything went well with you and Sandy. I *know* it will but I'll be waiting for your call."

The moment I saw Sandy that afternoon I began to understand everything. He was supposed to be one of the biggest men in the field, but he arrived in an outfit that had to be seen to be believed: high cowboy boots, a fuzzy Greenwich Village sweater, a magenta shirt and a silver ID bracelet.

I was instantly reminded of that questionnaire in the Fifth Avenue penthouse. That blank space for homosexual experiences, the blank space that had bothered my hyphenated ex-Benedictine friend—I got the feeling Sandy was ready to help me fill it in. He may have

265

had another wardrobe and another manner for the classroom, the faculty meetings, or the psychology lab. But with me he exhibited a come-on as obvious as any I had ever gotten from one of my overheated parishioners in the confessional.

I didn't know what to say to the man. He must have been thoroughly briefed about me, and I blushed, wondering whether this was a test in clinical psychology or a genuine stab at a job.

He kept lighting his pipe every thirty seconds. When I pulled out a cigarette to calm my nerves, he fell all over me lighting it. He talked vaguely about his good friend at a state university in the West.

"He has a great deal out there, if you happen to be the outdoor type," Sandy said.

I had to bite my tongue to keep from admitting I was. After two minutes with Sandy, I was through with the whole deal. It had taken me too many years to stop impersonating a priest. Now I didn't want to slide sideways into another role. I'd rather work in the Washington Market.

"Hey, Father!"

My head turned automatically. The crate of avocados slipped off my shoulder. When I tried to catch it with the small of my back, the wire bailing ripped at my sweater, dug into my wrist, and drew blood.

"Hey, Your Reverence!"

I ducked behind the truck and reached into my back pocket for a handkerchief to stanch the blood. The silk pants were all I had; luckily I hadn't torn them. I tied up my wrist and dragged the crate into the back of the fruit and vegetable stall.

"Hey there, Father!"

I had to be cracking up, imagining things. Three o'clock in the morning on a slow night at the Washington Market. Nobody would possibly find me or recognize me here. There was nothing to give me away except the pants and the black shoes.

I walked back to the truck to unload the rest of the avocados. As I turned to make the hoist to my shoulder, out of the corner of my eye I caught sight of a black figure: grey hair, red jowls, rimless glasses, a paunch, and the Roman collar. He lunged across the street, staggering, plunging in and out of a shoulder-high aisle of orange crates. Two men were playing a cruel kind of tag with him, ducking around the crated fruit, hooting at him, taunting him.

"Hey, Father, there's a greasy old broad back here. She really needs saving. Whyn't you see what you can do?"

A truck rolled up West Street just as the drunken priest lunged from the curb to escape his tormentors. The headlights caught him and the huge van airbraked to a halt. The driver's curses mingled with the hoots and hollers from the curb. I winced as the paunchy figure in the Roman collar lifted his right hand in benediction in front of the halted vehicle. I turned my head away and covered my ears. He was chanting in Latin, kneeling in the street.

"Get that bum outa here!" a voice shouted.

A small knot of workers and market roustabouts had collected on the corner. Two of them danced into the street, lifted the kneeling priest by his elbows and carted him off, kicking and chanting, to the curb. The truck rolled into gear and drove off with the driver hurling curses.

"Where's the greasy pig?" someone hollered. The market hands surrounded the staggering priest. Moving in formation, they lifted and dragged him toward the cluttered alley behind a row of stores.

My hands were shaking. I went back to the truck and hoisted another crate of avocados. I winced when the sharp edges dug into my shoulder. While I was in the back of the store unloading I could hear the continued shouting, hooting, curses; then came the shrill sound of a woman's voice, half screaming, half laughter. Four-letter words drowned her singing.

All the loading platforms seemed deserted, not a single supervisor in sight. Chubby had wandered off to the diner for coffee. It was the dull end of a slow night, recess time. The hotel and restaurant buyers had come and gone. Aging delinquents were exploding on the playground. From the alley you could hear the cheers:

"Attaboy, Father. Go! Go! Go!"

"Shake it up, Flo baby. That's it. That's it. That's my greasy girl."

My knees were getting mushy; my teeth were chattering. I had the shakes and the chills, just like the night on the Jersey shore with Sherry. I knew what was happening in the alley. But what could I do to stop them? If I called the police I'd be in trouble. There was no phone in the stall anyway. I'd have to run to the diner. The call would cost ten cents I couldn't afford. Chubby would be there and I'd catch blazes for leaving the stall.

Every sign of life seemed to have disappeared from the street. I walked to the corner. The brightly lit stalls were empty. Nobody was working. Everybody had congregated in the alley. Maybe something like this went on every Thursday. Maybe it was some kind of carnival that went on every spring. What was the old priest doing here in the first place?

My whole body was shaking now. When I grabbed my elbows to stop the shivering, I could feel the cold sweat trickling from my armpits. My shirt was wet to the waist. I ran back to the stall to slip on my suit coat or find that dirty old blanket. Are you out of your skull? That one-hundred-eighty-dollar black silk jacket would be a dead giveaway. You might just as well arrive in a cassock and surplice. I hung the coat back on the spike and raced across the street into the dark alley.

A dozen hangers-on from the market were hunched in a loose circle. Three of them waved broken barrel staves, slamming them into the cement as they collapsed with laughter. A young Negro with a goatee rolled a copy of the *Daily News* into a tight torch and set it aflame. The fire made weird shadows, and bits of charred paper curled through the smoky air. The pavement was littered with cucumbers and bananas that had been hurled at the couple and then squashed by the hecklers. The sodden priest was on his bare knees, crawling in search of something. His glasses! The terrible toothless tart was dangling his rimless glasses in front of her skirt.

"Here we are, lovey-love," she cooed.

One of the roustabouts had the priest's pants in his hand, now waving them in the shadows, now snapping them at his tousled grey head.

I stood there, teeth rattling, knees shaking, but nobody gave me a second look. I tried to turn away my head but my neck was rigid.

Then men took turns tossing bananas at the poor witch. The sound of money tumbling onto the cement sent her sprawling, crawling. When she turned on her knees, one of the stage managers reached out deftly with his barrel stave and indecorously lifted her soiled skirt. Rubinoff and his magic violin! The man with the torch moved closer, squatting and grinning to illuminate the gutter scene. My body recoiled and I turned away, leaning against the rough brick wall. I grabbed my elbows to slow down the convulsions. I wanted to get out of there but I knew if I moved or breathed I would vomit.

"What the goddamn hell kind of goddamn circus

you goddamn creeps think you're running here, god-dammit?"

It was Chubby's commanding growl, shouted from somewhere in the darkness. Now I'd be in trouble for leaving the store.

"Look, Chubby, *look!*" one of the barkers shouted. "The old bag is sick and His Reverence is pushing her up to St. Vincent's Hospital!" The bystanders doubled up laughing, slamming their sticks on the cement.

"I said break it up, you miserable bums!" Chubby commanded. "Give the poor bastard back his goddamn pants."

The alley was suddenly silent. The ringsiders started melting away. Chubby kicked angrily at the broken cucumbers. The spoiled priest was mumbling something in Latin.

"I said give the poor bastard back his *pants*," Chubby hollered. "Come on now, you wise guys. Pick the bum up and pour him into them. Who's got his mother-fucking money?"

The toothless tart was on her feet, running. One of the barkers scrambled after her.

"Never mind her," Chubby ordered. "Drag him to a goddamn cab and get him the hell outa here."

They lifted the poor priest to his feet. Chubby stood facing him, his five foot six, two-hundred-fifty pounds reeking with authority.

"You heard what I said, Father?" he lectured. "I want you to stay the hell outa this goddamn market. I catch you down here one more goddamn time loaded and looking for trouble and I'll get my friend Cardinal Spellman after your ass. Awright?"

The priest hung his head but said nothing.

"Awright. You'll end up in Africa or China or some goddamn somewheres."

Chubby was walking off when he spotted me. Then he turned and stared. I was still standing propped against the cold bricks, shaking and shuddering. He walked over and grabbed my quivering elbows like an intern checking an emergency accident case. He stood on tip-toe and reached for my forehead. My hair was soaking wet. He slapped my cheeks back and forth between his open palms like a trainer reviving a punch-drunk lightweight. Then he whammed me on the side of the face. The slap burned the chill out of me.

"And you, goddammit," he said in a harsh whisper, "you get the hell back to the goddamn store before I murder you."

Then he turned and waddled off. I trailed him sheepishly across the street to the store, still shaking and shivering. He grabbed a crate of avocados from the parked truck, slammed them on his shoulder angrily, then dragged another crate along beside him with his powerful left arm. Like a kid imitating Papa, I tried to duplicate the feat. But I lost my balance, the crate teetered on my shoulder. Quickly I dropped the second crate to save the first one from smashing in the street. Chubby turned disgustedly and slung the crate into the rear of the store with one easy motion.

"Whyn't you grab that goddamn blanket and sling it around yerself. You trying fer Chrissakes to get pneumonia?"

I looked again but I didn't see a blanket. Before I could open my mouth, the rough texture slammed me in the face.

"Stay in the back here, wrap yerself up and sit down fer Chrissakes."

"Thanks, Chubby," I said, as soon as my teeth stopped chattering. "I don't know what came over me."

"Yeah," he said. "I *know* you don't know. You don't know from nothing. That's why I'm telling ya fer Chrissakes. Didn't you eat nothing all day or something?"

"Sure."

"With the loot you got last night, you could at least get a decent meal for a buck somewheres. Whyn't you go where I told you?"

"I meant to, Chubby. But I was way uptown and I had this engagement."

"Yeah?" he said impassively as he walked over and held his hand on my forehead again. "No fever. Ya been shittin' regular?"

"Yes, thanks."

"Where'd ya sleep?"

"Well last night as a matter of fact. . . ."

"I don't want no stories. Don't give me no stories. Just tell me where you slept at."

"Abingdon Square Park."

"That outdoor shit is okay for some guys but you ain't up to it, pal."

"It was okay. Perfectly all right," I said. "I'm sorry about leaving the store unattended. I don't know what came over me."

"Ya want me to tell ya?"

"I don't mind."

"Yer like a nosey little kid. Ya don't know how to mind your own business."

"Oh, come on. If there's anything stolen or missing you can take it out of my pay."

"Look, pal. I didn't bitch that you wasn't minding my store, pal. I said you wasn't minding *your own* business."

"I don't think that's true, really."

"If it ain't true, then why are you blushing?"

I fumbled for a cigarette. Before I could find a match, Chubby had his Zippo lighter flaming in my face.

"Look, pal," he said, looking straight at me. "Don't think you're the first down-and-out priest I ever seen

272

around here. There's something about this asshole end of town. You guys seem to turn up here regular."

I was relieved in a way the big secret was out. I was only curious how I had given myself away.

"I had you figured for a doctor or a priest last night when I first seen ya."

"You did? I guess this suit gave me away."

"It wasn't the suit for Chrissakes. Every cheap hood is wearing them expensive silk suits now, pal. Clothes don't mean nothing. Look at your hands. Who gets blisters from loading crates one night?"

My fingers were covered with scrapes and tears and blisters. And the gouge on my wrist.

"Besides," he added, "for an Italian, pal, you talk funny."

"*I* talk funny?"

"Yeah, it ain't natural the way you talk. What you say, there ain't no real *feeling* to it. You don't even know how to curse and swear, fer Chrissakes."

"Maybe I'll learn that around here."

"Forget it. You won't be here that long."

Well, I thought, there goes my first real job. I didn't even last two full nights.

"I'm sorry, Chubby," I said.

"It's okay for a couple of weeks or so to scrape together eating money. Or if you got the idea of learning how to open your own store. Otherwise I don't like the idea. You can't settle none of your shit by hiding out working down here fer Chrissakes."

"I guess not."

"I'm telling ya," Chubby said flatly. Maybe I hadn't lost the job. If I could hang on for even a week it would be something, fifty dollars maybe.

"I'll speak to my brother-in-law and have him ask around," Chubby volunteered. "He might be able to line up something for ya. But first fer Chrissakes get

273

yerself a place to stay. How much loot you got left?"

I reached into my pocket and counted the change.

"Seven dollars and forty-five cents."

"You got seven dollars and sleeping in a goddamn park fer Chrissakes. What are you saving the goddamn money for?"

"Well," I began, "the police impounded my car."

"Yeah?" said Chubby. "What kinda car?"

"Mercedes convertible," I said.

"Bless me Father and kiss my ass!" Chubby exploded. "How much you owe on it?"

"It's all paid for. It was impounded for illegal parking."

"So you need fifteen bucks to get a five-thousand-dollar sports car out of hock. And I'm worrying about your troubles."

"Ten dollars towing charges brings it up to twenty-five."

"Excuse my arithmetic," Chubby snorted disgustedly. "A five-thousand-dollar automobile and you ain't got no money. How come?"

"Well, the best priest I ever knew taught me never to hang on to money."

"Yeah?" Chubby sneered. "Some of them are mighty high livers, fer Chrissakes."

"Not Father Joseph," I protested. "He died with only fourteen dollars to his name. As soon as he got any money he gave it away. And he taught me to do the same thing."

"But you hung onto enough to buy this five-thousand-dollar sports car."

Chubby stomped his hat into the floor and ground it under his heel. "So you got a five-thousand-dollar car and I'm going to bug my poor brother-in-law to get you a job. Well, exactly what kind of trouble was you in?"

"When?"

"When? When you *left*. I take it you left, *right?*"
I nodded. Chubby was moving into the areas where
the psychiatrists, my confessors, the bishop, my family,
and my friends had never managed to touch. And the
strange thing was, I welcomed the intrusion. I would
gladly have paid him twenty-five an hour, if I had had
it. Instead he was paying me a buck fifty an hour and
treating me on his time.

"Yes, I left," I began. "I just couldn't take it anymore.
I had planned to become a chaplain in the Air Force.
Everything was all arranged. I thought that would be
an easy way out for everyone—my family, the people
in the parish. Then I realized I was merely delaying
the inevitable. I thought it would be more honest just
to ask for a leave of absence instead. The bishop okayed
my request. I left everything I own at my parents'
home in Jersey City. I didn't want to tell them anything definite. They may think I've gone to Texas with
the Air Force. I don't know. I thought I wouldn't
worry them until I got a job and got on my feet. I
knew it wouldn't be easy, but I didn't think it would
be this hard."

"You didn't steal no money?" Chubby asked.

"No. Obviously not."

"You didn't get drunk and play the horses?"

"No."

"Nobody's after you, no cops or nothin'?"

"Not that I know of."

"You ain't on the lam from Kings Park or Bellevue
or one of them fancy bughouses?"

"No."

"Ya ain't got the clap or nothin' like that?"

"No."

"Your Mercedes don't need no heavy repairs. The
top still goes up and down automatic?"

I nodded and laughed.

"You didn't knock up no young broad and cut her

up and dump her in the river or nothing like that?"

"No. Nothing like that."

"No women problems?"

I didn't know how to answer that. There was a short pause as I scratched my head. Chubby offered me a cigarette. Then came the light.

"Listen, pal," he confided. "If you'd said no to that I'd have to call you a liar and throw you outa here."

"I was with a woman the other day," I began. "Completely. For the first time. You might call it my first worldly experience."

"I know what you mean, fer Chrissakes," Chubby interrupted.

"You don't believe me?"

"Why shouldn't I believe you fer Chrissakes? Most guys wouldn't admit nothing like that even if it was *true*, fer Chrissakes. So why shouldn't I believe you? How old are you fer Chrissakes?"

"Thirty."

"Jesus Christ, pal, that's quite a wait. Quite a wait."

"Maybe that explains why I nearly got sick tonight. It happened the other night when I was with this woman. Then tonight when I knew what was happening in the alley—like a nervous convulsion almost."

"You never had no kina fits when you was a priest?"

"Never."

"Jesus Christ, I never heard of a thing like that. But I never heard of a guy getting his first lay at your age either, pal, fer Chrissakes. I never knew nobody who was in jail that long."

I stood up, folded the blanket and grabbed the broom. It was time to clean the back room, even up the crates of fruit, sweep the debris, get ready to close for the night.

"How long was it exactly?"

First I counted on my fingers. Then I tried to remember: this is the spring of 1956. I left for the semi-

nary in the summer of 1946. But before that there was
two years at Seton Hall which was practically the same
as seminary. And before that Our Lady of Mt. Carmel. . . .

"How old was you when they hooked ya?"

"I was pretty young," I said finally.

"It figures," Chubby said.

mcmlxvi

LAST YEAR at holiday time, when my parents came down to visit their grandchildren for a few days, Mother brought along a tiny black jewelry box. "I think Joan should have this," she said. There were tears in her eyes when she handed it to me.

In the box was an engagement ring, with the stone that had been in the center of my chalice, the chalice I had held in my hands during the innumerable Masses I had said during my days as a priest.

None of my family had come to my wedding. There was an eight-year period during which my father had forbidden me entry into their home. When our first son, Chris, was born, Dad had said: "I have no son, therefore I have no grandson." But the wounds began to heal, and by the time Paul was born my Mother brought me the chalice. "Sell it and use the money for the children," she said.

My parents still lived at the old homestead in Jersey City, a few blocks from Mt. Carmel Church where Father Moscati had been killed, where Father Artioli had succeeded him, where I had decided to become a priest, where I had said my first Mass. They hadn't been able to pull up stakes and start over somewhere else, as I had. They had had to listen to all the gossip, endure all the snubs, and submit to all the petty humiliations that righteous parishioners dished out. Even after ten years, one family whose son had become a priest still refused to speak to my parents in the street. All the honors accorded them were forgotten.

The stories and the rumors were beyond belief. It was believed that my departure had been caused by a combination of insanity, larceny, adultery and other unmentionable mortal sins. The simple truth was more than anyone could face.

Family humiliation and panic reached its peak a few months after my departure. Bernie was to be married, and it was to be the biggest affair since my ordination. Mother didn't want anything to mar the occasion.

Friends who still thought I was stationed somewhere in Texas couldn't understand why I couldn't get a few days leave to officiate at my brother's wedding. The truth was that I was still unloading vegetables at the Washington Market. After a solemn council it was decided I might come to the wedding, on condition I arrive dressed as a priest. The family considered it blasphemy for me to show up in anything but a Roman collar; I considered it blasphemy to wear one.

After days of indecision, I finally agreed to make a brief appearance. I felt like the biggest fraud of all time. When I walked in, family and friends crowded around me. My appearance in that little collar was taken as proof that I was not guilty of any of those whispered mortal sins. But I had to disappear as mysteriously as I had reappeared. When Kay was married I just stayed away. It was too late for any more impersonations.

Monsignor Artioli attempted a family reconciliation; my father wouldn't hear of it. Once a priest, I was

279

supposed to stick it out. After a while Bernie and I managed to get together and he called one night to tell me Dad was in the hospital. I decided to try to see him. When Dad was told I was outside in the corridor, all he said was "What's he doing out there? Tell him to come in!"

As a priest I had spent money like a drunken sailor and given it away like a conscience-stricken dope pusher. During my first year as a civilian working for a living, I earned barely two thousand dollars. I had to scuffle every day for food, clothing and shelter. I learned what the inside of a pawnshop looks like. Nothing in my two decades of training and education was of any use to me in the world where I now lived.

I was constantly playing it by ear, improvising as I went along, competing with fellows fifteen years younger than I in the rugged New York rat race. Somehow I got a toe-hold in the advertising business; then I worked a little in radio and TV. There I got educated by being conned, swindled and out-foxed. Finally I discovered that there is one thing for which an ex-priest is qualified: he ought to be able to sell something besides salvation. So I settled down and became a very good salesman. Then I realized that if I could sell for somebody else, I should be able to sell for myself. So finally I started a little business and after a shaky beginning managed to make a comfortable living and be my own boss. Occasionally I try to pick up some extra money working for other companies, but I still have trouble when people hear I'm an ex-priest.

After floundering around for five years, always on the verge of messing up my new-found personal freedom, I finally met Joan. A beautiful girl from an Italian Catholic family, she had been bruised by an early, unhappy marriage. She had the saddest eyes I'd ever seen, like a Spanish statue of Our Lady. And she was uncannily close to being the composite dream girl of my seminary fantasies.

We had a strange problem in common. According to Holy Writ, she could never remarry, since her divorce was not recognized by the Church. I could not marry at all. Any ceremony we went through could never, in the eyes of the Church, be anything more than "an attempted marriage."

But the eyes of the Church did not matter very much to us. So we attempted marriage. And we have attempted two handsome bambinos as healthy and appealing as the cover of any anti-birth control pamphlet.

Marriage made my excommunication from the Church automatic, *late sententiae*. Sometime later, if and when my "attempted marriage" becomes a cause of scandal for the faithful, I can look forward to the ceremony of a public excommunication. Joe Doakes, an obscure divorced Catholic, can "attempt" marriage without Rome taking any notice of him. But when Henry Ford II, a much publicized convert of Monsignor Fulton Sheen, divorces his wife and marries again, Rome is forced to make his excommunication official and public.

Years ago, when I left the priesthood, the entire issue of clerical celibacy was a closed question, conveniently brushed under the rug four hundred years before by the Council of Trent. The average Catholic assumed that it had always been that way. Eyes were closed and ears were deaf to the very real problems it presented for a young man growing into maturity as a human being and trying to be an honest, healthy, Catholic priest.

Now the question of clerical celibacy has been opened with what amounts to an ecclesiastical explosion. Only the personal intervention of Pope Paul VI kept the item off the agenda of the Second Session of Vatican II. Dutch-born Bishop Koop of Brazil spearheaded the forces working toward open reformation at the Vatican Council. His case for repeal of the celibacy rule was eloquently stated in a treatise published in the influential Paris newspaper *Le Monde*. Prominent Catholic laymen from twelve nations, including the United States, signed a petition to the Vatican imploring a change in the Canon Law that imposes celibacy on the clergy. It became known that the Holy Office presently has on file ten thousand requests from priests all over the world asking for dispensation from their celibate vows. Considering the fact that all doors in Rome are known to be closed, it is amazing that as many as ten thousand priests have been driven to take this desperate measure. Recent figures presented to the Conference of United States Bishops indicate that one out of every five priests ordained in the United States eventually leaves his calling and disappears, as I did, into other areas of American life.

Suddenly the press—Catholic as well as secular—has discovered the issue. Things we used to whisper about in the seminary, like the existence of Via Coeli, the retreat for fallen clergy, are now the subject of articles in family magazines.

The question is open in such a way that it can never be closed without a resolution. The final word from the Vatican Council summed it up: "Indeed, celibacy is not demanded by the very nature of the priesthood, as is apparent from the practice of the early Church where, besides those who, with all bishops, by a gift of grace, choose to observe celibacy, there are also married priests of the highest merit."

At last Rome has faced the obvious: the Church canon on celibacy is an obstacle to the reunification of Christendom. If and when Eastern and Roman rites are joined, as now seems inevitable, there cannot be one rule for priests of Eastern Europe and another for priests in the West, Africa, Asia and the Orient. It is merely a matter of time.

Meanwhile, one of my ambitions is to find some way of using my own experience to help others in the same position. I knew how many of my fellow priests were wavering and struggling with similar problems. When I took the plunge, somehow the troubled ones always seemed to find me.

At first they were merely curious to find out if I could survive. It was usually obvious that I was not making out too spectacularly—once, after a priest's visit, I found a twenty-dollar bill tucked in the pocket of my jacket. In advising others who are thinking of leaving, my main concern is usually whether they will be able to support themselves.

On later visits from troubled clergy, the conversation usually got round to more basic subjects. My priest friends wanted to meet some of my girl friends, or they wanted to use my apartment to meet a girl of their own.

After I was married, I enjoyed inviting clerical friends to the house. Joan was very patient about being on exhibit: she always wanted to be especially gorgeous and to cook exceptionally well, to convince them their world might not end if they were to be honest about their problems and do as I had done.

One evening Joan and I stopped at a place that had been one of my favorite hangouts during my last days at St. Rocco's. Father Jim and I had been regular customers, in civilian clothes. The same bartender was there and I introduced him to my wife.

"Well, what do you know!" he said. "Your friend Jim was in here the other night with *his* wife."

Father Jim still wears the collar. He has often talked about leaving the priesthood to marry his steady girl-friend, but he has never had the courage nor the honesty. "There, but for the grace of God, go I."